THE DESTINY OF WESTERN MAN

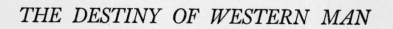

THE DESTINY
OF
WESTERN MAN

BY W. T. STACE

NEW YORK

REYNAL & HITCHCOCK

16862

Preface

Almost all the political controversies which are argued in newspapers, in magazines, on platforms, and even in treatises on political science, are concerned not with ends but only with means, not with the ultimate goals of political action but only with the machinery for their attainment. This is because the ends or ultimate ideals are generally agreed upon, are taken to be axioms which are common to all parties. "We hold these truths to be self-evident," says the Declaration of Independence, "that all men are created equal; that they are endowed by their Creator with certain unalienable rights; that among these are Life, Liberty, and the pursuit of Happiness; that, to secure these rights, Governments are instituted among men, deriving their just powers from the consent of the governed." This is not the creed of a party. It is the creed of all parties, a statement of their common ends. It is taken for granted that liberty, justice, equality of opportunity, the happiness—so far as possible—of all individuals, are *good* things, ends to be aimed at by the state. These are "self-evident" axioms. Political parties differ only as to what practical measures are best fitted to attain these ends.

Even if the professors of political science should argue in

v

their textbooks such questions as whether it is better to have a written constitution, as in the United States, or no written constitution, as in Britain; whether the chief executive of the state should remain in office for a fixed term of years or resign when he no longer retains a majority of the votes of the people's representatives; whether he and his cabinet should or should not be members of the legislative assembly; whether it is better that judges should be elected or appointed; whether proportional representation would improve our constitution; even these questions, comparatively remote and academic as they may appear to most people, are still concerned only with subordinate questions of machinery. For the parties to these disputes all agree on the supreme ends, the ideals of the democratic way of life.

So long as there is thus a common ground between political disputants, the usual methods of political controversy may well suffice. The political scientist can continue happy in his chosen field of ways and means, ignoring questions about ends. But what are we to do if a party, a program, a people, should arise which does not admit the validity of our axioms, which denies the desirability even of those ultimate goals of our policy, such as liberty and the happiness of individuals, which we had all along supposed to be "self-evident"? What if they impugn our entire conception of the good life, that which we call the democratic way of life? How are we then to argue our case? How are we to show that our political philosophy is right, and theirs wrong? An entirely new sort of problem now arises. For there would seem to be no longer any common ground as between the disputants. And a rational argument of any kind presupposes a common ground between the parties.

This is what has now happened in our world. The totalitarian peoples dispute our axioms and deny what we

had taken to be the supreme values of political life. They
do not admit that "all men are created equal." They do
not agree that the individual has any "unalienable rights."
They do not think that liberty—at any rate in our sense—
is a good thing. The happiness of individuals, they pro-
claim, is a poor and contemptible end. Thus our controversy with them is not about means, but about ultimate
ends and ideals. They have developed, it seems, a different
conception of the good life from ours. Our conception of
the good life—which is also, as I maintain, the inward spirit,
the ethos, of the age-old civilization of the western world—
has incarnated itself in our institutions. And their conception of the good life is rapidly incarnating itself in a new
set of institutions, a new kind of civilization.

In these circumstances the methods of the orthodox political scientist avail nothing. Given the ends, he knows how
to argue questions of the means. But if the ends are disputed, he has nothing to offer. How futile it is, for instance,
to argue that the various decrees and laws of a totalitarian
state destroy liberty and undermine the rights of individuals! For in the totalitarian state these liberties and rights
are not admitted to be ultimate political aims. And thus to
criticize an alien standard of the good life on the ground
that it is not our standard, to judge *their* methods by *our*
ends, is uselessly to beat the air.

There are only two courses open to us. We may admit
that, as between these two sets of ideals, the democratic and
the totalitarian, there is no common ground, and therefore
no possibility of rational argument. We have one idea of
the good life, we shall say, and they another. And since
there is no common standard, there is no possibility of
showing that one is superior, the other inferior, one right,
the other wrong. They are simply different, and that is the

end of the matter. In that case our preference for democracy, we shall have to admit, is in the end nothing but an irrational prejudice. Our reasons are mere rationalizations. The preference of the other side for totalitarianism is also, of course, mere prejudice. And there is no way of settling between two sets of equally irrational prejudices except the way of force.

This despair of reason, this profound unfaith in the rationality of our ideals, this deep defeatism in regard to our values, is, in the most up-to-date intellectual circles, the fashion of the moment. Those who discuss the issue of democracy versus totalitarianism are divided into two classes, those who merely abuse totalitarianism for not being democracy—those, that is, who just do not see the point of the problem—and those who, seeing it, say that there is no solution because there is no common standard by which to judge the two sets of ideals.

This latter way of regarding the matter may at least seem impartial, since it admits that both the democratic faith and that of the totalitarian peoples are alike mere matters of private preference and personal taste. But in reality it has not even this doubtful virtue of impartiality. Actually it is already an abandonment of democratic ideals and an espousal of the totalitarian *Weltanschauung*. For democracy is founded upon faith in reason. Belief in the rule of reason in human affairs,—which we get from the Greeks—is the indwelling spirit of western civilization, and is also the ultimate basis of democracy. To believe in democracy means to believe that human problems must be solved, not by passion, or brute will, or force, but by reason alone. Totalitarianism is in fact a revolt against this western tradition of the rule of reason in human life. It is an upsurging of irrationalism. That is why it is a rebellion against civilization.

That there is, as between the two ways of life, no method of decision save that of force, that of the blind irrational will, is precisely the totalitarian belief.

Is there any *rational* way of showing that democratic ideals are better, that the democratic faith is true? Is the matter open to *argument?* Can a *reasoned* justification of our conception of the good life be given?

My belief is that it can. But the path is no easy one. The waving of democratic banners, the beating of drums, the abusing of our opponents, will not help. Nor will any customary platitudes about freedom avail us. We shall have to force our way back to the first principles of human living. For we can no longer take as admitted the old axioms and "self-evident" truths of democracy. It is precisely these which are being attacked and which call for justification. Therefore we have to dig deeper, *below* the old axioms, to discover the ultimate principles on which the axioms themselves depend. And since it is our conception of the good life which is denied, there is nothing for it but to try to discover what reasons we have—apart from tradition and blind faith—for thinking it good. And this cannot be done without examining the notion of goodness itself. We have to dig down to the roots of the tree of good and evil.

The attempt, of course, involves denying the common view that, as between the democratic and the totalitarian sets of values, there is no possibility of finding any common ground. It involves asserting that there is discoverable —however deep down and hidden from the sight of most of us it lies—a point from which the two theories begin to diverge, to branch off from one another, a common place of meeting from the ground of which rational argument can proceed. To discover this is precisely the problem.

Not to make a mystery of the matter, the principle of

the solution is extremely simple, however difficult may be its application in the particular case. Every set of ideals, moral or political, is an outgrowth of some theory—whether explicitly set forth or unconsciously assumed—about *the nature of man*. Therefore to discover whether a set of ideals is true or false we have to ascertain upon what theory of the nature of man it is based, and whether that theory is true or false.

Not that we shall ever, of course, succeed in convincing our totalitarian opponents by any such argument. They do not appeal to reason any more. It is for our own sakes that we make the attempt. We can, in the deep places of our own spirits, justify the faith which is in us. We can replace our own blind allegiance by reasoned understanding. And by doing this we increase our own spiritual strength.

I record my thanks to my friend and colleague Dr. Norman Malcolm for suggestions which were valuable to me in connection with the writing of chapter IX.

Princeton University,   W. T. S.
  August, 1941.

Contents

PART ONE

Good and Evil

CHAPTER I

THE SKEPTICAL ATTITUDE

CIVILIZATION is organized goodness. Here and there in the world an exceptional individual, like a sport of nature, achieves a degree of personal and private excellence so great that he towers head and shoulders above his fellows. The names of such men endure in history as those of heroes and saints. But there exists also a common level of goodness to which ordinary men in any given society may be expected to attain. The organization of this goodness in institutions and customs is the civilization of that society. It follows that we cannot understand the idea of civilization, cannot measure the worth of one civilization against that of another, without first understanding the idea of goodness. We have to begin with the question: What is goodness?

Art, science, philosophy, and religion are also characteristic products of civilization. In appraising a civilization we take them into account. But these presuppose and are themselves based upon some set of ideal ends, some set of beliefs about the nature of the good life. Art is in general a mode of expressing these beliefs and ends. Religion is plainly concerned with them. Science may be pursued either as an end in itself or as a means to material advancement; in either case it is cultivated because it is thought to minister in some way to the good life. Hence however important its science, philosophy, art, or religion may be as products and measures of a civilization, what is fundamental is its conception of goodness. Whether we regard a civilization on the side of its cultural achievements or on the side of its institutions, its laws, its customs, and its political concepts, it is in essence nothing but the expression of some conception of goodness.

In this book I shall have occasion to speak constantly about morality. Indeed, in a sense, the book will be about nothing else. But I wish that I could find some other word to express the same idea. For the word morality, as it is often used, carries with it associations the very reverse of what I intend. It stands, in many minds, for some narrow bigotry about life. It suggests sermons prosy or merely fatuous. It has a puritanical ring which is apt to cause a shudder. Around it floats the aroma of pedantry and pedagogy. Often enough it means nothing more than the outworn conventionality or respectability of the age just past. Against morality in this sense we rebel. For every generation is in revolt against its immediate predecessor—or at least appears to itself to be so. It is morality in this sense which becomes for us an effigy to burn in the market place.

I wish I could find another word. But I cannot. I might invent one, after consulting Greek and Latin dictionaries. But then I should have on my hands some barbarous neologism, some inhuman-sounding technical term which would stamp me forever as the professional pedant. I shall have to use the old word. And all I can do to save myself from disastrous associations is to say at the outset what *I* mean by it. Morality then, I will say, means for me the principles of the good life. And I mean by the good life the life which men themselves feel to be good, healthy, satisfactory, and happy. Everybody, I suppose, wants to live what he feels to be a satisfactory human life. In this sense everyone wants to live a good life. And if morality simply means the best way of living it, there can hardly be a prejudice against morality. Anybody who says that he does not want morality in this sense, or that he rebels against it, or wishes to expel it from life, will be saying what is irrational and has no sense.

Why is the word healthy included among the adjectives descriptive of the good human life? What will be the principles of a healthy life? Will they not be rules of diet, exercise, and medical welfare? And are these to be called moral rules? What I have in mind is the healthy personality rather than the healthy body; I mean to suggest the Platonic idea that morality is the health of the soul, immorality its disease. But even if bodily health be included here, I am not sure that I object. Why should not the precepts that we ought to eat green vegetables, or that we ought to keep our windows open at night for fresh air, be called moral rules? Certainly they belong among the principles of the good life since, if they are neglected, our lives will be sure to become—in one way or another—bad and unsatisfactory lives.

Perhaps this is a kind of snobbishness, this looking down upon the body which is implied in the refusal to apply the word moral to anything other than the affairs of the soul. It is doubtless of greater moment that we love our enemies than that we wash our hands before meals; certainly it is more heroic. Yet washing too contributes to the good life. And it is not certain that the soul and the body can be divided, even distinguished. The body at any rate is a part of me, of the me which wishes to live a satisfactory life. It is entwined with my personality. And even if you define moral rules as those which apply to the personality, the soul, the mind, or what you will, you cannot keep the body out of its affairs.

This snobbishness about morality is among the causes of its unpopularity. It insists upon being soulful. It is a high-flown affair. And so it gets disconnected from the common lives of common men which are neither very soulful nor very high-flown. It gets itself disliked.

I do not believe that there is any sharp division between the rules of physical health and what are conventionally called moral rules. In the end they belong in the same bag. This, at least, will be one of my main contentions. But it is true that it is both possible and convenient to make a rough distinction. And it is true that by a convention of our language the word moral is in general pre-empted as a description of those rules of the good life which concern the personality rather than those which concern the body. I agree to be bound by this convention, and to use the word morality in the commonly accepted sense. But I disavow the snob's motive. And I disassociate myself from the view that it is ridiculous to bring under one rubric the precepts of the moralist and those of the physician. I shall insist that, in the end, they *must* both be brought under one rubric if we are really to understand what morality in its essence is. For both are aimed at good, healthy, sane, happy, valuable human living. Thus they both have the same general end, and both have—I shall try to show—the same sort of final justification. Hence if anyone asks whether the inadvisability of a diet composed exclusively of shellfish is a moral idea, I shall say: Yes, in the large sense, it is, since it has to do with the living of the good life. But in the narrower sense of the word morality, which I shall myself adopt for convenience, the idea is not moral, but rather perhaps medical or dietetic.

Why do I include the word happy in the description of the good life? Does this imply what is commonly called "utilitarianism" or "hedonism," the view that the sole end of life is "happiness," and that happiness means the greatest possible number of "pleasures" and the minimum amount of "pain"? By no means; and I refuse to be dragged into the arid wastes of this discussion. If anyone says that happiness or pleasure is the sole end of life, I suspect that he is led to say this because he is using these words simply as blanket terms to cover everything in life which is good; so that his theory is only a tautology. Or, if anyone denies this theory, I suspect that he is led to deny it because he uses the words happiness and pleasure in a narrower sense which excludes many of the things which are good. And for this dispute I have no relish. But I include the word happy in my description because in my view the moral life is the life which we feel to be satisfactory for a human being; and I do not believe that a man can feel his life to be thoroughly satisfactory if he is unhappy—whatever this term may mean.

There is another ambiguity about the word morality. Usually it is taken as not including politics. But plainly politics has to do with the best way of living our lives. The principles which make for the good life in our individual and private relationships with one another constitute what is conventionally called morality. Political principles concern the best mode of living in so far as our lives are molded by the fact that we live in large groups. No one who wants to know how best to live can leave out the question whether it is better to live in a democracy or under a dictatorship. Therefore the question whether democracy or dictatorship is the better form of government is a moral question. For such reasons the Greeks took it for granted that politics is a branch of morals, and in this respect I shall follow the Greek example.

I shall have to discuss in this book the heritage of our civilization. But the concept of civilization is itself a moral idea. I do not know how to define the term, but whatever else it means it at least implies an attempt to live in a *better* way than did our uncivilized ancestors. To be civilized means in some way to live better; and if moral ideas are those which concern the good life, then civilization is a moral idea. Moreover, I believe that different civilizations are essentially expressions of different moral ideals. It is evident that the totalitarian conception of the good life is quite different from our democratic conception, and that the form of government, the laws, the customs, and the institutions which the totalitarians are seeking to introduce are all attempts to actualize their peculiar moral ideal; likewise that our democratic institutions and our forms of government are expressions of our peculiar idea of the good life. If this is so, then the justification of any particular civilization, the determination of its historical world-value, will in the last analysis consist in a justification of the ethical ideal which it embodies.

We wish to know whether our western Greco-Christian civilization is really, inherently and in its own right, superior to the civilization of the new order which the totalitarian powers are seeking to thrust upon the world. We know already that *we* prefer *our own* order. But is this merely because it is ours, because we are accustomed to it, because it is our tradition, because our blind emotional reactions favor it? Or is it really and in itself superior? Is our preference a mere matter of personal taste? Or is it capable of *rational* justification? This is, in essence, the question which I shall be asking, and I think that there is in the end only one method of answering it. We must first extract from our western democratic civilization its essential ethos, the theory of the good life which it actualizes. We must do the same thing, so far as we can, for totalitarian civilization. We must then compare the two philosophies, the two types of moral ideal, and we must seek to determine, on rational grounds and apart from personal and emotional preferences, which of them is true and which is false; or perhaps one should say, which contains more truth, which more falsehood.

This involves the profoundly difficult problem: how to find a rational and impartial criterion for judging between two disparate types of moral ideal.

It will be denied by many that there is the slightest possibility of finding such a criterion. For how are we to judge, as between two moral ideals, which is the better, except by employing some standard of better and worse? And where is this standard to come from, if not from one of the very two moralities which are being judged? Yet if it does come from one of them, we are obviously involved in a vicious circle. Of course, if we judge the two civilizations by some standard derived from the Greco-Christian idea of the good life, we shall decide in favor of the Greco-Christian civilization; but if we use a standard derived from the totalitarian conception of the good life, we shall decide in favor of the totalitarian type of civilization. On the other hand, the idea of a standard which is not derived from either, but which stands above both, seems impossible. What are we to do in this impasse?

Moreover, our whole enterprise implies the assumption that there is such a thing as truth in moral principles, that some moral ideas can be called true, others false. We are going to ask, it seems, whether the ethical ideal which is embodied in our western civilization is more *true* than the ethical ideal which is the substance of a possible new type of civilization. But what is the meaning of truth when that word is applied to a moral principle? Is there really any such thing? Can one say that a moral idea is true in the same sense that a scientific principle—say the law of gravitation—is true?

The assumption which I am making—namely that there is truth or falsity in moral ideas—is one which not only can be, but has been and is, widely denied. I shall call the denial of it moral skepticism. Moral skepticism may be defined as the denial that any moral principles are true.

Such skepticism, if well-founded, would block completely the enterprise which I am undertaking in this book. It would invalidate the entire argument which is to be unfolded in the following chapters. For if *no* set of moral ideas is true, then plainly we cannot measure the worth of civilizations by the truth of the moral ideas which they embody. Either civilizations are not in fact one better or higher than another—in which case we have no real right to think ourselves better than barbarians—or their comparative superiority or inferiority has nothing to do with the truth of their immanent moral ideas. I shall accordingly begin by taking up this problem.

Perhaps the first recorded appearance of moral skepticism in history is a type of opinion which is to be found among the Greek Sophists. According to one version, as recorded by Plato, man is by nature like any other animal. In the essential laws of his conduct he resembles a cock, a tiger, or a horse. The only natural principle of behavior is therefore that each man should gratify his desires and his instincts, should get all that he can for himself to the utmost of his power and regardless of the interests of other persons. Following this rule the strong will get the most, the weak little or nothing. The desires of men are, of course, many and complicated, while those of the animal are simple and few. But this makes no difference to the fundamental law of nature which is that each shall grab what he can for himself. This is the only principle of conduct which has any sanction in nature.

But in actual society we find that this principle does not operate to the full. It is restricted and hampered by the agencies of law, morality, and religion, and by the notion of 'justice' which they foster. This idea of justice tends to protect the weak from the strong. It teaches that the weak have 'rights' as against the strong. This is a new idea, new in the sense that it is not found in nature but has somehow been invented by man. How has this happened? How did law, morality, religion, and the idea of justice arise?

Callicles, one of the Sophists, gave the following answer to the question: "The makers of laws," he said, "are the majority who are weak; and they make laws and distribute praises and censures with a view to themselves and their own interests; and they terrify the stronger sort of men, and those who are able to get the better of them." [1] Thrasymachus, in the "Republic," gives in a sense an opposite account of the matter. For he asserts that it is the strong who make laws and invent the idea of justice in their own interests.[2] But in spite of the apparent opposition, the two opinions join in the fundamental belief that justice and morality are fraudulent ideas put forth by one set of people

[1] Plato, "Gorgias," in "The Dialogues of Plato," translated by B. Jowett, volume 1, page 543; Random House, New York, 1937.
[2] Plato, "Republic," in "The Dialogues of Plato," translated by B. Jowett, volume 1, page 603; Random House, New York, 1937.

to deceive another set. In the one case they are devices of
the weak to protect themselves against the strong. In the
other case they are devices of the few strong men for
keeping the many weak in subjection. Both opinions are
skeptical in that they deny any real truth or validity to
moral principles.

Philosophical egoism, as preached by Hobbes in the seventeenth century and by a great many other people before
and since, is also a kind of moral skepticism. It is not pure
skepticism, but it has a skeptical flavor. It may be said to
consist essentially of two assertions: (1) that there are true
moral principles, but (2) that they are all founded on pure
selfishness. This is not pure skepticism because it admits
moral principles. But its second assertion gives it a skeptical
twist. Morality, it says, is only intelligent selfishness. Thus,
though it admits morality, it denies the nobility of being
moral. The good man is not more noble than the bad man—
he is only cleverer; his motives are the same, but his method
is different. Both men have the same ends, their private
advantage; they differ only as to the means. There is no
such thing in the world as a genuine disinterested goodness.
What is denied is that the difference between the good man
and the bad man is what most people would understand as
a *moral* difference; it is merely a difference of intelligence
or cunning. This opinion is founded upon a false account
of human motives. It proceeds from an abstraction, like the
economic man. It oversimplifies human nature. But just because of its false simplicity it keeps on cropping up in the
history of thought.

Forms of skepticism more characteristically modern are
the theories of morals propounded respectively by the
schools of the so-called ethical relativists and logical positivists. The theory of the first is largely the result of the in-

vestigations of anthropological sociologists. It emphasizes
the immense variety of so-called moral codes in the world—
particularly those of uncivilized peoples—and the impossibility of reconciling them or finding in them any common
core of ethical thought or feeling. It is a delusion to suppose
that human beings are universally agreed on any single
question of right or wrong. There is nothing, thought
wrong in one country or age, which is not thought right in
another. The customs of a people can make anything whatsoever appear right or wrong to that people. The conclusion is that there is no universal or common moral standard
by which all these particular codes can be judged. Each is
its own standard. Each is good for itself and from its own
point of view. There is no possibility of saying that one
is better or higher than another. There is no possibility of
saying that one moral principle is true in a sense which
would imply that another and opposite principle is false.
In a sphere of universal relativity, where all is shifting,
where there are no objective standards, truth and falsehood
have no meaning.

Those who call themselves logical positivists tend to
come to very similar conclusions, but on somewhat different grounds. They emphasize that in the sphere of the
sciences nothing can be called true which is not at least
theoretically capable of being verified by observation. No
one has actually observed the change of biological species
involved in the evolution of man from his simian ancestors.
Yet it is the sort of thing which could have been observed,
and the details of which could have been recorded, by an
imaginary observer if he had lived a few million years, or
by a series of observers handing on their records to one
another. Again, no one has ever seen the back of the moon.
But to say that the statement "the moon has a back" is a

true statement means that, if one could travel in a space-ship to a certain position in space, one would be able to observe certain phenomena. Even the statement that elec-trons exist must either mean that they could be observed in certain conditions (very difficult to imagine), or it is not, in the strict sense, true. If the scientist disallows even the theoretical observability of his electrons, then we shall have to say that the statement that they exist is only true in the Pickwickian sense that it affords a useful means of predict-ing certain facts which *can* be directly observed.

Now it is obviously impossible, by watching a human action, actually to observe its rightness or wrongness. I can *feel* it to be right or wrong, and I can no doubt in some sense observe my own feelings about it. But I cannot ob-serve the moral characters of the act as actual objective qualities of it. Suppose I see a man stab another with a dagger. There are all kinds of things which I can observe: the gleam of the dagger, the swiftness or slowness of its movement through the air, the expression on the murder-er's face, the groan of the victim, his fall to the ground, and a thousand other things. But I cannot possibly observe the character of wrongness which the action is supposed to have. This is an attribute which I may perhaps attribute to it as a result of my own feelings of anger or disgust. But it is not an attribute which I can find in the outward physical act itself.

The reason for this is obvious. When I say that the action is wrong, what I mean is that it is one which *ought* not to occur. And if I say, of another action, that it is right, what I mean is that it is the sort of action which, in my opinion, *ought* to occur. But it is plain that I can only observe what *is* the case, never what *ought* to be the case. If I look at something through a microscope I can, no matter how skilled an observer I am, only see what actually *is* there before my eyes. It is plainly impossible that I should ever observe what is not there but only—in my opinion—ought to be there.

Nor is this equivalent to saying that only statements about physical things can be true. It is not necessarily materialism—although it is often interpreted in that way. For even if I suppose that there are nonmaterial entities which can be observed—by a spiritual eye, perhaps—it will still be true that I can only observe the characters which they actually have, not characters which they merely ought to have.

Thus since rightness and wrongness are the sort of things which could never conceivably be observed, statements such as "this is right" or "this is wrong" cannot be called either true or false. They are not actual attributes which things or actions objectively have.

Logical positivists usually go on to say that ethical statements, since they do not refer to objective facts about anything outside us, only express our own feelings or emotions. When I say "this is wrong" the only meaning the statement has is "this disgusts me," or "this makes me angry," or "I don't like this." They are really to be compared with statements like "this sugar is nice." Nobody supposes that the sugar has a quality of niceness in the same sense as it has a quality of whiteness. "Sugar is nice" is merely a way of saying "I like sugar." It is really a statement, not about the sugar, but about me or my feelings.

On this view there is nothing which is really, in itself, right or wrong, good or bad. Hence a moral principle cannot be, in any real sense, true. Nor can it be in any real sense false. For it merely expresses our own subjective reactions to things and situations in the world. But truth and falsehood refer only to statements which tell us that something is, or is not, the case in the world. Moral principles are merely emotional. And emotions are neither true nor false. They simply exist.

Moreover, emotions and feelings vary from person to person and from culture to culture. Actions which disgust us may very well delight the inhabitants of New Guinea. Hence the same action which they call good we should call bad. And we come round to an opinion very much like that of the ethical relativists. There are no *true* principles of right and wrong because there are no objective standards. And hence there is no real meaning in inquiring whether a moral principle is true or not. It can at most amount to an inquiry whether we like that principle, or perhaps whether most of the members of the society to which we belong like it.

There are many different kinds of moral skepticism, and a few of them have been very briefly illustrated. If any of them are true, there can be no use in asking our question whether the ethical principles which underlie our Greco-Christian civilization are truer than those which underlie totalitarian civilization. We shall only be able to say that we prefer our own kind of civilization, but we shall not be able to give any valid reasons for this. We shall have to admit that our preference is in the end perfectly irrational and incapable of justification. And there are many people who would in fact say this. I am not one of them, and I do not accept this conclusion.

It is part of my thesis that some moral principles are true, others false. And I believe that the words true and false here mean exactly what they mean in science, or in common-sense language. I believe that a moral principle can be true in exactly the same sense as the law of gravitation is true.

But it must be confessed that this is a very bold statement. There *seems* to be some difference between scientific and ethical statements. For it does look, on the face of it, as if a principle such as "we ought to be unselfish" cannot be true in quite the same sense as the law of gravitation is true. It seems to be a different sort of statement. And yet we vaguely feel that there must be *some* sense in which Christian moral principles, say, are truer or better or higher or more valid than the moral principles of Australian savages. We feel dissatisfied with the various skepticisms. However good their reasoning, they leave us with the sense that something profoundly important has been left out by them. What is this something? In what sense are we to interpret our strong feeling that there is, there must be, some way in which moral ideas are valid, have some kind of objective justification?

The only way in which we can decide this, I think, will be to examine the origin and nature of our ideas of goodness.

CHAPTER II

THE ORIGIN OF THE IDEA OF GOODNESS

THE first inquirers into the validity of moral ideas were Sophists such as Callicles and Thrasymachus. And it seems to me important to realize that, whatever we may think of their conclusions, their *method* of inquiry at any rate was correct. Their conclusion was that moral principles are not valid, not true; they are false, fraudulent. Their method was to inquire into the *origin* of such ideas as that of justice. How did this idea ever arise? Since it does not exist in nature, i.e., in the subhuman world, they argued that it must have been the invention of some man or men. *It had a human origin.* Following this clue they surmised that it was the weak—or the strong, it does. not matter which—who spread about this idea of justice for the purpose of gaining their own ends. And since this was the origin of the idea of justice, it could be seen at once that it had no genuine validity, being in essence nothing but a method of outwitting one's rivals in the struggle of life. This theory was hasty and based upon entirely insufficient inquiry. But if we are to judge of the truth, or validity, or objectivity, or value—whatever we may discover these vague terms to mean—of ethical ideas, it is certainly vital to know how they arose, whether they bear upon them the stamp of a human or a divine origin, whether they are natural, supernatural, or artificial. Thus the question of the origin of morals is not, as we ask it here, a question of their history—at any rate not of their detailed history—but rather of their inner nature.

There are two theories of the origin and nature of morals; or rather there are many theories, but all of them belong to one or other of two types. The first is the theory of *morality as imposed*. The second is the theory of *morality as immanent*.[1] According to the latter, morality is immanent in man; in some way it grows out of, and expresses, his own nature. Its origin is from within himself. According to the former, moral principles are imposed upon man from some outside source. Their origin is external to him.

European ethical thinking derives from two sources, Greece and Palestine. The immanentist stream of thought comes from Greece, the impositionist stream from Palestine. For the Greeks morality grew out of human nature. For the Hebrew prophets it was imposed upon man by Jehovah. This latter idea was taken up into the Christian tradition. With the triumph of Christianity over paganism Greek immanentism was practically wiped out. Imposition theories dominated the whole thought of Europe through the Middle Ages and down to the present day. Almost all ethical philosophies of modern Europe have been variants of the imposition theory. Very recently there have been signs of a revival of immanentism.

[1] I have adopted the antithesis of "immanent" and "imposed" from a chapter in Whitehead's "Adventures of Ideas" (Macmillan, 1933). But in Whitehead it has nothing to do with the theory of morality. It is used by him in connection with natural laws such as the principle of gravitation.

Morality as Imposed

The simplest theory of this type, the origin and exemplar of all such theories, is the view that moral principles are commands arbitrarily imposed upon men by God. According to the crudest form of this view God is pictured as a potentate giving laws to His subjects.

The question then arises whether God commands morality because it is good, or whether it is good because God commands it. The latter view puts God above morality, and so makes Him nonmoral in His own nature. Cruelty or lying are vicious because God says so, but if He had happened to have commanded them, instead of forbidding them, they would have possessed the character of virtues. The former view puts morality above God, thus making Him subject to a law of which He is not the author. Morality is then not only superhuman, but superdivine. It takes much theological ingenuity to wriggle out of this dilemma. But owing to the general decline of supernaturalism, the theory of morality as the imposition of a divine autocrat no longer exerts much direct influence.

Nevertheless it molded the general European climate of opinion. With it as a background nearly all European ethical philosophizing has been carried on. Its influence can be traced even in secular theories which seem to repudiate, or at least to ignore, all religious presuppositions. These secular theories leave out God as the imposer of morality, but the general idea of imposition remains. If not God, then some other external agency imposes moral principles upon us.

Thus indirectly the influence of the theological theory has been, and still is, enormous. It is the original pattern of all imposition theories. Nonreligious theories of this type have come into existence just because the original theological theory has decayed. They are secular substitutes for it. Through long ages of religious faith it had come to be taken for granted that moral principles must be thought of as commands laid upon man from the outside. The Greek immanentist view was overwhelmed by Palestinian and Christian influences, was swept aside, buried, and almost forgotten.

Through the early Christian epoch and throughout the Middle Ages the imposition theory reigned supreme—in its theological form. And it bred in European man a habit of mind which has persisted with the decay of religious dogma and still remains. It is extraordinarily difficult for us now to cast our thoughts in any other mold. Imposition has become a fixed idea, a need. There must be an outside source of moral principles. If it is not God, it must be something else. It is for this reason that the notion of what is called objectivity became of supreme importance in modern discussions of morals. The great problem was supposed to be whether, and in what sense, moral laws could be objective. To be objective meant to be outside us in the same sort of sense in which objects in space and time are outside us, and in which God too is outside us. Thus it was assumed that unless the source of ethical principles is external to man, they could not be valid or true. And this tacit assumption is an offshoot of Palestinian impositionism.

Thus there arose a variety of theories which, though purporting to be based upon independent scientific or philosophical grounds, are in reality attempts to satisfy a habit of mind engendered in us by centuries of religious thought. As psychologists tell us that a crude animal desire may be sublimated into some ideal aim, so are these theories sublimations of the crude belief that morality is a set of arbitrary commands laid upon us by a God conceived as like an oriental potentate.

One such theory is that morality is somehow rooted in the structure of the universe, or in the Absolute, which is the metaphysician's substitute for God. Since it seems clear that moral laws are not to be found, like the law of gravitation, in the physical world; since morality is in some sense spiritual, the world itself—in order that moral laws may be supposed to be inherent in it—is said to be spiritual in its essence. This theory of morals, known as idealism, is plainly an attenuated version of the theological theory, and a form of impositionism.

At the beginning of the twentieth century a school of thinkers made their appearance in England and America who became known as the realists. They were opposed to the idealists. Some of them held that goodness is a kind of *quality* which things or states of affairs may have. They were supposed to have this quality in something the same sort of way as things may have the qualities of yellowness or hardness. Morality is founded upon the recognition by the mind of this objective quality of goodness in things. This is plainly to put morality upon a nonreligious basis (although there is no reason to call it antireligious). Yet it does not shake itself free from impositionism. For the source of goodness is still external to man's mind. It is a character of things in the external world which imposes itself as a brute fact upon the mind just as does a physical property of matter. Thus this theory is simply a secular form of impositionism, and is, in spite of its freedom from the concept of God, a lineal descendant of the view that God imposes the moral law upon man.[1]

[1] This paragraph, with its summary and rather crude exposition of the realist view, would probably not be a correct representation if taken as

At the root of all such theories is a superstitious view of the world. I do not mean that belief in God is a superstition. But the view of God as an arbitrary potentate issuing commands—and it is from this view that all imposition theories are lineal descendants—is a superstitious view of God. God may be, in some way, the Author of the whole world. What is superstitious is not this belief, but the belief that one can pick out from among all the phenomena of the world certain particular phenomena—because they happen to be surprising, or terrifying, or mysterious, or admirable —and suppose that they are due to an immediate act of God in a sense in which this is not true of the rest of creation. Nobody ought to call Sir Arthur Eddington unscientific because, or if, he believes—rightly or wrongly—that the Originator of all things is a Divine Mind. But if a scientist should explain a particular physical phenomenon as being caused by an act of God, instead of by an antecedent physical cause, he would be immediately and rightly condemned. And just as it is a mark of primitive thinking to explain a clap of thunder as caused by God's anger, instead of by electrical charges, so it is equally primitive and superstitious to explain moral principles as caused by God's wishes and commands, instead of by psychological principles in man's own mind. In this sense the theological theory of imposition is superstitious. And in spite of the nontheological character of modern imposition theories, the aroma of superstition hangs around them as it did around their theological ancestor.

It is interesting to inquire whether Kant's theory of morality belongs to the impositionist or the immanentist

---

a statement of the theory of Professor G. E. Moore, the founder of the school. But it is a fair statement of the view as maintained by many of his followers.

tradition. At first sight there would appear to be a difficulty in classifying him. According to his view the source of morality is reason. Now this was also the view of the greatest Greek philosophers, and in a sense Kant is here following the Greek or immanentist tradition. For the gift of reason is a human attribute. It is part of human nature. Plato would have called it a "part of the soul." But when we read Kant we find that for him reason is not a human thing, but an impersonal abstraction. This is the source of the ambiguity which causes us to hesitate concerning the heading, immanentist or impositionist, under which to place Kant. According to him, morality depends on reason in the following way. He supposed that every immoral action involves a logical contradiction in the principles on which we act. When I do wrong, therefore, I contradict myself, and am in that sense irrational. When I do right, on the other hand, no contradiction will be found in the principles on which I am acting. In this case, therefore, I am acting self-consistently and therefore rationally. Hence right action is action in accordance with reason. Wrong action is illogical, inconsistent action, which infringes the principles of reason.

For instance, a man who refuses to help those who are in distress will nevertheless expect others to help him when he is in distress. This involves an inconsistency or contradiction in his principles. For his refusal to help implies the principle "no one ought to help others in distress." But at the same time he thinks, when it comes to a case in which he is in trouble himself, "people ought to help others in distress." Thus the man contradicts himself. For his act implies two principles, one of which contradicts the other.

Subsequent criticism has shown, I think, that Kant's theory cannot be maintained, and that logical contradiction is not necessarily involved even in actions which would be universally condemned as immoral.

But we are not concerned with the criticism of Kant's views. The question of interest for us is whether this theory is impositionist or immanentist. And in attempting to answer this question we seem to be embarrassed by the ambiguous position of reason. According to Kant, morality originates in reason. It is an expression of man's rationality. And this looks like an immanentist theory. For reason, one supposes, is simply one element in human nature, like emotion, desire, will, or sensation. So that morality, because it is an expression of man's reason, is an expression of his inner psychological nature.

But Kant's own explicit statements warn us that this is not his view. No doubt he would admit that there is a sense in which reason is an element of the human mind. But by reason here Kant means the laws of logic. And the laws of logic are laws of the universe in general, not mere psychological laws. For instance, it is a law of logic that a thing cannot both have an attribute and not have it. This is the famous law of contradiction which, it can easily be shown, is basic to all reasoning. But although we must think in accordance with this law if we are to think correctly, the law itself is a law about the world outside us. The leaf cannot be both green and not green. The wheel cannot be both circular and not circular. This law thus applies to leaves, wheels, and all other things in the universe. There is nothing psychological about it, except that we have to think in accordance with it if we are not to make mistakes. Now it is on reason, or logic, in this objective or non-psychological sense that Kant bases morality.

That he is not basing morality on human nature is clear from such statements as the following: "Moral philosophy does not borrow the least thing from the knowledge of man himself." [1] Statements of this sort abound in his writings. The elements of human nature, such as feelings, inclinations, sensations, desires, so he is constantly telling us, are variable. But morality must be, according to him, a universal law, absolutely the same for everyone, the same indeed for every rational being in the universe. For this reason, morality cannot be founded on the shifting characteristics of human beings, since this would give us, not morality, but many divergent moralities.

Thus it is clear that for Kant reason is put at the basis of morality precisely because it is *not* merely a part of human nature. He compares morality to mathematics. He thinks that it is forced upon us from the outside in identically the same sense as the principle that $2 + 2 = 4$ is forced upon us. Moral principles would not cease to be true if human nature were to change any more than arithmetical principles would. They would not cease to be true even if the human race were wiped out of existence. Thus morality does not arise out of human nature. It is imposed upon us by the nature of the world. And Kant appears after all as an upholder of the theory of morality as imposed.[2]

Morality as Immanent

Greek ethics was overwhelmingly immanentist. And the greatest exponent of the theory of morality as immanent

[1] Kant; Selections, by T. M. Greene, p. 269, Scribners.
[2] It may be objected that according to Kant's doctrine of the "autonomy of the will" the moral law is self-imposed. This matter is too technical and difficult to be discussed here. However, I have not overlooked the point. And it seems clear to me that the autonomy of the will does not take Kant's theory out of the category of impositionism. The "self" which imposes the moral law is not anything which can be called human nature or an element of it. It transcends all particular individuals, and is an inhabitant of another world.

who ever lived was Plato. There are to be found in Plato, it is true, strong suggestions of the opposite theory. These suggestions are all connected with the famous theory of ideas or forms. It is not necessary for us to examine them. Suffice it to say that for Plato the form of the good is an eternal and immutable reality, which exists timelessly in the world, and which is independent of the existence of men, or of other living things, or indeed of particular things of any kind. Men, and indeed all created things, can strive to pattern themselves after the likeness of the form of the good. In this way goodness appears as something external to man and not arising out of human nature. And it may fairly be said that this is a form of impositionism. Yet in spite of this, the theory of morality as immanent is not only found in Plato, but moreover it reached in his dialogues a peak of development never excelled before or since. He is, and will probably always remain, the greatest prophet of the immanent view.

In what I shall have to say here I shall leave out wholly that entire side of his philosophy which tends towards the theory of imposition. And if my aim were to expound the philosophy of Plato, I should be open to the charge of drawing a one-sided picture of it. But I am concerned only to explain the theory of morality as immanent. And for this purpose it is unnecessary to examine that part of his teaching which tends towards impositionism.

Nor shall I consider the question whether Plato's own thought, including as it does two opposite tendencies, is radically in contradiction with itself, or whether there lies in it any principle of inner reconciliation. This again is of interest only to Platonic scholars; I will merely suggest that we ought not to expect or demand too great a measure of consistency in a mind so supremely fertile in ideas of all kinds as that of Plato. Somewhere or other in his writings we can find the suggestion of almost every philosophical tendency, thought, idea, and attitude of which the human mind seems to be capable. They are, as Whitehead has re-marked, "an inexhaustible mine of suggestion" with a "wealth of general ideas scattered through them." The in-clusion of inconsistent ideas is likely to be a part of the price we pay for this wealth.

In spite of Plato's occasional suggestions to the contrary, the characteristic view of the Greeks was immanentist. Plato was indeed a Greek to the marrow. Yet his was also a universal mind which transcended the limits of race. Greek ethical thought in general was bound to be imma-nentist because the background of it did not contain the idea of a single righteous supreme God. This idea has been the natural precondition of the theory of morality as im-posed. As we have seen, all theories of this type are lineal descendants of the Palestinian cosmology. Greek religion was, in the first place, polytheistic. Thereby at once the gods appear as mere parts of the world, not as first princi-ples of it. They are not above the universe, but in it. They are not pristine sources of anything, and therefore not of goodness. Secondly, these gods are not in any sense righteous. The Greek philosophers were constantly com-plaining of the immorality attributed to the gods by the poets and the popular religion. They lied, stole, cheated, and committed adultery. Not from such a source could it be supposed that morality is derived. Thus it was inevitable that morality should be ascribed to a human, not a divine, origin. It did not descend upon men from outside. It must have grown out of human nature itself.

This ethical humanism accorded well with the paganism of the ancient world. Paganism is nothing but the natural self-expression of the unabashed man, who delights in his own human nature and believes in it, to whom it has not yet occurred to stand ashamed or frightened before a judge who imposes commands upon him. The Greek gods were themselves joyful pagan superheroes disporting themselves on hilltops. Paganism and humanism are in essence the same thing. And both were rendered impossible, were rooted out of the world, by the triumph of Palestinian ideas of man's relation to the universe. Greece was finally conquered, not by Rome, but by Palestine.

The famous controversy whether man is by nature good or by nature evil still divides us, and achieves its peculiar poignancy in our minds by reason of the fact that there are both Greek and Palestinian elements in our culture which we have failed to reconcile and which are still at war with one another in our hearts. For it is characteristic of the immanentist theory of morals to hold that man is by nature good. This is not an accidental connection of ideas. It is necessary. For the goodness which is morality cannot grow out of human nature if that nature is not in itself implicitly good. But in the Palestinian view man is by nature "desperately wicked." And this again is not accidental. If morality is externally imposed upon man, this takes for granted that it is not in him naturally and originally. Also for this reason paganism is associated in our minds with the joy of life, Palestinian philosophy with its gloom. Christian apologists are apt to assume that a gloomy puritanical morality is not necessary to Christianity, but a distortion of it. A distortion, or at least an exaggeration, it may well be. But puritanism emphasizes that morality is put upon us by force, against our natural wills, and that it must in consequence be unpleasant. And it cannot be denied that the seed of this lies in the theory of morality as imposed. A joyful Christian

morality, such as that of St. Francis of Assisi, has something
of paganism in it. Also the never ending question whether
the good man is he whose goodness seems spontaneous,
temperamental, natural to him, or he who through strenu-
ous battling of the will has overcome the forces of evil
within him, derives from the coexistence in our civilization
of these same unreconciled Greek and Palestinian elements.

In baldest outline the history of ethics has three stages.
It began in the Greek world with the view of morals as
immanent. Then came the era of theology and the conse-
quent theories of morality as imposed. This stage has lasted
nearly two thousand years until well within our own times.
The third stage seems to be now beginning. It consists in a
return to Greek humanism, not of course to the wooden
reproduction of any particular Greek theory, but to the
underlying spirit. It consists in a return to the general view
of morality as immanent. This tendency is evincing itself,
as we shall see later, in the writings of many contemporary
thinkers, who are, in respect of detail, widely divergent
from one another.

We must return to the beginning of the subject. The
first immanentists were the Greek Sophists, of whom we
may take Callicles and Thrasymachus as typical. They appealed to the nature of man. They taught that this nature
is in essence identical with that of the animal. Man is simply
an animal. But the law of the animal world is that the
strong should seize whatever they can while the weak
perish. This was the only law of conduct sanctioned by
nature, and since man is merely an animal, it should apply
to him too.

But then it is evident that other and very different ideas
have arisen among men, ideas of justice and law and so-
called morality. How are these to be accounted for? They

too must somehow be explained as originating in human nature. It is true that the Sophists stressed the antithesis between nature and law. Law and justice were not natural but artificial. In this sense of nature, morality does not arise out of nature. But it does arise, the Sophists thought, from human nature. The artificial, in fact, is simply what is produced by what is peculiar in man's nature, what he does not share with the animals. For in spite of their general assimilation of the human to the animal, they had to admit that there is some difference. But what they seized upon as peculiar to man, that which differentiates him from the animals, is that he is capable of fraud and cunning in pursuit of his ends, while the animals are not. The ends of men and animals are the same, to grab each for himself whatever he can. But the animal is directed to his ends by mere impulse, the man by intelligence which he uses, however, only to outwit his neighbors. Thus the Sophist theory of morality was that it grew out of human nature, and out of what is specific in human nature; but that this is merely the capacity for cunning and deception. The Sophists did not express themselves precisely in this way, but rather in terms of the antithesis between nature and law. This is, nevertheless, the upshot of their philosophy.

There were two ways in which this theory was crude and defective, and the advance of later Greek immanentism consisted in the progressive elimination of these defects. The first defect was that the Sophists had failed to mark the difference between *invention* and *expression*. They thought that morality is an invention of human intelligence, whereas in fact it is an expression of human nature. An invention is something which, having issued from the mind, detaches itself from us and becomes external. An expression remains a part of that which it expresses. Man invented the steam engine, but the steam engine is in no sense a part of man. An expression is organic to what it expresses and cannot be separated from it. In this sense a flower expresses itself in the beauty of its petals, an artist in the beauty of his art. Although a poem may be printed in books which circulate a thousand miles from the poet, yet this mechanical reproduction, the printed page, is not the true poem. *That* consists in the poet's own utterance as it issues in words which he sings or chants or speaks or merely imagines in his heart, and afterwards records on paper.

The Sophists thought that morality is a contrivance, a device, an invention. It is a trick which certain clever men had thought of to deceive people, as one might contrive a snare to put out in the woods to catch animals. If this were so, morality could not be anything good *in itself*. For it would be a mere instrument. The good presumably would be that towards which it was instrumental—the riches, the power, the satisfaction of our desires which it helped us to obtain.

The superiority of the later view, the developed view that morality is an *expression* of human nature, is that it makes provision for our feeling of the goodness of goodness. For the self-expression of an organic being is an end in itself for that being. It is the triumph of that life, the supreme happiness and success of it. Therein it achieves itself. The plant, if it could feel, would find joy in its flowering, apart from any external ends. The phrase about the flower "wasting its sweetness on the desert air" reveals a blindness to the secret of life. For the flower does not grow to be put in a vase in a lady's boudoir. It achieves its goodness and its happiness in the tiny universe of its own self-expression. Unseen in the desert it does not "waste its sweetness." Rather it wastes its sweetness in the boudoir. Those who deeply sympathize with flowers feel a pang at this violation of their being. And it is because the supreme good of each life lies in its self-expression that poets, painters, and musicians are willing to starve in garrets rather than deny their art. This too is the reason why we feel that morality is an end in itself, and why we use phrases such as that we ought to do what is right for its own sake, and that virtue is its own reward. These sayings will be true if moral goodness is a genuine expression of human nature—which is the true and developed immanentist doctrine.

This was the secret which Plato perceived as against the crude and immature immanentism of the Sophists. It is the nerve of the argument by which he seeks to establish his famous doctrine that the good man is necessarily happy. Even if his goodness gains no external reward, even if it leads to nothing beyond itself, he has, according to Plato, his happiness in the mere fact of being good. Why? Because morality is simply the harmonious functioning of all the elements of human personality, which is another way of saying that it is the proper expression of man's self.

The full details of Plato's theory cannot be given here; we must rest with the outstanding points. Human personality, he thinks, has three essential "parts." A modern would not use this word parts, owing to its spatial implications. We should perhaps speak of the elements, or aspects, or faculties, of the mind—although to the word faculty objection has also been taken. But we need not here concern ourselves with fine verbal points; and it will be convenient to use Plato's own term.

The three parts of the soul, then, in his view, are reason, spirit, and appetite. None of these terms is defined with scientific precision. But their meaning is fairly clear. Reason is intellect or intelligence. It is the faculty of knowing and thinking. It is that which men possess and animals do not. Appetite refers either chiefly or wholly to such physical, sensuous appetites as hunger, thirst, and sex. Spirit is the principle which makes men or animals spirited, in the sense in which we talk of a spirited horse or a man of spirit. It is, according to Plato, the root of ambition, bravery, and love of honor.

This tripartite division of personality is no doubt open to criticism on various grounds of psychology. For instance, what Plato calls spirit ought surely not to be classified as a distinct faculty or part of the mind along with reason and appetite. It is a quality rather than a faculty. No one would think of calling stubbornness, cleverness, stupidity, or determination a faculty of the mind. They are qualities. And spiritedness seems to go along with them rather than with reason and appetite.

Again, Plato's classification is certainly not complete and all-inclusive. To give only one instance, where is one to place sympathy? It is not a character of reason. It is not a physical appetite. And I cannot see that it has anything to do with spirit. Sympathy is, of course, emotional in character. And there is no clear place for the emotions in Plato's scheme, though they have something in common with appetite and something in common with spirit.

These criticisms, however, are of very little importance in assessing the value of Plato's contribution to the theory of morality. For, as we shall see, his general idea of the essential nature of morality will stand, even if the psychological details cannot be maintained. His general idea of morality was that it consists in the harmonious working together of the different parts of the soul, so as to achieve the welfare of the whole. Each part has its proper function. And harmony, or in other words morality, arises when each part performs its proper function and keeps to that alone. The function of reason is to control, to rule; of the appetites to be controlled, to obey; and of spirit to be the "ally" of reason and to see that its commands are carried out. *Morality is thus the harmonious working of human personality through the proper functioning of each of its parts.*

The notion of *proper function* is of central importance here. It may best be explained by referring to the functions of our physical organs. No one would deny that each organ of the body has a proper function. For instance, that of the heart is to pump blood, that of the lungs to purify the blood, that of the stomach to digest food, etc. If every one of the bodily organs fulfills its function in the economy of the whole, we have what we call a state of health. If not, we have ill-health. Plato's belief is that exactly the same applies to the mind or personality. And morality is to the mind exactly what health is to the body. If the parts of the soul function each according to its nature we have morality; if not, immorality.

What ground can Plato possibly have for asserting that the function of reason is to govern, of the appetites to be governed? One may answer by asking what ground we have for saying that it is the function of the heart to pump blood or of the stomach to digest food. The answer in this case obviously is that in normal and healthy men we find the heart and the stomach actually doing these things; and that if, in some particular case, they do not do them, we find that sort of unsatisfactory state of the body which we call ill-health. Just so, Plato argues, you find in normal and healthy-minded men that their appetites are ruled by their intelligence; while on the contrary a man who is ruled by his appetites is precisely what we call a bad man or a man suffering from ill-health of the soul. Suppose a very thirsty man in the presence of stagnant water. The appetite of thirst impels him to drink. His reason warns him not to. It is clear in this case that his reason ought to govern his appetite; and in the normal and healthy-minded man it does so. Only in the mentally and morally inferior man will appetite win. Again, the thief is the man whose desire for gold runs away with him; the honest man controls his desires through his intelligence.

This leads Plato to the view that the good man is he in whom reason controls appetite, the bad man he in whom appetite controls reason. This is his view of the essences of morality and immorality respectively. And further, control of appetite by reason means in practice moderation in the indulgence of the appetites. Control of reason by the appetites means excessive indulgence. The drunkard is ruled by his desire for drink. The temperate man will allow this desire a moderate amount of satisfaction, but he keeps it well in control; and what controls it is in the end his intelligence or reason. Thus moderation in all things, the golden mean, becomes the Platonic, as well as in general the Greek, moral ideal.

There is much in the line of thought thus rapidly sketched which is debatable. As to the psychology it is open to question whether reason can properly be said directly to influence desire. And even if it can, the rule of reason over passion, and the ideal of moderation, though they may be important elements of human goodness, are certainly not the whole of it. Can the heroic self-sacrifice of the Christian saints and martyrs, and of the Founder of the Christian religion, be brought within the limits of the Platonic formula? I think not. Some of these doubtful questions we shall have occasion to discuss in subsequent chapters; for the moment, we may pass them by in order to consider the great elements of truth which Plato's theory certainly contains.

First of all, this is a genuine immanentism. Morality is not conceived as a sort of strait jacket clapped upon man by an external agency; it is the product of human nature itself. It arises out of the interrelation of the internal factors of man's peculiar personality, his reason, his appetite, and his spirit.

Secondly, it advances beyond sophistic immanentism by making morality a genuine expression of human nature, not a mere invention. Human goodness is now seen as that mode of life in which a human personality is operating naturally and normally. If one examines its parts and their functions, one finds that its *nature* is that reason should rule over appetite. It is the nature of a plant to have its roots in the ground, its leaves and flowers in the air. And this is so because the proper functions of its parts, roots, leaves, and flowers, are what they are. To reverse this position, to put the roots in the air, the leaves and flowers in the ground, would constitute an unnatural condition for the plant. Just so, to reverse the natural positions of reason and appetite, to put appetite above reason, is an unnatural condition for a man. Morality is therefore the expression of man's essential nature.

Thirdly, the Platonic view gives a meaning to the conception of the truth, or objectivity, or validity, of moral principles. We saw in the first chapter that although we have a vague feeling—as against the moral skeptic—that moral principles must be in some sense true or valid or objective, we were utterly unable to attach any definite meaning to this idea. Plato supplies at least a possible answer to our problem. For him a moral law is true in exactly the same sense as a law of physics or biology or medical science is true. "The heart *ought* to pump blood" means for medical science "the pumping of blood by the heart is a condition of physical health, and if the heart does not pump blood an unsatisfactory and unhappy condition of the body (which we call disease) supervenes." This is true in the common-sense meaning of the word true; and its truth can be proved (or disproved) by the ordinary rules of observation. "Men *ought* to be truthful, honest, temperate, moderate, and in general moral" means, for Plato, "Morality is a condition of the satisfactory state (= health) of human personality, and if a man is immoral, an unsatisfactory and unhappy state of his personality results." If this is true at all—its truth may of course be denied, but this is not the point—it is true in the ordinary common-sense meaning of the word true; and its truth can be proved (or disproved) by observation of human life and of the effects on men of morality and immorality respectively. Thus while sophistic immanentism makes moral principles false and fraudulent, Platonic immanentism makes them true. Moral skepticism gives way to moral faith.

The second defect in the sophistic account of morality, which is also corrected by Plato, is its obliteration of the difference between human nature and animal nature. Immanentism means that morality is an expression of human nature. This makes it clear that if we are to give an adequate account of morality we must first possess an adequate conception of human nature in all its fullness. Now man has much in common with the animals. But his nature is also certainly very different from theirs. To ignore the differences and simply to equate human nature with animal nature will therefore necessarily give rise to a hopelessly inadequate view of morality. And this is precisely what the Sophists did.

According to them a man is just like a cock, a tiger, or a horse. Therefore his conduct ought to be governed by the same principles as theirs. Each ought to grab for himself whatever he can, regardless of the claims of others. In the resultant struggle of all against all the strong must and should crush out the weak. For this is the universal law of nature.

It is, of course, true that a man is like a cock, a tiger, or a horse. But if this is to be regarded as a complete account of human nature, it is simply infantile. In the first place, a cock, a tiger, and a horse are all different from one another. We may, however, pass that over, and concentrate on the more important point, which is that, in spite of obvious resemblances, a man is enormously different from any of them.

What are the chief differences between men and animals? They are doubtless many; but the later Greeks, especially Plato and Aristotle, hit upon what appeared to them to be the main point when they said that man is distinguished from animals by the fact that he possesses reason, or intelligence, while the animals do not. The other differences, in all probability, flow from this. Thus man builds houses, wears clothes, lives in organized societies, invents machines, uses fire, manufactures tools. Animals do none of these things. But all these specifically human activities are made possible by the fact that man possesses reason. Therefore reason is the essential quality of man, that which most clearly marks him off from the animal. Men, like animals, possess appetites. But what is specifically *human* about man is his rationality.

Greek humanism, when it reached its full development in

Plato and Aristotle, was humanism, not animalism. Morality, since it is to be an expression of human nature, must give scope for the exercise in conduct of *all* the parts of that nature. Appetite is certainly an essential part, and it must therefore have its proper place. This consideration prevented the Greeks from embracing the moral ideal of asceticism, which seeks to stamp out the animal appetites altogether. But it also meant that reason, which is peculiar to man, must have its proper place in the good life.

What is its proper place? We have already seen how Plato answered this question. The proper function of reason is to rule all the other elements of personality. And we have seen some of the reasons which Plato put forward for this conception. We must now glance at another point.

The Greeks found in human nature at least these two elements: appetite which is the animal part, and reason which is the peculiarly human part. Both must express themselves in the good life, if it is to be an adequate expression of human nature as a whole. But do they merely lie alongside one another, on the same level, co-ordinate, of equal value, so that they both have the same right to influence and direct human life? To this question they answered with an emphatic "no." Reason, they asserted, is "higher" than the appetites and passions. It is more valuable. It is nobler. It is the noblest part of man. Therefore it ought to control the man. It ought to control the appetites. For the appetites, as being inherently "lower," ought to be subordinate to it. This is a characteristically Greek idea, and it is plainly one of the reasons why Plato identified morality with the control of appetite by reason.

What justification can there be for asserting that reason is higher than the other parts of human nature? Indeed we ought to ask what *meaning*, even, there is in the expression "higher than" in this context. These are exceedingly difficult questions to answer, and we shall be compelled to consider them in the course of our argument. At present we are merely noting the idea as one which has entered into the history of our civilization. It has been, in fact, one of the basic ideas on which European civilization has been built. The Greeks originated it, but they neither analyzed it, nor made any attempt to justify it. They probably considered it obvious that men are higher than animals, that their superior worth must be due to their possession of something which animals lack, that this something is plainly reason, and that therefore reason must be higher than that which man shares with the animals, namely his appetites.

It has been noted that ethical theory began with immanentism among the Greeks; that then, under the influence of Palestinian cosmology, there followed two thousand years of impositionism; and that recent thinkers have tended to exhibit a revival of the immanentist theory. This revival made its first appearance, perhaps, with the so-called utilitarians, Bentham and Mill. Morality is by them defined as whatever sort of action tends to increase the general happiness of mankind. In the working out of this idea they made various rather crude mistakes. But we are not concerned with the criticism of them. The only point for us here is that presumably what tends to increase human happiness will depend upon the qualities of human nature. This theory, therefore, implies an immanentist view of morals.

But if we wish to see modern immanentism in full play we must turn to the ethical relativists and logical positivists whose views have already been briefly mentioned. They all hold, of course, that there is not a single type of morality suitable for all men, but that there are many moralities, none of which can properly be said to be better or higher than another. At the moment I am not concerned with this part of their theories, but with the fact that the theories plainly rest upon the basis of immanentism. For these philosophers think that moralities are not imposed from the outside but are developments of the natures of the people who live under them; morality is a *human* thing. It is true that, on their view, a morality is in some sense imposed by society upon the individual. But it arises out of the nature of the men in that society, and is therefore, in the last analysis, immanent.

If we are to think that man, after two thousand years of Palestinian impositionism, is now at last freeing himself from its influence, and that a new era of immanentism is just beginning (and I do mean to suggest this), then it is extremely interesting to notice that just as Greek immanentism began with moral skepticism in the Sophists, so modern immanentism is beginning again with moral skepticism in the ethical relativists and positivists. Will history repeat itself further? As Greek immanentism passed from sophistic skepticism to the moral faith of Plato—while yet not ceasing to be immanentism—will modern immanentism pass from the skepticism of the relativists and positivists to moral belief, still based, however, upon the theory of morality as immanent? I hold that this will and must be the case; or at least that it must happen if our civilization is not to perish. I hold that these contemporary relativistic theories are indeed immanentism, but crude and immature immanentism. And this is to be expected at the dawn of a new epoch.

I will close this chapter by noting what I think are the

two main differences between the new immanentism of the twentieth century and the immanentism of Plato.

First, Plato founded morality upon what is common to all men, on what he believed to be a *universal* human nature. Plato was well aware of national and tribal differences of custom, or at any rate of the differences between Greek and barbarian. But he thought that all men exhibited a certain common basic psychological structure—that of reason, spirit, and appetite. If morality were based upon such a common structure, it would, of course, be universal. There would be one common human morality.

But modern relativists, on the contrary, either deny a common human nature of any kind, or they think that morality is not an expression of it. Rather they suppose it to be the expression of the special and peculiar emotional reactions of different races and tribes. One tribe resents a certain type of action and calls it immoral. Another reacts to the same type of action with a pleasurable emotion and calls it good. Thus their moralities differ, and as there is no common denominator they cannot meaningfully be compared. There is not a *human* morality expressive of *human* nature. There is a European morality, a Chinese morality, a Hottentot morality, etc. And these are merely expressions of the peculiar emotional idiosyncrasies of all these different peoples. But it can hardly be doubted that there is such a thing as human nature, a common psychological ground plan of man as man—we can hardly deny, for instance, that reason and desire are in some sense common to all men. The moderns are accordingly open to the charge that they seek to base morality on what is accidental and superficial in man rather than on what is deep-seated and essential. The question will be whether, as a matter of empirical fact, morality actually is the expression of deep common elements or of superficial regional idiosyncrasies of feeling. On this it is better that we should not at present pronounce an opinion beyond saying that the moderns, in taking the latter view, seem to be making a large and rather light-hearted assumption. Plato took the opposite view, and it is at least possible that he may have been right.

The second difference between the developed Greek form of immanentism and the modern version lies in the fact that morality according to the former is the expression of the *whole* of human personality, while according to the latter it expresses only a small part of man's nature, namely his emotions. In Plato's theory it is reason, spirit, and appetite working harmoniously together which produce morality. And these three are supposed to constitute the entire personality. But the relativists and positivists, or most of them, make emotion the sole root of morals. Reason has nothing to do with it, nor has any other "part" of our nature. This again seems rather a light-hearted view. For morality is a purely human thing, not shared with the animals; while animals do have emotions. Reason is certainly, as the Greeks insisted, what is above all peculiar to man. And one might therefore suspect that reason has at least something to do with morals, that it is probably in some way at the base of morality.

CHAPTER III

HUMANISM

IN CHAPTER II, I contrasted the two types of theory regarding the origin of our moral ideas. And I stated, or at least implied, some of the grounds on which the theory of morality as immanent is, in my opinion, to be preferred. The theory of imposition is seen as the product of a superstitious world-view. No one would now seek to explain tides or other natural phenomena as due to the interference of God. It is taken for granted that we are to seek their causes in nature itself. Morality is, after all, one of the things which exist in the world along with tides and thunderstorms. And its causes should likewise be sought in nature, not in a special act of God. It is true that morality is above nature if one means by that word only what is sub-human; and the word nature is often used in this sense. But if by nature one means whatever exists in the world of space and time, including man and his works, then morality is surely natural. And the place in which one would plainly expect to find its origin is human nature.

This is ethical humanism, by which I mean nothing else than the theory of morality as immanent. It is the natural and naïve view. I mean it is the view which men would always naturally have taken had not their minds been diverted, or rather perverted, from it by a special historical cause. This is the reason why ethical thinking begins with it as a matter of course—among the Greeks—and now in the contemporary era as naturally returns to it when the depressant of Palestinian cosmology is being lifted. The Greeks did not think that it had to be *proved,* for it had not then occurred to anyone to doubt it. They simply took it for granted. And now, when the era of the theological explanations of natural facts is disappearing, the mind of man returns to it as a spring goes back to its normal position when a weight is lifted from it.

There is, however, another very strong reason for espousing ethical humanism, which I have not so far mentioned. It is, in my opinion, the only view which enables us to refute the moral skeptic. If we accept the theory of morality as imposed, I do not know how this is to be done. And I do not think that anyone else knows either. We should have to proceed, I think, by trying to *prove* the spiritual nature of the universe, or the existence of whatever we regard as the agency which imposes morality upon us. I do not believe that any such proofs can be given. And the attempt to give them will land us, to say the least, in a morass of metaphysical subtilties. But the refutation of moral skepticism which can be offered on the basis of humanism is, at any rate, straightforward. It remains on the level of observable facts which are open to the inspection of every man. I do not mean that the refutation will be absolutely coercive, watertight, certain, impossible to dispute. This is too much to hope. There will always, of course, be room for criticism and for differences of opinion in matters of this kind.

Moral skepticism is, in essence, the assertion that *there*

are no true moral principles. Or in some cases, what it asserts is that *moral principles are neither true nor false.* It will admit that there are moral principles in the sense that men have certain ideas which are called moral principles. But these are merely subjective ideas or feelings in people's minds. They are not true in the sense in which the principle of gravitation, or the doctrine of evolution, or any other scientific or even common-sense truth is true. The skeptic may say that moral ideas are fraudulent and deceitful, as the Greek Sophists did. Or he may say that they are merely the expressions of subjective emotions, as the relativists and positivists tend to say. But in one way or another moral skepticism always involves the view that moral ideas and principles are not, in any proper sense of the word, true. This accordingly is the position which has to be overthrown.

The Refutation of Moral Skepticism

It may be taken as an axiom that *no animal can live without action.* For even to eat is to act. Another axiom is that *no action is possible in any animal save on the basis of a distinction between the good and the bad, the better and the worse.* It is solely on account of the good and the bad that an animal acts. Hunger is bad; a square meal is good. A certain temperature is good; some other temperature— too hot or too cold—is bad. The animal eats, drinks, moves, acts, to obtain the good or the better and to avoid the bad or the worse. Putting these two axioms together we get the result that *no life is possible without making a distinction between goodness and badness.*

It is indifferent to this argument whether the good and the bad are called objective or subjective. It is also indifferent whether, in the animal life, the same things are sometimes good and sometimes bad, or whether one thing is always and for every animal good and another thing always and for every animal bad. All that is asserted is that *some* distinction between good and bad is essential for every life.

I am not so simple as to suppose that this argument alone proves the existence, or the necessity, or the truth, or the validity of what are ordinarily called moral principles, and so refutes the moral skeptic. For morality, in the narrow sense in which that word is ordinarily used, is a human thing and does not exist for animals. And the argument, if it were supposed to prove the validity of moral principles, would prove too much, since it would apply to animals as well as to men.

But what the argument does show is that *for every animal, and not only for man, there is a good life and a bad life.* There is a good dog life, and a bad dog life; a good cat life, and a bad cat life. A good dog life will be one which that animal feels to be satisfactory *for him;* and this will be a life replete with the things which are, *for him,* good. So of the cat; and so of every animal. If one wants a concrete illustration one may say that, for a dog, plenty of physical exercise, good food, opportunities for play, opportunities for the satisfaction of sex, a comfortable home and a kind master, seem to be the main factors of a good life. But a life in which the dog has no exercise, grows fat and wheezy, is stuffed with overrich food; or one in which he has no home and is starved—these will be examples of bad and unsatisfactory dog lives.

It further follows that for every animal there must be *principles* of the good life. By a principle I mean a rule which, if followed, tends to lead to a satisfactory life, while the breach of it will tend to lead to an unsatisfactory life. For instance, it is a principle of the good life for the dog that he ought to take plenty of exercise. This is not, I believe, a necessity for the cat—at any rate not in the same degree; but it is a necessity for the dog. It will be a principle of the good life for the lion that he ought to eat meat; for certain other animals that they ought not to eat meat.

Notice that in all these cases we use the word ought. The dog *ought* to exercise, the lion *ought* to eat meat. Now ought is the key word of morals. All moral principles are statements that we ought or ought not to act in certain ways. The fact that the word ought is also used in stating principles of the good life for animals is extremely significant.

Note further that the principles of the good life for animals are *true;* and true, not in any metaphorical or derivative way, but within the ordinary meaning of the word. That dogs ought to take plenty of exercise means that this is a condition of their good health, and that lack of exercise will tend to cause an unsatisfactory state of the dog's body and therefore of his life. This is true, and its truth may be observed by watching what happens to dogs who are given, or are not given, exercise.

Since there are principles of the good life for the dog and for every other animal, there must also be principles of the good life for man. And these principles of the good human life will be true in the everyday meaning of the word truth. Now according to the humanistic conception of morals which we have adopted, morality simply means the principles of the good life for man, or as an alternative definition the principles of living which will ensure what men themselves will feel to be a satisfactory human life. Therefore there must be true moral principles.

Accordingly it cannot be true to say that there are no moral principles, or that no moral principles are true. To say that there are moral principles, but that they are all fraudulent, all deceitful inventions of some to get the better of others, must be false. For this is not the case in regard to the principles of the good dog life. That the dog ought to exercise and not eat great quantities of rich food is not a fraudulent idea. It is not an attempt by the dog's master to deceive the dog for the master's benefit. Much less is it a fraud put upon the dog by other dogs.

Likewise it cannot be true to say that moral principles are neither true nor false, that they have no meaning, that they merely express emotions, or that they are only 'postulates.' No one would say these things of the principles of the good dog life.

Commentary on the Refutation

First: The refutation depends wholly upon the humanistic or immanentist definition of morality as that set of principles which will ensure a satisfactory human life. If this is rejected, the refutation has no cogency. If anyone says that for him morality does not mean the rules for living a satisfactory human life, then I have no idea how to establish the necessity, or truth, or validity of moral principles in his sense of the word moral.

Second: According to the argument, the truth of moral principles is to be understood in the same sense as the truth of scientific propositions, or of the statements we make in everyday discourse about everyday matters. And their truth is to be verified, i.e., either proved or disproved, in the same way, namely by observation. It is not denied, however, that in practice the truth of moral principles will be very difficult to verify. The truth of the statement that water, at a certain atmospheric pressure, boils at 100° Cen-

tigrade is comparatively easy to put to the test. The truth
of the statement that lack of exercise will lead to ill-health
in a dog is more difficult to prove, and cannot be established
with the same degree of accuracy, because the conditions
and events which have to be observed are much more complicated. The truth of the statement that observance of
moral rules tends to produce a satisfactory—and their
breach an unsatisfactory—human life is still more difficult
to test, and can at best be established only very roughly,
because the conditions and happenings of human life are
almost infinitely complicated. But in all these cases the
truth of the statements means the same thing, and is verifi-
able by the same method, namely observation of what
happens in certain conditions. Therefore the practical difficulties in the way of establishing the truth of particular
moral principles have no bearing on the argument of the
refutation.

Third: But the great objection which will certainly be
raised to the argument will be that it is absurd to compare
moral rules to rules about the exercise and diet of dogs.
The latter are mere rules of physical health. And whatever
moral principles are, they certainly are not that. Morality
is something which exists only for human beings. There is
nothing even faintly analogous to it in the world of animals. Yet my entire argument has depended upon comparing men to animals and supposing that the principles of the
good life for man have the same sort of origin and justification as rules of physical health in dogs and cats and lions.
And this, frankly, is absurd.

I think myself that those who argue thus have failed to
learn the lesson which is taught us by the biological doctrine of evolution. Their view is a remnant of the habit of
mind which arose out of belief in the doctrine that man is a

special creation. The lesson of evolution is that we can no longer believe in any sharp line of division between the man and the animal. The human has grown out of the animal; and everywhere, in matters of the soul as well as in those of the body, there must be, or has been, a continuous shading from one to the other. The human mind has evolved out of the animal mind. We say that men have reason, while animals have none. But the seeds of reason must be discoverable in the minds of animals. It is absurd to think that morality has no evolutionary precursors, no roots in the animal world. Morality too must have grown out of the principles of the good life which existed for our prehuman ancestors. But the principles of the good life for them no doubt consisted almost entirely of mere rules of physical health, for the reason that their lives were lived almost exclusively on the physical plane. We require very different rules, which we are pleased to call moral, because our lives are *not* lived exclusively on the physical plane, but on what we call the higher plane of mind and personality.

But the detailed answer to the objection which we are considering is as follows. We established that there must exist principles of the good life for every animal. It is now important to notice that these principles are quite different for different animals. They are all doubtless what we should in general call mere physical rules of health. But still they differ from species to species. Thus the dog ought to take plenty of exercise. But this is apparently not true for the cat, or at least not true to the same degree. It is a principle of the good lion life that he ought to eat meat. But it is a principle of the good camel life that he ought not to eat meat. Fish must live in water, birds in air.

On what do these differences of principles depend?

Plainly on the differences between the *natures* of these animals. The dog must have plenty of exercise because of the nature of dogs; cats can do with little because their natures are different. The nature of the camel is different from that of the lion, and this accounts for their different rules of diet.

No doubt this is rather a vague way of stating the truth. We ought, in order to be more accurate, to substitute for the word nature some term which would be less vague. Perhaps we ought to say that the differences of health rules depend upon differences of anatomical structure or something of that sort. But it cannot be denied that the special anatomical structure of an animal is part of its nature—which means nothing else, after all, but its essential characteristics. And I prefer to use the word nature here for a reason which will appear in a moment. Let us agree to say, then, that the differences between the principles of the good life which apply to one animal and those which apply to another *depend upon differences in the natures of the animals.*

It will follow from this that just as the principles of the good dog life depend upon dog nature, those of the good cat life upon cat nature, so the principles of the good human life will depend upon human nature. And just as the difference between the principles of the good dog life and those of the good cat life depend upon the specific differences in the natures of these animals, so the difference between animal principles of the good life in general and human principles of the good life must depend upon the difference between animal nature and human nature. Now the objection which we are discussing stresses that what we call moral rules are enormously different from what we call rules of health. This is, however, exactly what we should on my theory expect, since human nature is enormously different from any animal nature. This consideration will provide us with the key for solving the riddle why men have what we call morals, while animals have only rules of physical health.

What are the fundamental differences between animal nature and human nature? Speaking in a general, and no doubt rather vague way, we may say that men have minds, reasoning powers, personalities, even souls if we like an old-fashioned word, in a way that animals do not. Though animals are conscious, and in that sense have minds, yet I hope the reader will understand what I mean if I say that they live purely physical lives. Men, on the contrary, though they also live physical lives, live much more what I may call the life of the mind. Let us express all this by saying that while men have personality, animals have none. (Of course there is a sense in which we speak of a dog as having personality, but then we are using the word in a different sense.) Let us say also that animal nature has only one component, the physical, while human nature has two components, the physical, and also that component which we call personality or soul.

If we are correct in supposing that the principles of the good life for any animal depend on, grow out of, and express the specific nature of that animal—and this is our general humanistic supposition—then as a result of the considerations mentioned in the last paragraph we shall have the following consequence. The rules of the good life for an animal will express only his physical nature and provide only for his physical welfare. But the rules of the good life for man will be of two kinds—those which ensure the welfare of his physical body and those which ensure the welfare of his personality or soul. The former will be rules of physical health. The latter will be rules for the health of personality, or moral rules. The good life for man includes both.

Fourth: If we consider moral rules to be rules for the health of the personality as distinct from the body, will not even this yield much too wide a definition? Not only will it include what are ordinarily called morals, but also the principles of politics and even esthetics. Perhaps we may add that it will include even the rules of football and chess, the principles of engineering, the techniques of the carpenter and tinker. For art, too, contributes in one way or another to a good and satisfactory human life—and so do engineering, football, and chess. And as they belong—with the possible exception of football—to the life of the mind rather than to the life of the body, they will have to be considered the concern of moral principles and not of the principles of physical welfare.

But I do not consider this an objection. On the contrary, I rejoice to have discovered a conception of the good life so all-embracing. Or is the objection merely the verbal one that I am using the word morality in a much wider sense than that in which it is commonly used? If so, the matter is soon set right. All we have to do is to explain our meaning clearly. And we may express the matter thus. To begin with, there are principles of the good life for man. This is our widest genus of value. It will include the principles of the best way of doing all the things which enrich the lives of men, from being saints to playing football, from composing music to compounding delicate-tasting sauces. Since all these principles are principles of the good life, they may all be called moral, if one chooses to use the word in so extended a sense. But of course this would be quite without the sanction of any common usage. Anyhow, whatever word we use, this highest genus may be subdivided in various ways. There will be rules for the body and rules for the soul. The former will include the principles of medicine, sanitation, physical culture, diet, and what not. The latter will doubtless also be subdivided. The soul too has different aspects or elements. The political or social nature of man will give rise to political and social principles. His esthetic nature will give rise to esthetic principles. What are generally called moral rules, in the narrow sense, will perhaps consist chiefly of those principles which concern man's conduct of his affairs in daily life in his relations with his neighbors. Where exactly the line is to be drawn I do not know, and it does not seem to me to matter. For all such divisions are arbitrary and are made only for convenience.

Proceeding on these lines we shall have something of the following sort:

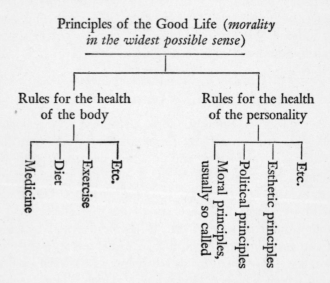

Principles of the Good Life (*morality in the widest possible sense*)

Rules for the health of the body

Rules for the health of the personality

Medicine
Diet
Exercise
Etc.

Moral principles, usually so called
Political principles
Esthetic principles
Etc.

This is not intended as an accurate classification, but only as a rough diagram to illustrate the essential idea. Indeed if that idea is correct, an exact classification is probably impossible, or would at least be a matter of drawing arbitrary lines of division. For the essence of the idea is that all rules for the good life arise in the same sort of way, as expressions of different aspects of the nature of man. But since there are no sharp lines between these aspects, there cannot be any sharp lines between the different kinds of rules.

Fifth: The argument of the refutation proves (assuming it to be valid) that there must be true moral principles. It has no tendency, however, to show *what* particular set of moral principles are true. For instance, if the question be whether we ought to follow Christian ethical rules or those of some different and opposing system such as that of Nietzsche, the argument so far throws no light on this. To answer such a question we have to go on to discover criteria for judging between rival moral codes. I accordingly proceed to attempt a solution of this problem.

The Criteria of Good and Bad Moralities: and of Higher and Lower Civilizations

A civilization embodies some particular conception of the good life. To achieve the good life in the sense thus conceived is the ideal or end or aim of that civilization. For instance, the civilization of the democratic west aims at a certain way of life which it considers good. Totalitarian civilization aims (as I shall try to show in due course) at quite a different way of life. It has a different conception of the good life; or if we like so to express it, a different morality. How then are we to judge, as between civilizations, which is higher, which lower, which is better, which worse? Obviously the fundamental question will be whether the conception of the good life entertained by *this* civilization is better or higher than the conception of the good life entertained by *that* civilization. In other words, we shall have to compare their moral ideals.

It is true that another question will also sometimes arise. Two civilizations, or at least two societies, may be inspired by the same idea of the good life. They may both be trying to achieve one and the same ideal. In that case we shall have to ask which of them embodies or achieves this ideal more thoroughly and successfully. This, however, is not the sort of question I propose to discuss anywhere in this book. For it does not concern ultimate ends. It is sociological or historical, not philosophical. Accordingly I mention this question only to exclude it from our purview. We may suppose, for instance, that the civilizations of the United States and Great Britain have roughly the same general ideals. They are both Christian civilizations. They both seek to work out, each in its own way, ideas such as individualism and democracy. And we may certainly ask which has been the most successful in achieving these ends. Perhaps there may be no clear answer. Perhaps each has achieved its ends better in some respects and worse in others. Owing to this, and owing to the complicated character of the data, there may be such enormous practical difficulties in making a meaningful comparison that we may dismiss the question as impossible to answer. But great as may be the practical difficulties, there are no difficulties of principle in such a question if we assume that the moral ideas of the two civilizations are the same. However, where ultimate ends are opposed—which I think is the case, for instance, as between democratic and totalitarian countries—there is a difficulty of principle. For we have to decide

which of the two ideals, which of the two conceptions of
the good life for man, is the truer. And it may seem that
there is here no common ground between the two by
reference to which such a dispute could be decided. This
is the kind of question with which I am concerned in this
book.

There is also another kind of question which I wish, at
least in part, to exclude from consideration. It may be said
that a civilization has to be judged not merely by its moral
ideas but also by its achievements in art, literature, science,
philosophy, etc., and that therefore our method, confining
itself as it does to moral issues, is too narrow to yield any
significant result. This, however, is only partly true. For in
large measure the art, science, literature, and philosophy of
a people are themselves expressions and products of its
ethos. In its art and literature its views of life find articulate
utterance. Its science is used—except by the very few who
cultivate it as an end in itself—as a means for achieving or
obtaining the things which it thinks good. Even its philosophy, though much of it may seem remote from practical
issues, is largely determined by its theory of life. Hence
we really go to the root of all these aspects of a nation's
cultural life when we examine its conception of the good
life. This is not indeed the whole truth. And in so far as
it is untrue, in so far as a nation's intellectual achievements
are independent of its ethical beliefs, I have to exclude
them from consideration in this book. But I do not myself
feel that the result will be for that reason insignificant.

It is important that we should understand clearly the
difficulty of principle which arises in connection with the
attempt to discover criteria for evaluating rival conceptions
of the good life. There are many thinkers today who will
deny that such an attempt can possibly succeed. And their

argument will be somewhat as follows. Suppose we try to show that the Christian conception of morality is truer or better or higher than the moral ideas of Nietzsche. The Christian ideal is selflessness. The Nietzschean ideal is the exact opposite, self-assertion. Christianity praises the self-denying virtues—humility, gentleness, charity, and the like. Nietzsche condemns these very qualities as forms of weakness and slavishness, and praises their opposites—proudness, hardness, aggressiveness, and so on. Christianity would have us succor the weak and lowly. Nietzsche would have us ruthlessly crush them out as hindrances to the advance of the evolutionary process. Which of these two conceptions of goodness is the truer?

As soon as we attempt to give an answer to this question, we are met with the query: by what standard are we to judge? We can, of course, use the Christian morality itself as a standard; and if we do that we shall doubtless condemn the Nietzschean morality as evil or at any rate inferior. But this will obviously be a hopelessly circular argument. It assumes at the outset the very thing which was to be proved, namely that the Christian moral ideal is the true one. We shall be involved in the same circle if we use the Nietzschean morality as our standard and judge the Christian morality by that. For in that case we assume from the outset that the Nietzschean morality is the true one. We might, of course, try to find some third standard by reference to which to evaluate both the Christian and the Nietzschean ideals. But this will only increase our difficulties. What third standard are we to take? Is it to be the moral code of the Chinese, the ancient Greeks, or perhaps some new set of moral ideals made up in our own heads? Whatever standard we take, we are committing the same fallacy, that of assuming that one standard is the best and

that we already know which it is. We shall be assuming
that we already know the very thing which we are setting
out to discover, namely which is the best moral standard.
We can never escape from this circle. We can never show
that one morality is better than another except by taking
that morality itself as the standard on which our judgment
is based.

It seems to follow from this that we never can say, with
any real meaning or truth, that one morality is better than
another. And if it is true that different civilizations are
embodiments of differing conceptions of the good life, i.e.,
of different moralities, it will follow that no one civilization
is really any better or higher than another—except, of
course, that we shall be able to judge one better than the
other if they both aim at the *same* ideals and if one achieves
them more fully than the other.

This reduces us to moral skepticism again. For it means
that we cannot really say that there is some set of moral
principles which is true, and that if another set of such
principles contradicts it, this second set must be to that
extent false.

And it means also that the fundamental question which
I am posing in this book is at bottom senseless. American
civilization is a branch of the Greco-Christian civilization
of the western world. This entire Greco-Christian civilization, I shall try to show, is founded upon a certain set of
ethical ideas. A new type of civilization, represented by
the fascist powers, is springing into existence. This, in my
view, is not an attempt to find better ways of realizing the
ethical ideals on which our western civilization has been
built; it is an attempt to realize wholly different ethical
ideals, a different and opposed conception of the good life.
The present struggle of civilizations is a struggle between

opposed conceptions of the good life. If we are to fight for ours, do we not wish to be assured that our conception of the good life is really higher and better than that against which we are struggling? If it is not, then we are merely struggling to preserve a civilization which has no real justification in the nature of things; which embodies, not a set of sacred ideals, but only a set of irrational prejudices which we happen to have inherited from our forefathers. And the question will certainly arise, is it worth while?

Yet this is the position to which we shall be reduced if we admit that it is impossible to find criteria for evaluating civilizations and for judging as better or worse the conceptions of the ethical ideal which they seek to embody.

Now if we have been right in assuming the general position of ethical humanism, the position that morality is an expression of human nature, then there *must* be something wrong with the argument that we cannot judge between moralities without assuming as a standard one of the very moralities which is to be judged. For this latter argument logically implies moral skepticism. But we have seen that, if ethical humanism is true, moral skepticism must be false. For it was the acceptance of humanism which led to the refutation of skepticism. Therefore, since humanism implies that the skeptical belief that it is impossible to judge between moralities is false, it seems to follow that humanism itself ought to be able to provide us with the criteria of good and bad moralities and of higher and lower civilizations. And I believe that this is the case.

I cannot refrain from appealing also to our natural feelings in the matter. When it is suggested that Christian ethical ideals are not in any real sense better or higher than the moral ideas of a New Guinea savage we instinctively feel, I believe, that there must be something wrong in such a view. When clever arguments are presented to prove it, we may not be able to put our finger on the fallacies in them. We may become confused and may not know what to say. But we are not convinced. When I say "we" I mean those of us who, amid general sophistication and bewilderment, have managed to retain some measure of natural human feeling and good sense, have contrived to keep our heads level and our feet on the ground. This, however, is a digression from the logical argument in which we were engaged.

Humanism does in fact imply criteria for evaluating moralities and civilizations. These criteria will certainly be very general; they will not be very precise or exact. But they will not be useless. The generality and lack of precision are to be expected from the nature of the subject. We can exactly measure spatial magnitudes with scientific instruments. But we cannot exactly measure any human things. We have to be content with such degree of precision as the subject admits.

The creed of humanism may be expressed in three main propositions:

(1) that morality is an expression or outgrowth of human nature or personality.

(2) that it consists in those principles of conduct which lead to the most satisfactory life for man, having regard to his special nature.

(3) that human personality, though it is no doubt in one sense unitary, contains a variety of "parts" (Plato's word), or aspects, or faculties, or elements,—such as reason, desire, emotion, will, sensation, etc. This is not intended as a complete or accurate catalogue of the elements of human personality—to give such a catalogue would be a task for

psychology—but merely as an illustration of the idea by means of rough examples.

I think I ought to add that there is also implied in humanism, or at any rate in the criteria which follow, a fourth proposition which is (4) that each of the elements of human personality has a proper function to fulfill. This is of vital importance because the notion of the *properness* of the function is really the basis of the idea contained in the conception of the moral "ought." No doubt the legitimacy of this fourth proposition may be, and will be, questioned. I have already, in discussing Plato, stated the justification of it in essence. And I shall return to a further discussion of it in a later chapter.

The criteria of which we are in search are corollaries of the above four propositions. They are as follows:

(1) *A better or truer morality is one which more adequately expresses human nature; an inferior morality is one which expresses it less adequately.*

(2) *A better or truer morality is one which assigns to each element of personality its proper function, place, and importance, in human activity; an inferior morality is one which fails to do this.*

Failure may consist either in perverting the functions or in suppressing some element of human nature, or in not allowing it sufficient room or place to fulfill its proper function.

(3) *A better or truer morality is one which leads to a more satisfactory human life; an inferior morality is one which leads to a less satisfactory human life.*

Why should we have three criteria, and not merely one? And what are we to do if, in applying them, we find that they clash? This would be the case if a particular morality, judged by one of the criteria, had to be given a high place;

while judged by another of the criteria, it had to be given a low place. The answer to this question is that the criteria cannot clash because they are not really three different ideas but three different expressions of the same idea. They imply one another since they are merely three diverse ways of stating the single general creed of humanism.

Objection may be made that the criterion in its third form is really circular. The word satisfactory is here merely a synonym for good. And if this is realized, it is seen that what is asserted is merely that a good morality is one which leads to a good life. And this seems a circular definition.

Philosophers have argued at great length about the exact meaning of the word good. I do not propose to follow them in this inquiry. I define a good life as a satisfactory life. And I mean by a satisfactory life one which the liver himself intuitively feels to be satisfactory. Whatever may be the proper philosophical analysis of the notion of good-ness or satisfactoriness, men do in actual fact know whether their lives are satisfactory or not. Every animal knows this about himself. A dog knows the difference between a good and a bad dog life—though he certainly could not define or analyze the meanings of these terms. And a man too knows whether his life feels satisfactory to him.

Nor is this at all the same as the hedonistic principle that the only good life is the life which is filled with pleasures. I am far from saying that pleasure is the only good. It may be for all I know that pain, or a certain amount of pain, or pain in certain circumstances, is a good. And it may be that there are many other good things besides pleasure. But what this means, in terms of my doctrine, is simply that men do not feel that a life consisting wholly of pleasures and devoid of these other good things would be a satisfactory life.

Again, Nietzsche pours contempt on the belief that happiness is the only end of man. For happiness he wishes to substitute power. What this means for me is that, according to Nietzsche, men feel a life devoted to the pursuit of power to be a more satisfactory human life than a life devoted to the pursuit of happiness. There is nothing in the humanistic theory which I am advocating which would render it impossible for Nietzsche to be right. Whether he is right or not depends on whether it is true that a life devoted to power is what men feel constitutes a satisfactory human life. Again, the question is asked: why, if happiness is the only end, would most men prefer to be Socrates unhappy rather than a fool happy? The question does not embarrass the humanist as such. If it is a fact that men do not feel that the life of the happy fool satisfies them, then that life is not what I call the good life, however replete with pleasures it may be.

The question what is the proper analysis of the idea of the good means, I suppose, what is it that *makes* men feel that one kind of life is satisfactory while another is not. And as to this I have—at any rate in this book—no theory to offer. And the reason is that, although I recognize the interest and importance of the question, it does not affect the particular inquiries with which I am here concerned. I am concerned to discover criteria by means of which we can distinguish a good from a bad morality. One criterion is that a good morality is one which leads to the sort of lives which men feel to be satisfactory human lives. What makes them feel this, or why they feel it, does not for my purposes matter. In practice one knows the difference between the satisfactory and the unsatisfactory without any theory of the nature of goodness, just as one knows on sight the difference between black and white without any theory of the nature of color. And this practical knowledge of the distinction is all that is required for the working of my criteria, which is all that I am concerned with in this book.

What has now become of the alleged difficulty that it is impossible to judge between moralities without using as our standard or criterion one of the very moralities to be judged, and so arguing in a circle? In spite of this we have suggested criteria. And it might perhaps be suspected that in doing so we have somehow dodged or evaded the issue, or that the fallacy of the circular argument, though it does not seem to have been committed, must really be concealed somewhere or other in our results.

The suspicion is unfounded, and the explanation is quite simple. We certainly have to judge between moralities by means of some standard. And our suggested criteria constitute our standard. But the alleged difficulty was that we have to judge by means of a *moral* standard, which would mean assuming the truth of some particular morality. Now our criteria, although they are standards, are not *moral* standards, and therefore they do not assume the truth of any particular morality.

One has only to glance at the actual wording of the three criteria to see that no particular morality, such as the Christian or the Greek or the Chinese, is assumed in them. There is not a word in them about the special ideals, such as self-sacrifice or moderation, which may be characteristic of these moral systems. What is assumed in them is a theory *about* moralities, the humanistic theory. This is not itself a particular morality, nor even a theory about a particular morality. It is perfectly general. It is a statement about the origin and nature of *all* moralities, and it could have been framed if the Christian morality had never existed, or if the Greek morality had never existed, or if one had never even heard of the Chinese. These criteria, therefore, do not commit the fallacy of assuming the truth of some particular morality.

But still it may be asked: How is this possible? How can we judge between moralities by means of standards which are not themselves moral? Surely there must be something wrong here? The answer is that, according to humanism, moralities have a *function*, that of adequately expressing human nature in conduct and thereby producing satisfactory human lives; and that they can be judged by their degree of success in performing this function. This is what is expressed in our three criteria. If the question were asked which of two knives is the better, we should inquire what is the general function of knives. On learning that their function is to cut, we should judge the best knife to be the one which cuts best. This is the method which we are adopting here.

The root of the difficulty which we had to face was that in order to evaluate moralities we had to discover some common ground of them all on the basis of which to judge them. It was then assumed that the common element must be itself some moral ideal or standard—which it was plainly impossible to find. But this assumption was quite false. The common element of all moral ideals is not itself a particular moral ideal but the general function of all moral ideals as such; just as the common element in all knives is not a particular knife, but the function of knives. Hence it is by the function of moralities that they are to be judged, not by a particular moral standard.

Perhaps it would be well at this point to attempt a concrete illustration of the sort of way in which the criteria can be worked. The illustration will have to be very rough and ready, because I do not wish to be involved, at this stage, in a discussion of the details of particular moral ideals and their detailed merits. Consequently what I shall say will not aim at doing justice to the particular case which I shall use as an illustration, but only at exhibiting the sort of method to be used.

Suppose the question to be which is the better: a morality which allows a controlled and moderate indulgence of the bodily appetites (such as the Greek), or an ascetic ideal which seeks to stamp out the passions and appetites altogether, or at least to do so as far as this is consistent with the bare maintenance of life. The statement of the case in such terms is probably unfair to both ideals. But for the sake of giving a simple example I express it thus. Our criteria will declare, I think, that of these two the ascetic ideal is the inferior. For the physical appetites are a part or element in human nature. They must therefore be allowed a proper and adequate rôle in the moral life. The essence of the ascetic ideal (as stated above) is to refuse them as far as possible any representation or expression in morality. This morality is therefore not an adequate expression of human nature, since it definitely aims at suppressing one of its elements. It must accordingly be condemned.

This example brings out very clearly the dependence of our criteria upon the humanistic or immanentist theory of goodness. For what seems to be at the root of asceticism is the view that the passions as such are evil, or at least have some evil element in them. Thus it believes that human nature, or at least a part of human nature, is inherently bad. But it is of the essence of humanism to believe that nothing in human nature can be *in itself* bad, but that badness arises through an improper relation between the elements of human nature, or perhaps through an improper proportion in the amount of expression allowed to the different elements. Of course, if the humanist theory is rejected, our criteria, and also any judgments which are reached by means of them, will have to be rejected too.

In the belief that morality is an expression of human nature an assumption is involved which ought to be made explicit—namely that there is such a thing as human nature. This means that for all human beings, however great their differences of race, color, creed, culture, or modes of thought, there is a ground plan which is everywhere the same. It is what is human as distinguished from what is American, French, Hottentot, or Laplander. It is not assumed, of course, that all men are alike. The differences are not denied. The houses in the world are of many kinds, very unlike. Some are large, some small. Some are made of brick, some of stone, some of wood. They are of different colors and shapes and designs. Yet they all have a common pattern in that all have roof, walls, foundations, doors, windows. Or if there are a few freak houses which lack one or other of these elements, it may at least be said that to have them is in general the common pattern of normal houses. So, it is assumed, though men differ vastly in many respects, yet there is in general a common human structure. This common structure is human nature.

Since the principles of the good life must be the expressions of the whole human being, body and soul, a common bodily structure and a common psychological structure will be required. The existence of a common physical structure cannot be doubted. Men differ in color, size, type of hair, and so on. But all have a spine, heart, lungs, arteries, veins, liver, stomach, noses, eyes. There may for all I know be freaks without spines; but they are freaks, and this does not alter the fact that having a spine is part of the ground plan of the human body as such. On this ground plan of the body are founded those of the precepts of bodily health which are universal in the sense that they apply to all normal men of all races and periods. A doctor can prescribe as easily for the indigestion of a Negro as he can for that of a white man. Appendicitis in a Chinaman yields to the same medical treatment as appendicitis in an American. The main rules of health are the same for all men (though we need not deny that minor differences of treatment are called for on account of minor differences of physical disposition) because all men have the same fundamental physical structure.

Moral rules in the narrow sense are outgrowths of the mind or personality of man. In this case therefore the conception of human nature implies that there is a ground plan of the personality or soul, as there is of the body. If there is no such common structure of men's minds, then there cannot be such a thing as a distinctively human morality, a morality consisting of precepts which are universal in the sense that they apply to all normal men. In that case we shall have merely a chaos of different moralities—an American morality, a British morality, a Chinese morality, a New Guinea morality, and so on. And even this implies that there is a common psychological structure of American men, another of British men, and so on.

It seems to me in the highest degree unreasonable to suppose that, although there is a common anatomical structure of men's bodies, there is no common psychological structure of their minds. The very fact that there exists a science of psychology—however unadvanced it may be as compared with other sciences—presupposes the existence of such a common mental structure. If none such existed, if there were only German personality, British personality, Chinese personality, then instead of one science of psychology we should have many different sciences of psychology,

German, British, Chinese, and the rest. If there were no common psychological structure of men, this would introduce chaos into our thinking about human things. I do not see how there could be any understanding of one nation's art or culture by another. It is difficult to see how men could ever learn each other's languages, communicate with one another, understand each other even in the simplest matters of daily life.

And if we look at the matter from the point of view of evolutionary science, the result will surely be the same. There is only one species of man now on this earth, *Homo sapiens*. There must be specific characters common to all members of a species. No doubt the species is classified biologically by its physical, not its mental characters. So that the classification of man as a single species directly implies no more than a common physical structure. But the mind of man must have evolved along with his body. And we should certainly expect, on general evolutionary grounds, that there would be a common structure of men's minds. At least the burden of proof would be upon those who assert otherwise. That evolution which has produced similar physical structures will also probably have ensured similar psychological structures.

It is doubtless much more difficult to specify the details of the common structure of human personality than it is to make corresponding specifications as regards the body. We must not expect the same degree of precision. But there are certain facts which are surely fairly obvious. For instance, reason is as much a part of the ground plan of man's mind as a spine is of his body. There may be men born without reason, as there may be men born without spines. Yet being human means, among other things, being rational. Again, the possession of will (however that elusive term may be defined), of passions, appetites, emotions, sensations, is common to all men. That all men have emotions would still be a common human element, even if specific emotions differed in different regions and races. That all men have likes and dislikes would be a common element, even if they all liked and disliked different things. But as a matter of fact the ground plan of human personality extends much further into detail than that. Thus it is not only the case that all men have emotions, but they all have the same kinds of emotion. For instance, love, hate, jealousy, fear, anger, are shared by all men in greater or less degree, and are parts of the common human pattern. Also such appetites as hunger, thirst, and sex are parts of it.

It is true, of course, that men love different things, fear different things, hate different things. They also differ in the strength and proportions in which the elements of human personality are mixed in them. Some men are more full of hate, some of fear, some of love. But these facts no more destroy the truth that there exists a common structure of human personality than the physical differences between men—differences of size, strength, color, physical constitution—destroy the truth that there exists a common structure of the human body.

The supposition of Lévy-Bruhl that primitives use a different logic from ours would, if true, have some slight tendency to throw doubt on our assumption. For it might show that there is not one common human reason, but at least two, and perhaps many. But Lévy-Bruhl's suggestion is not now, I understand, looked upon with favor by anthropologists, but is rather regarded as an exploded hypothesis. And apart from this I will venture to say that it is in any case a nonsensical hypothesis. Logicians speak of the law of contradiction—the law that two statements which contradict each other cannot both be true—as a fundamental law of reason. There could not be a race of man who possessed a kind of reason different from this. For to think on the basis that two statements which contradict each other can both be true is not another kind of reason; it is simple irrationality. Of course we all, and not only primitives, do often believe contradictory propositions at the same time. This is because we are all muddled and inconsistent, more or less, in our thinking. And primitives are very likely more muddled than we are. But this is not because their minds have a different structure of reason, but because they have not yet learned to use their reasoning powers as well as we have. That I use my hands and fingers —in a game of billiards, for example—less skillfully than another is not a proof that he and I have different kinds of hands and fingers.

We may take it then that there really is a common structure of human personality just as there is a common structure of men's bodies. And just as *universal* rules of physical health are founded upon the common bodily structure, so *universal* moral rules will be founded upon the common psychological structure. Not to overeat habitually is a rule of health which applies to all men in all countries and ages. It is not true for Americans and false for Italians. This is because the digestive apparatus is in all men substantially the same. Not to tell lies, not to thieve, not to be cruel or adulterous or dishonest—if these are precepts by obeying which all men would benefit—as surely they are, even if all men do not know it—these moral principles must rest upon the basis of some common element or elements of human personality.

The suggestion that there is a universal morality does not mean that there are any moral ideas which all men hold in common. This is sure to be the objection—that the inhabitants of America, China, New Guinea, Togoland, all have utterly different moral codes. The objection is completely muddleheaded. Our suggestion is not that any moral principles are universally *believed*, but that certain moral principles are universally *true*, whether they are believed or not. For explanation we may turn again to the analogy with physical rules of health. The doctor knows that there are certain rules of health which all men ought to follow. There is therefore a universal medical science. But this does not, of course, mean that all men, and all races of men, and men in all ages, have believed in the same precepts of health or the same rules of treatment. It is true for all men that bad sanitation causes epidemics of disease, and that bad sanitary arrangements ought to be avoided. But that certain uncivilized peoples have ideas of sanitation very different from ours, or no ideas at all, does not affect the truth of true sanitary principles. They are true whatever particular men or races of men may happen to believe about them. Should we deny the existence of a body of universally true medical principles on the ground that some peoples have thought that applying urine to the eyes is a cure for blindness, while we do not believe this? Precisely as stupid is the argument of the ethical relativists that there cannot be universally true moral principles because different people have such widely different moral ideas.

The moral teacher is the physician of human personality. If he says that, for the sake of the health of their souls, men should love one another, should curb their passions, should be truthful, honest, upright, and sincere, he may be right or wrong—just as the doctor may be right or wrong in his advice about the body. But if he is right, then these principles may well be universal, true for all men, whether men know them or not, whether they believe them or not, whatever they believe.

The opinion of the ethical relativists—which is, of course, a form of skepticism which would make nonsense of our whole enterprise in this book—seems generally to proceed upon several false assumptions. They hold, rightly, that morality is a human thing, based upon human nature and not imposed from an external source. But they then assume, falsely as I hold, that it is an expression not of the whole of human personality, but of only one part of it, the emotions. I do not mean that all relativists would put their case precisely in this way. Some doubtless would refuse to say this. Nevertheless to rest morality solely upon man's emotional nature is a tendency which most of them seem in general to exhibit. Now it seems to me that Plato's view —though it may have erred greatly in the details of its psychology—is much nearer the truth. According to him, morality expresses the harmonious relationship of *all* the elements of man's nature. His particular account of this nature was that it consisted of reason, spirit, and appetite. We need not accept this psychology, although there is obviously some degree of truth in it. But we may accept from Plato the general view that, whatever may be the true account of man's nature, morality is the expression of the whole of it.

To consider one point only for the sake of example: surely Plato was right in thinking that reason must at least have something to do with morality. The capacity for being moral is one of the characters which mark off man from the animal. But it is reason or intelligence which especially and essentially distinguishes men. It is therefore at least a probable view that other distinctively human characteristics, such as the capacity for morality, flow from, or in some way arise out of, man's rational nature. Yet this is excluded from morality by the relativists. They wish to found this exclusively human thing, morality, on a part of personality, namely emotion, which man shares with the animals. Their view might be correct. But on the face of it this does not seem likely.

The other false assumption which the relativists make is that morality, or rather moralities, are expressions of the superficial differences of men, and not of their deep-seated resemblances. Why should such an assumption be made, and does it seem inherently likely? There does not seem to be any empirical evidence for it. And apart from evidence, the natural presumptions seem to be against it. After all, morality everywhere concerns the most profoundly important things in human life. It is not a matter of trivialities. But the important for man is everywhere correlated with the deep-seated in man, the trivial with the superficial. To deny me the satisfaction of some personal idiosyncrasy of mine may annoy me. But to violate my fundamental human traits, my reason, my love, my joy in my family and children—this will disrupt, at least for a time, my whole being. These are the matters which are the substance of morality. The relativist assumption is that morality is wholly concerned with what is only skin-deep. All experience protests against such a distortion of the facts.

We may surmise that rules of conduct commonly accepted are likely to be of two kinds. Some will be based on our common humanity, others on various regional and ephemeral characters of local populations. We have this sort of thing in matters of bodily health too. There are some medical principles which depend on the facts of our common structure, and these will be universal in their application. Others may possess only a limited applicability because they are based on peculiarities of some persons. All men ought to eat green vegetables, but the inadvisability of eating sugar applies only to diabetics. If this is the case as regards human personality also, we may expect that there will be a certain body of rules of conduct which are universal, while others will be merely local because they express regional idiosyncrasies. Differing marriage customs would perhaps be of the latter type. But what we recognize as deep-rooted moral laws would belong to the first kind. The error of the ethical relativists perhaps consists in the fact that they fail to make any such distinction, and falsely suppose that all principles of conduct are of the second type.

It is only on the basis of a belief that at least the most important moral principles are an expression of a universal human nature that we can hope to find a rational justification of our belief that one morality, one civilization, one conception of the good life for man, is better than another. And unless we can believe this, it is obviously useless to proceed with our attempt to show that the principles on which our western democratic civilization has rested are superior to those on which rests the totalitarian civilization which is now threatening us.

PART TWO

Civilization

CHAPTER IV

THE GREEK CONTRIBUTION TO CIVILIZATION

A CIVILIZATION is an attempt to express in institutions what the people living in a certain area or age think to be the good life. Civilization is therefore an ethical concept, and every civilization is the embodiment of some ethos. The ethos is the soul, the institutions and customs are the body, of the civilization. Where civilizations differ and conflict, if the differences are not superficial but fundamental, it is because the embodied ethical ideals differ and conflict. Wars between countries which harbor the same ethical ideals, and so fall within the boundaries of the same civilization, are really civil wars. But a battle between civilizations is a battle between ethical ideals.

In this and the following chapters I shall discuss the fundamental attitudes to life, that is to say the ethical ideals, which have entered into the substance of western civilization. I shall consider them here as they are in their naked state, prior to their incarnation in the ordered institutions of civilized communities. Taken thus naked, they appear as ideals of personal and private living, as moral ideas in the ordinary sense. How they came to be the substance of institutions and political theories will be the subject of Chapter VII.

The phrase "western civilization" is intentionally vague. It stands for something of which the boundaries are essentially unclear. Hence it cannot be made very precise. In a very general sense it means European civilization during the Christian era. In a more special sense it means the democratic civilizations of western Europe and America. But it would be a mistake to limit it exclusively to countries which happen to have supported a democratic form of government. For countries which have not created for themselves the outward forms of democratic institutions may nevertheless have been imbued with the inward spirit and ethos of what we are calling western civilization. This inward spirit, I hold, naturally and necessarily expresses itself in democracy when it is fully developed. But this only happens where conditions have been favorable. Elsewhere we shall find stunted forms of what is, nevertheless, the same type of civilization. The democratic way of life has been Europe's special and distinctive contribution to the world. Hence the more democratic parts of Europe are the more characteristically European in their civilization.

Historical students may point out that, even in the so-called democratic countries, democracy—as we now understand it—hardly existed until very recent times. What democracy was there before the French Revolution? Even if we go back to Magna Carta, this is but a few hundred years ago. Mussolini speaks of 1789 as the "year commonly referred to as that which inaugurated the democratic and liberal century." [1] How then can we identify democratic

[1] Mussolini, "The Doctrine of Fascism" translated by Cope; Vallecchi, publisher, p. 34.

civilization in any sense with European civilization during the Christian era?

But the question has nothing at all to do with dates. The spiritual forces which have molded the west are Christianity and Greek philosophy. The fusion of them provided the ethos of European civilization. This ethos, I hold, necessarily developed into the democratic way of life—at least it so developed where conditions were favorable. This development was not an historical accident, but a logical necessity. For the democratic ideal is a necessary and logical development of the Greco-Christian ethos. It makes no difference whether the growth to full stature of the ethical idea of Europe took nineteen hundred, or only ninety, years. The seed grows into the flower. And be the growth slow or swift, the seed was there all the time; and the flower was in the seed. And if the flowering of the European ethical idea took nineteen hundred years, this shows nothing except the slow working of ideas in human history. To give but one instance of this slowness, the abolition of slavery was immanent in the Christian ethic from the beginning. But it was not till the nineteenth century that it got itself realized in practice.

To say all this is not to beg the question of the value of democracy, nor to prejudge the issue between it and its rivals. For it is a mere historical statement of fact, the truth of which might be admitted by an opponent of democracy. It is alleged merely that democracy is the characteristic product of European civilization. Whether that civilization is superior or inferior to some other which actually exists, or which may be proposed, is altogether another question.

The view that a civilization is always the expression of an ethical idea does not necessarily imply any particular philosophy of history. It does of course imply that ideas influence events. Even the Marxist does not deny this, though he apparently wishes to minimize the importance of ideas. But that ideas *do* shape human destiny is palpable, whatever the Marxist may say. It would be monstrous to deny either that Christianity is a set of ideas, or that it has influenced history. Or, to take a quite different kind of example, the steam engine was originally an idea in someone's head. And that idea has greatly changed the world. Whether ideas may not themselves be determined by some special sort of conditions, such as economic inequalities, is another question. And it is a question which I do not propose to discuss, beyond saying that it seems to involve a gross oversimplification of the facts. Human ideas are determined—in so far as they are determined at all by forces outside man himself—by man's whole environment, of which economic conditions are only a part. Why should this part be selected as the *sole* or even the *chief* determinant of ideas? Even in the purely material sphere there are other important determining factors. Wordsworth's ideas were largely a product of the fact that, from his childhood up, he found himself surrounded by *mountains*. Climate, too, is important. How much of Indian philosophy, with its dreamy ideals and its Nirvana, may not have been due to the enervating influence of heat? But we need not pursue these inquiries. Enough if we recognize that ideas enter into history, whatever the causes of the ideas.

Nor do our statements imply any particular psychological or metaphysical theory about the nature of ideas. So far as anything in this book is concerned, the reader is welcome to believe that ideas, and the minds in which they exist, are nonphysical entities which are outside space—as some philosophers and religious persons think. Or he may, if he prefers it, suppose that ideas are nothing but disturbances of brain molecules. He may call himself an idealist or a materialist or a behaviorist. Perhaps ideas are merely physical events in the brain. But even so, men have ideas, and their ideas influence history. Or perhaps ideas are only movements of the legs and larynx—as behavioristic psychologists seem to think. Still there *are* ideas. And ideas work in the world. And this is the only hypothesis about ideas which it is necessary to accept for the purposes of this book.

There are three distinct types of ethical idea to be found in the history of European thinking. They have their roots in the past, but all three are active and working in the world today. They have not remained isolated from one another in separate world-compartments. They have acted and reacted upon one another. Sometimes one has blended with another; sometimes one has battled with another. European culture has been the product of their interplay. The first of the three has its origin in the Greek ethics of *reason and moderation;* the second in the Christian ethics of *sympathy and selflessness;* the third in the Nietzschean ethics of *will and power.*

According to the view outlined in the last two chapters morality is an expression of human nature. From this there follows an important consequence. *Different or rival types of ethical ideal are always based in the end upon different or rival theories about human nature.* If you start with a certain theory of human nature, you will derive from it a certain distinctive moral ideal. If you start from a different view of human nature, you will necessarily develop a different moral ideal. The kind of morality you espouse will depend in the end upon the kind of view of human nature you hold. I do not mean that the theory of human nature which is at the root of a morality is necessarily held consciously by those who support the morality. It may be, or it may not. It may be quite unconscious. But if so, it is implicit, nevertheless, in the attitude to the world of men which is adopted by those concerned.

This truth is expressed in the three pairs of correlative words by which the three European moral ideas are above described, namely reason and moderation, sympathy and selflessness, will and power. In each case the second of the two correlative words expresses the moral ideal, while the first gives the key to the theory of human nature on which the ideal depends. Thus moderation is the Greek ideal of life, but the word *reason* is a signpost to the Greek view of human nature. This emphasized reason as the essential characteristic of man, and subordinated to it all the other elements of human psychology. The Greek theory of man was that he is a *rational* animal; and Greek ethics depended wholly upon this view. Similarly selflessness is the Christian ideal of conduct, but this is based upon an emphatic assertion of *sympathy*, rather than reason, as the central and controlling fact about man. It is sympathy, according to Christianity, which ought to rule over the other elements of human personality. That this is the essence of Christian ethics will be shown in the sequel. According to the Nietzschean type of ethical thought power is the ideal, the supreme end of human life. But this view has for philosophical. basis a particular theory about human nature, namely that will, not reason or sympathy, is its essence; and that *will*, not reason or sympathy, should rule the other factors of personality.

The first and third views of human nature may be sharply contrasted. That reason is lord over will—this is the Greek theory of man's nature. That will is lord over reason, this—derived from Schopenhauer—is the Nietzschean view. These two theories of human nature flatly contradict each other; and we shall have to ask what are the grounds for each, and which is true. There is an obvious issue here. The Christian principle of sympathy seems at first sight to stand in no specific relationship to this issue, to be an irrelevant psychological side show. We shall find that this is a false appearance, and that a profound relationship is involved.

In the development of European civilization what has been the actual interplay between these three types of moral idea? The answer is briefly as follows. All that is most characteristic in western civilization derives from two sources, Greek ethics and Christian ethics. These two, in a manner to be later described, have blended or fused with one another. Ours is a Greco-Christian civilization, not simply a Christian civilization as is often supposed. The Nietzschean ethical tradition is, or has been, a vocal opposition in Europe, a heresy. Although we give it the name Nietzschean, because Nietzsche was its most famous modern representative, it has its roots much further back in European thought. Indeed it had its representatives even in the ancient world, for the thought of Thrasymachus and Callicles, of which some account has already been given, has much in common with that of Nietzsche. But whether in the ancient world or the modern, the Nietzschean kind of ethical theory has always been regarded as a heresy. I do not mean to imply by this that it is false, or not valuable. That question must not be prejudged. Heresies sometimes turn out to be the truth. I am merely stating the historical fact that in Europe, ancient and modern, the Nietzschean type of ethical view has always been a minority tradition.

To say that our civilization is Greco-Christian, or Christian, does not mean that the men and women who compose it live up to Christian (or Greek) moral ideals. For this would be plainly untrue. People everywhere fall below the high ideals which they sincerely profess. That ours is a Greco-Christian civilization means (1) that in so far as our actual conduct is influenced by any moral ideals at all—and in spite of the cynic such influence is in fact very great—they are Greek and Christian ideals. And it means (2) that the ideas on which the institutions and customs of our civilization are based—the ethos of our civilization— are ideas derived from Christian and Greek ethical attitudes. The latter of these two meanings is the one which is of importance to us in this book. For it concerns the distinctive character of our civilization as a whole, whereas the former meaning concerns only our conduct as private individuals.

The Greeks contributed to western culture the thought of the rationality of man, and the ideal that his conduct should be guided by this rationality. Of the various psychological elements of human nature they picked out reason and asserted that it is, and ought to be, the supreme ruler over all the others.

We have already glanced at Plato's theory of human nature, and seen how his ethical ideal depends upon this theory. He maintained that the soul is divided into three parts, reason, spirit, and appetite. Each has its proper function and place in the economy of the whole personality. The function of reason is to rule the appetites, while that of spirit is to be the ally of reason and to enforce its commands. Reason is thus essentially higher than either spirit or appetite. It is the highest part of human personality. It is and ought to be the ruler of man and of all human affairs. This theory—that reason is the highest element in us, and that it ought therefore to direct us in our private conduct and in all our human relations, personal and political—may be called the theory of *the primacy of reason*. It is, of course, independent of the rest of Plato's psychology, his views of spirit and appetite. Whatever may be the elements of personality apart from reason—whether they be spirit and appetite, or will, emotion, desire, or what not—reason is king of the soul and ought to rule over the rest: this is the doctrine of the primacy of reason.

Our task is to explain the fundamental ethos of western civilization. When this ethos is taken naked, bared of all extraneous details, freed from its involvement in the welter of historical accident, it is found to consist in only two or three extremely simple ideas. The first of these ideas—the key ideas of our civilization—is that of the primacy of reason. This came from the Greeks, and especially from Plato. It is the Greek contribution to our world. Since Plato's time it has flowed in the main stream of European thought down to our own day. It has embodied itself in the western tradition, in our customs, laws, and institutions. It is thus one of the root ideas of our culture. And it is well that we should spend a little time analyzing it and examining its logical foundations. For on our estimate of its truth will in part depend our final estimate of the value of western civilization.

On what grounds did Plato, and the Greeks generally, hold that reason is higher than the other parts of human personality? The Greeks used, in general, two arguments to prove this.

First: The first argument was based upon the fact that reason is what is *specific* to man, what distinguishes him from all other animals. The capacities of desire, emotion, appetite, will, sensation, and so on, he shares with the animals. Reason is his alone. It is therefore the highest part of him.

The argument, stated thus baldly, is undoubtedly bad. That a certain factor x is peculiar to one species does not of itself imply any superiority in that factor. The rhinoceros, so far as I know, is the only animal which has horns on the top of its snout. But this does not make the possession of horns on the top of the snout an especially noble characteristic. Moreover, man has other peculiarities not shared with the animals. He is, I believe, the only animal which has highly developed earlobes. But this does not impart any peculiar glory to earlobes, or make them higher or better than the eyes, stomachs, or livers which man shares with the rest of creation.

Evidently in the argument as I have stated it there is something left out. And I think it is easy to see what this is. The Greeks took it for granted that *man is a higher being than the other animals*. And if we add this, the argument becomes plainer. For if man is a higher being than any other animal, what makes him higher must be something which he alone possesses, while the other animals do not. But what is specifically peculiar to man is his reason. This therefore must be what makes him higher. And this can only be because reason is in itself higher than those psychological elements, such as appetite, sensation, desire, emotion, which man shares with the animals. Reason then must be the highest part of him.

In considering the value of the argument thus stated, we may waive the objection that highly developed earlobes, laughter, and the wearing of clothes are also peculiar to man; and that logically speaking it might be argued that he owes his superiority to one of these rather than to reason. For the objection is captious. It can probably be shown

that many of the points in which man differs from other
animals are the result of his possession of reason. So that
the possession of reason is the real fundamental difference.
And some of the differences, such as the highly developed
earlobes, are accidental trivialities; and no one would say
that man's superiority is due to them.

What we have to concentrate attention on is the belief
that man is superior to other animals. What meaning are
we to attach to this statement? What is the meaning of
these words higher and lower, or superior and inferior, in
this context? And if we suppose that some meaning can be
given to the statement that man is higher than the other
animals, what evidence can be offered to show that it is
true?

Such words as superior and inferior, better and worse—
value words we may call them—only have meaning provided they refer to some definite scale of values. It is not
perhaps necessary that when we use such language we
should always know, in the sense of having clearly before
our minds, to what scale of values we are referring. A great
deal of vagueness in our thinking is consistent with mean-
ingfulness, and even with truth. But if our value judgments
are to have any meaning at all, there must at least *be* a
scale of values to which they refer—even if we are not
quite clear what it is. It must be possible that, if we thought
clearly enough, we *could* point out the relevant scale.

To what sort of scale of values, then, can we be referring
when we make such statements as that men are beings
superior to animals? The special point that I wish to make
here is this: that it must necessarily be some *nonhuman*
scale. We must be referring to some notion of value as
not arising out of human nature, as not being relative to
any special human characteristics or human needs. We

must be referring to some objective or cosmic standard. In short we must have in mind the conception of value as imposed, not as immanent.

For if we accept the humanist doctrine of value—moral value at any rate—as immanent, then what we mean by "good" is only "good for man" or "good from a human point of view." On the immanentist doctrine the good life for man is quite different from the good life for a cat. And what is good for man may be bad for a cat. Thus our scale of values is a human one. But if we are referring to any such scale as this when we say that men are superior to animals, it is obvious that our statement means nothing since it is a mere tautology. It means only that men are higher than dogs *from a human point of view*. They might well be lower from a canine point of view.

If we are to judge meaningfully that a man is superior to a dog, it is obvious that we require a common measure. The man-measure of value will not do. Nor will the dog-measure. Nor will any other measure which is relative to the nature of any particular being. Hence what we require is an absolute or cosmic measure.

The conclusion is that the belief that men are superior to other animals must refer to an absolute, nonhuman, and cosmic scale of values; that it can only be justified if there is such a scale; and that, unless we accept such a scale, our belief in the inherent superiority of man cannot be given any intelligible meaning.

It is of the essence of humanism that good and evil are purely human conceptions. Goodness is not something imposed upon us by the universe. There is no cosmic scale of values. But Greek thought was immanentist or humanist through and through. It is true, as already pointed out, that the opposite tendency of thought, the theory of im-

position, also appears in Plato. But this does not do away
with the overwhelmingly humanistic character of Greek
thought in general, and even of Plato's philosophy in
particular. The Greeks, therefore, had in general no right
to their belief that man is superior to the other animals.
And as this was an essential premise of the argument in
favor of the primacy of reason which we are considering,
we must conclude that at least that argument falls to the
ground. And even if we are wrong in attributing inconsistency to the Greeks, we have of our own accord to draw
the same conclusion. We, at any rate, have accepted the
humanist account of value. And therefore we cannot admit
the validity of that argument in favor of the primacy of
reason which bases itself upon man's superiority to the rest
of creation. For this conception has, for us, no meaning.
Accordingly I shall henceforth treat this argument for the
primacy of reason as invalid.

Second: There is, however, a second argument in favor
of the primacy of reason to be found in Plato. And this
argument is entirely independent of the meaningless conception of man's inherent superiority. It turns upon the
notion of proper function. Plato argued that just as each
of the organs of the physical body has its proper function,
so has each of the parts or elements of human personality.
And the proper function of reason is to govern and control
the other psychological elements. Plato reaches this conclusion by simple observation. We know that it is the
proper function of the heart to pump blood simply by
observing the fact that this is what it does in normal and
healthy men, and by further observing the fact that if the
heart fails to perform this function satisfactorily, the man
becomes unhealthy or dies. Just so Plato seeks to show by
observation that it is the proper function of reason to rule

the whole man. For this is what reason actually does in men who have a normal and healthy personality, in men whose lives are considered satisfactory and therefore good. If men are ruled by their appetites, on the other hand, we find that their lives are of the kind which are considered unsatisfactory or bad. From this it follows that reason is higher than the other elements of personality in the sense that it is their natural ruler, in the sense in which the king is higher than his subjects.

I shall postpone to a later page the final evaluation of this type of argument. I will say here merely that, in my opinion, it is only through some argument of this kind that the conception of the primacy of reason—on which in part our civilization depends—can be validated. I do not mean that the details of Plato's thought can be accepted. But I think we shall have in the end to rely upon some version of the type of argument which bases itself upon the notion of the proper functions of the elements of personality.

Final consideration of this matter must be postponed. But in the meanwhile it will be useful to note that Plato's argument gives a definite and intelligible meaning to the notion of "higher than" and to the doctrine of the primacy of reason in general; and that the meaning so given is not inconsistent, but consistent, with the humanist account of value which we have accepted.

First, as to the meaning of "higher than." To say that reason is higher than the other elements of personality, such as will, appetite, or emotion, means only that it is the proper function of reason to control these other elements. It is higher than they are in the same sense that the brain is higher than the other nerve centers. No doubt a question can be raised about how reason *can* control elements such as desire, and whether in fact it ever does so. But that is another question; and one which we shall have to raise ourselves on a later page. Whatever the answer to it may be, it does not alter the fact that a definite meaning has now been given to the doctrine of the primacy of reason. We are not to interpret it as implying that reason is, in some mystical way, nobler than other psychological factors. It is simply higher in the sense that it is the natural ruler of them. If we want to add that it is *for this reason* to be regarded as nobler, there will perhaps be no objection—except that we shall not be adding anything of importance to the doctrine; we shall be merely adding honorifics. The fallacy of the first argument in favor of the primacy of reason consisted in saying that reason ought to rule because it is in some way intrinsically nobler. We avoid this fallacy if we reverse this statement and say, as is now suggested, that it is called nobler merely because it is the ruler.

The doctrine of the primacy of reason, when it is interpreted as is now suggested, is entirely consistent with humanism and does not imply any nonhuman or cosmic standard of values. It does not rest upon the basis that man is higher than the other animals. For what is meant is that if a man is to achieve perfect health of personality (which is morality) then his reason must be in control. Otherwise he falls into spiritual ill-health (which is moral badness). This truth depends upon nothing except man's psychological structure, just as the rules of physical health depend upon man's physical structure. It is not true for any nonrational being. Thus it is only *for man* that reason is the highest element of personality. The measure of value relative to which this judgment of the superiority of reason is made is the human measure. It is rooted in human psychology, not in the nonhuman universe. Reason ought to control men only because this control alone leads—in the special case of man—to a satisfactory life.

In the light of what has been said it ought to be clear that the doctrine of the primacy of reason may have two entirely distinct meanings—and it is most important to keep them separate in our minds. The first meaning is that reason possesses an absolute, inherent, and intrinsic value in itself, and that for this reason—because it is inherently nobler than will, emotion, appetite, etc.—it ought to rule over them. This meaning evidently influenced the Greek mind, since it is what is implied by the view that man, because of his reason, is higher than the other animals. It certainly influenced Plato himself in spite of his predominant humanism. In the modern world it was maintained by Kant; and is doubtless still maintained by many thinkers. But according to the analysis which I have given it is quite false.

The second meaning of the doctrine of the primacy of reason is only that for us, for men, reason is and ought to be supreme in our lives because only thus can human personality function in a normal, healthy, happy, and satisfactory manner. This is the view derived from Plato's humanism, and it is the only version of the theory which is consistent with immanentism. Whether it is ultimately true or not is a question which will require much further discussion. On it depends in large measure the question whether our type of civilization is capable of ultimate justification. For the moment I am explaining only the meaning of the doctrine, not arguing the question of its truth.

If the primacy of reason is one of the root ideas of western civilization, the question will then be asked whether western civilization rests upon its first or its second meaning. Is our civilization based upon the belief that reason is superior as having an intrinsic and absolute value in the cosmic scale of things? Or is it based only upon the belief that reason should govern human affairs merely because this alone will lead to a satisfactory human life? If the former, then the basic faith on which our civilization rests is one which cannot in my opinion be justified. We shall have to hold that it rests upon a falsehood, or at least upon a meaningless idea. If the latter, there is at least a possibility that further analysis may show that the doctrine of the primacy of reason is true.

The question now raised is not which of the two meanings has been most commonly maintained, as a matter of historical fact, by the thinkers of the western world who have been the representatives of our civilization. If this were what were being asked I do not know what the answer would be. Perhaps a majority of European thinkers have agreed with Kant in attributing an intrinsic cosmic value to reason. This is what we should expect in view of the fact that Europe for nearly twenty centuries has been under the influence of Palestinian impositionism. But the real question is not one of history; it is rather one of logic. Which of the two meanings of the primacy of reason is it logically necessary to hold if we are to succeed in our enterprise of establishing the truth of the basic principles of our civilization? Which of the two meanings does our civilization *require* if it is to establish its value in the world? The majority of thinkers may have *thought* that it required a belief in the cosmic superiority of reason. Or they may at any rate have believed in this cosmic superiority whether they thought this necessary for our civilization or not. And in both of these beliefs they may have been wrong.

To the real, that is the logical, question at issue, I shall answer that the only meaning of the doctrine of the pri-

macy of reason which is necessary for our civilization—
that by which it stands or falls—is the belief that reason is
superior, and should rule, in the sense that this alone will
lead to a satisfactory human life. It is upon this belief that
our civilization really rests. For the best civilization means
the best way of life *for man*. It does not mean the embodiment of absolute values, the flowering of cosmic nobility.
Or if it does mean this—as some, of course, will still wish to
urge—it is at any rate not necessary to show it. It will be
enough if we can show that the way of life which our
western civilization envisages as the best way—and I shall
try to establish that this is in the end simply the democratic
way—is really the best way in the sense that it yields the
most satisfactory human life as judged by purely human
standards. And for this no doctrine of the absolute cosmic
value of reason is necessary.

I shall therefore in the future presume (1) that by the
doctrine of the primacy of reason is meant only the humanist view that the control of all the elements of personality by reason is in accordance with the natural functions
of the parts of personality, and must accordingly lead to a
healthy state of personality, and therefore to a satisfactory
life; and (2) that our western civilization rests upon this
belief, and does not require for its justification any belief
in the doctrine of the primacy of reason in its other non-
humanistic and, as I believe, illegitimate sense.

I have called Greek ethics the ethics of reason and moderation. This implies that it contained two distinct ideas;
first, the idea of the primacy of reason; second, the ideal
of the moderate life. It is necessary to emphasize that these
are two ideas, not one, although the second is based—or was
supposed by the Greeks to be based—upon the first. The
first was, properly speaking, a contribution to psychology;

the second a contribution to ethics. The second was supposed to be logically implied by the first.

It is, however, the first and not the second of these two ideas which has been the special contribution of Greece to the civilization of the west. It is the idea of the primacy of reason which has guided the modern world in the formation of its characteristic democratic institutions. The ethical ideal of moderation has been of minor importance. The west has looked for its inspiration to the Christian ethical ideal of selflessness, not to the Greek ideal of moderation.

Not of course that the ideal of moderation is repudiated by our western culture. On the contrary, it is and always must be a guiding consideration of the good life. We, like other people, seek to be moderate in the indulgence of our appetites. We think temperance in all things to be a part of goodness. To be moderate is commonly equated with being reasonable. And being reasonable is commonly thought to be good. And it is probable that in all this we may rightly trace Greek influence.

But the ideal of moderation is not *distinctive* of the west. It does not give the characteristic and peculiar flavor of western, as distinct from other, ethical cultures. It is more or less universal, a characteristic of all stable and advanced civilizations. For instance, it seems to be much more the fundamental note of Chinese ethical culture than of ours. It is universal because no stable and advanced civilization can exist at all without it. It is present in our culture, of course. But what is peculiar and distinctive to the ethos of western civilization is the Christian ideal of selflessness.

It is extremely doubtful whether the Greeks were in fact right in supposing that the doctrine of the primacy of reason logically implies the ideal of moderation; or that the ideal of moderation is properly based upon the doctrine of the primacy of reason. What seems much more likely is that the special emphasis which the Greeks placed upon moderation was an outgrowth of their esthetic ideal of balance and harmony. The life of extremes repelled them because it is lopsided. It implies the overdevelopment of one part of the man and the underdevelopment of another. It thus violated their strong feeling for the importance of a balanced whole. But this is an esthetic idea, while the primacy of reason belongs to the spheres of psychology.

What happened, I think, was that the Greek philosophers, such as Plato and Aristotle, sought to rationalize their more or less intuitive preference for the balanced life by trying to connect it with the doctrine of the primacy of reason. They gave as the reason for believing in the moderate life their belief in the primacy of reason. But this was not the real reason. The Greek mind had at least these two strongly marked characteristics, an intense rationalism (belief in the supremacy of reason) and an intense estheticism. The Greeks sought to assimilate these ideas to one another by showing that the second was really based upon the first. And in this it seems to me they were mistaken.

The reason I say this is that the ideal of moderation does not in fact follow logically from the doctrine of the primacy of reason. And the Greek philosophers committed a fallacy in supposing that it did. Moderation is a precept based either—as with the Greeks—upon an esthetic sense of balance, or upon general utilitarian considerations. It is not, and cannot be, deduced *a priori* from reason. It is found in experience that excess does not lead to a normal, healthy, and satisfactory life. Neither does a deficiency of appetite or a complete denial of the passions. This is empirically found, and might logically be connected with any theory whatever about the place of reason in life. Thus it might be accepted by the Schopenhauerian who teaches that reason, so far from being supreme, is the mere bond servant of the will.

It is logically impossible to deduce moderation from the supremacy of reason. If, prior to any actual experience of life, a model of the human soul were to be constructed showing reason in control and the appetites controlled, it would be impossible to predict that reason would direct volition or appetite to the middle point. It might direct to excess or privation. There is nothing inherently rational, i.e., logical, about moderation. It is only by living our lives, by putting the model in motion, that we learn that it works best if the pointer is set somewhere in the middle of the dial rather than at either end. *After* this has been learned by experience we can say, if we like, that the moderate life is the reasonable life. And this means only that since the moderate life has been found by experience to be the most humanly satisfactory, therefore the intelligent, i.e., the reasonable man, will of course aim at this. Reason would have aimed at excess if that had been found to work better. Moderation is reasonable because it is best. It is not best because it is reasonable. To suppose the latter was the fallacy of the Greek philosophers. For in saying that the primacy of reason implied the ethical ideal of moderation they were saying that moderation is best because it is reasonable—which is to put the cart before the horse.

This conclusion is of some importance to our inquiry. For our western culture has taken from the Greeks the doctrine of the primacy of reason and made this doctrine part of the essential substance of our civilization. But western culture has *not* drawn the Greek conclusion that moderation is the highest ideal of the good life. On the contrary—though of course it admits moderation as a good thing—its supreme ideal is selflessness. And this, I shall try to show, is justified. Western culture has disconnected the doctrine of the primacy of reason from the ideal of moderation and connected it with the Christian ideal. This would have been logically incoherent—and our civilization would have been founded upon a contradiction—if the Greeks had been right in believing that the primacy of reason logically implies the ideal of moderation. It was therefore important to show that it does not. We shall find in fact that to connect the ideal of selflessness with the supremacy of reason is more logically coherent than to connect the ideal of moderation with it; because there *is* a logical affinity between reason and selflessness, whereas there is no such affinity between reason and moderation.

Though the theory of the supreme value of reason was not the real basis of the Greek ethical ideal, it did nevertheless in many important ways mold the lives of the Greeks. It explains the high esteem in which they held all intellectual pursuits. It was the Greeks who invented the idea of thinking for thinking's sake, of knowledge as an end in itself. For instance, as is well known, geometry had its beginnings in Egypt, but was there cultivated only in the interest of land surveying. It was the Greeks who disconnected it from its practical applications and made it a pursuit for its own sake. It was noble, even divine, to understand the properties of the circle, the triangle, the square. But to apply these divine truths to the solution of practical problems was thought by the Greeks to be a relatively inferior occupation. To know them, simply to contemplate them—this was the real good. No people in the world save the Greeks and those who have been influenced by the Greeks have ever valued pure knowledge for its own sake. Even the profound metaphysical speculations of the Hindus have always been connected with a practical interest, that of the soul's salvation from the world, from reincarnation, from craving, from sorrow.

Wherever in the modern world knowledge is thought to be *in itself* a valuable end, there the Greek influence is still at work. It permeates our universities. It has been the inspiration of all European science. Why is it that Europe has so amazingly developed pure science, while every other civilization in the world, however advanced ethically and esthetically, has practically no science at all? This has been entirely due to the Greek belief in knowledge for the sake of knowledge. And this in turn is an offshoot of the doctrine of the primacy of reason. If western civilization had followed the view of Professor Dewey and the pragmatists and regarded knowledge and thought as mere means to the solution of practical problems, we should have been today as lacking in science as are the civilizations of India and China.

CHAPTER V

THE CHRISTIAN CONTRIBUTION
TO CIVILIZATION

IF THE one source of the ethos of our civilization was Greek philosophy, the other was Christian ethics. Greece developed the ethics of reason and moderation. The ethical ideal of moderation was supposed to be founded upon a theory of human nature which saw reason as its central and governing factor. For the life in which the appetites were ruled by reason was by the Greeks identified with a life of moderation, a life which followed the middle path in all things. Now if one seeks a single word which will express the Christian moral ideal, one may find it perhaps either in the word selflessness or in the word love. And these two words, so far as I know, mean the same thing. I shall speak of selflessness as the Christian ideal. It is better, I think, than the phrase self-sacrifice which is also sometimes used. For the term self-sacrifice is scarcely applicable save to the heroic occasions of life. The supreme and final demands of self-sacrifice are seldom made upon us. But a man may be selfless in his every thought and act. Self-denial is also not a good phrase for the Christian ideal. It expresses a negative virtue, and sometimes the mere formalistic aping of goodness.

As has already been suggested, every moral ideal rests ultimately upon some view of human nature, some special belief about the psychology of man. The Greek ideal of moderation rested, or was supposed to rest, upon the theory of the primacy of reason. And we have now to ask what is the theory of human nature which is at the root of the Christian ideal of selflessness.

It is essential that we should discover the answer to this question if we are to succeed in our task of providing a rational justification of our type of civilization. For the Christian ideal has entered into the marrow of that civilization. Our failure to attain the ideal may be abysmal. But the life of love, charity, and selflessness is nevertheless our traditional conception of the good life. It is at the root of our institutions, customs, and laws. It is the fundamental inspiration of the democratic way of life. If these statements are doubted, a single instance may perhaps suffice to clear our vision. Suppose that for the Christian ideal of selflessness we should substitute in our civilization the opposite ideal of self-assertion—which is the principle of the Nietzschean ethics. Suppose that we took our new ideal seriously and pressed it to its logical conclusion. One of the first things we should have to do would be to abolish welfare institutions, hospitals, and the majority of charitable organizations. For these are all founded upon the Christian principle that the strong and able should succor the weak and lowly. They are founded upon the ideal of love and selfless service to others. According to the Nietzschean ethics, the weak and lowly ought *not* to be succored. They should be left to die out.

It follows that if we are to give a rational justification of

our civilization we must give a rational justification of the
Christian ideal of selflessness. We must show that it is a
true moral ideal, perhaps *the* true moral ideal. If it is a false
ideal—as Nietzsche suggests—then ours is a false and bad
civilization, and does not deserve to endure.

The only way of discovering whether any particular set
of moral principles is true or false is to examine the theory of human nature on which it depends. If the moral
principles have a false psychological basis, then they themselves will almost certainly be false. If they arise out of a
true theory of human nature, and if they draw the correct
deductions from that theory, they will be true. This is
merely another way of stating the humanistic criteria of
good and bad moralities which we have already discussed.
Morality is an expression of human nature. Hence the question in any particular case is whether the morality which
we are trying to evaluate is a true expression of human nature, whether it is based on a true and adequate psychology.

Thus we have the following situation. If we are to evaluate our civilization, we have to evaluate its conception of
the good life, that is, its moral ideal. In the case of western
civilization this will certainly mean evaluating—among
other things—the ideal of selflessness. But this cannot be
done without examining its psychological basis. And this
brings us to the question which we are now proposing to
ask: What *is* the psychological basis of the Christian ideal
of selflessness? On what theory of human nature is the
Christian ethic founded?

The question presents peculiar difficulties owing to the
fact that the founders of Christianity were not philosophers, not intellectuals of any kind, but men of the people.
Not, of course, that their ideals and ideas are any the worse
for that. But Plato and Aristotle, being philosophers, natu-

rally put the philosophical, or psychological, bases of their ethical ideals in the forefront of their writings. So that we do not have to search for them. But the case with Christian ethics is very different. There is nowhere to be found in the recorded sayings of Jesus, nor even in the writings of the more philosophical Paul, any hint of the philosophical basis of the ideal of selflessness. We have to divine it for ourselves.

If we cannot do so, we shall be—intellectually speaking—in a parlous state. For we cannot then discover any rational justification for the ideal of selflessness. In that case we shall have to regard it as a mere private preference of certain peculiar persons. These persons, we shall have to say, happen to like and admire selflessness, and to prefer it to the opposite ideal of self-assertion. But there will be no ground for supposing that their ideal is actually any better than the opposite ideal. Some men prefer beef, others prefer mutton. No one would say that one of these is right, the other wrong. There is no disputing about tastes. Are we to say the same thing about moral ideals, and about the civilizations which grow out of them?

It may be suggested that the theological doctrine of the fatherhood of God and the brotherhood of man is the philosophical basis of the Christian ideal of love. I shall not discuss whether this is true or not. For in any case it is not what we want. We are in search of the *psychological* foundations of Christian ethics; in other words the theory of human nature which it implies. Even if, in one sense, Christian theology is the basis of Christian ethics, in another sense it must be true that there is a psychological foundation. There must be a theory of human nature involved. And it is this, and this alone, which is of importance to us in our inquiries.

Since no answer to our question is to be found in the sacred writings, we have to discover it for ourselves. And the answer in outline seems to me to be as follows. As the Greeks emphasized reason as the great fact of human nature, so Christianity emphasizes sympathy. And as the Greek ideal of moderation was believed to grow out of the doctrine of the primacy of reason, so the Christian ideal of selflessness grows out of the belief that sympathy is the prime fact of human nature. Sympathy is the psychological source of selflessness, just as reason was believed by the Greeks to be the psychological source of moderation.

It is unfortunate that the word sympathy is apt to suggest something sickly and feeble. Sentimentalists wallow in mutual sympathy. And as some men keep holding out their hands to the world for gold, there are others who seem to go about begging for sympathy. And this tends to arouse our contempt. We feel it to be unmanly. There is undoubtedly plausibility in Nietzsche's condemnation of sympathy as sentimental weakness.

But it is true of all gracious and beautiful things that sentimentalists can ruin them with their fawning. Fine and noble in themselves, they can be sentimentalized into decadence and softness. Flowers are beautiful. But the esthete who lunches on the color and form of a daffodil disgusts us. Gentleness and charity and love and kindness are good. But there is, of course, such a thing as weak humanitarianism.

So when we say that the psychological principle of sympathy in human nature is the root of Christian ethics we must be careful not to associate with it the common sickly overtones. And perhaps the best way will be to give a definition of what sympathy actually is. We shall then be able to see that it is not, in essence, any of the decadent things with which it is commonly confounded. The best definition I can find is one which has been suggested to me by the writings of Bergson.[1] *Sympathy is the infectious character of feelings and emotions.* It is the fact that feelings and emotions tend to flow, or spread, from individual to individual. Thus panic in a crowd is an example of sympathy. The fear set up in a few individuals spreads like wildfire to the others. The fact that herds of animals can be stampeded proves that they, as well as men, are subject to the influences of sympathy. Many well-known phenomena of crowd psychology are also due to sympathy. In the theater the pity and terror which we should feel at tragic happenings on the stage if we were alone are enormously enhanced by the presence of the other members of the audience. An orator moves us very deeply in a crowd by words which would leave us more or less cold if we faced him in an otherwise empty hall. In all such cases we receive the emotions from two sources. We see the horrifying spectacle on the stage, or hear the moving words of the orator. The appropriate emotions are thereby directly engendered in us. But they also flow into us indirectly via the other members of the audience. In this way the force of the emotions is enhanced. This is also why in a company of people we may laugh uproariously at a joke which would only mildly amuse us if we were alone.

Doubtless some worthy psychologist will break in at this point to "explain" these facts by some physical or physiological principle or other. But we can ignore his explanations. They may perhaps be true, but they are unimportant to us. It is the facts themselves which concern us. This flowing or passage of emotions from one person to another

[1] Henri Bergson, "The Two Sources of Morality and Religion," page 45; Macmillan, New York, 1935.

is what I call sympathy. It is certainly a fact, as anyone may observe for himself in almost any social situation. It may have a physical or physiological explanation. But whether it has or not, or what the explanation is, will make no difference to anything that is said in this book. We shall talk, in the common language of men, about human sympathy. And everyone, I think, will understand what we mean.

All emotions and feelings of whatever kind are, so far as I know, subject to the kind of contagion which is here called sympathy. At any rate all the common ones, such as fear, anger, hatred, love, jealousy, are subject to it. But the sympathy on which Christian ethics is based is mainly the contagion of those complexes of feeling which we vaguely call happiness and unhappiness. That these are utterly vague words I well know. But I shall not attempt any analysis of them. I shall rely upon our intuitive understanding of them. It is just as much a fact that the happiness and unhappiness of those around us tend to make us happy or unhappy as that their fear tends to make us afraid. It is true that individuals differ in their sensitivity in this respect. Some are highly susceptible to the infection. These are the so-called "sympathetic" people. Others are relatively immune. These are the "callous" people. But no one is entirely immune, unless he is a psychological freak. Sympathy is as much a normal part of human personality as reason or appetite is. It is not entirely peculiar to man, being shared in some measure at least with the so-called higher animals. But in the human species it is enormously more developed than in any animal.

The stock example of common human self-sacrifice is that of the mother for her child. This is based entirely upon the psychological mechanism of sympathy. The feelings of

the child flow into the mother in a manner peculiarly force-
ful and unobstructed. His happiness makes her happy. His
unhappiness makes her unhappy. Therefore she labors for
his happiness. And so great is the contagion of feelings in
this case that the child's hunger may cause the mother more
acute suffering than her own hunger would. She is thus
faced with a choice between two evils, her own hunger
and the suffering caused to her through the channel of
sympathy by the spectacle of her child's hunger. Of the
two sufferings she will choose that which is the less. If her
own hunger is for her the less suffering, she will choose it,
and "sacrifice" herself for her child.

At this point the reader will perhaps be led to suggest
that what is here being stated implies the doctrine of egoism. Egoism maintains that all human action—even that
which appears to be unselfish—is in fact based upon selfish
motives. And it is now suggested that the mother's self-
sacrifice is caused by her own desire to choose the course
of action which results in the least suffering for herself.
And this, it seems, implies egoism.

We need not quarrel about words. And if anyone wishes
to call this egoism, he can. But what I wish to point out is
that it is not egoism in the usual meaning of that word, in
the meaning which it has, for example, when we say that
Hobbes was an egoist. It is in fact the very opposite of the
Hobbesian doctrine. For the true essence of egoism—in
the Hobbesian sense—is that it denies the existence of sympathy altogether; whereas the view I have stated makes
sympathy the sole psychological cause of self-sacrifice. I
shall elaborate this contrast. And I shall maintain that the
psychological principle which I have suggested is at the
basis of Christian ethics, while Hobbesian egoism is the
complete denial of Christian ethics. When in the future I

use the word egoism, I shall mean egoism of the Hobbesian type. And I shall assert that this egoism is false.

According to egoism, if a man acts unselfishly, this is because, consciously or unconsciously, he calculates on a return. He expects dividends. We help others because, and only because, we expect others to render help to us when we need it. Morality is only intelligent selfishness. The selfish or bad man is too stupid to see that, if he grabs everything for himself, others will treat him in the same way, so that he will get less in the end. The good and unselfish man is really just as selfish in his motives, but is wise enough to see that a policy of unselfishness (up to a point) will pay him better.

This is to assert that *no man ever considers the happiness of another person as an end in itself*, or treats it as such. We may define an end in itself as that which directly satisfies a desire, or that which is desired for itself alone. A means is that which is desired only because it leads to something else which is desired for itself. There is nothing especially mysterious or noble or exalted about ends in themselves. Thus if I take medicine to recover my health, I treat it as a means. But my small son who, when my back is turned, eats cough drops (though he has no cough) because he enjoys their taste, is treating the cough drops as ends in themselves. Means and ends are not mutually exclusive. A thing may be both a means and an end in itself to me at the same time. I may eat lobster salad and other pleasant foods both to preserve my life and because I enjoy their taste. As a preservative of my life they are means; as a source of immediate enjoyment they are ends in themselves.

Now what the egoist is in effect asserting is that the happiness of another, if it is sought by me, is sought always only as a means to other ends of mine. He denies that I can seek it simply because I enjoy it as I enjoy a lobster salad. And in doing so he overlooks the psychological principle of sympathy. What this principle tells us is that any emotion or feeling, or complex of emotions or feelings, may flow from another person into me, and may thereby become my feelings. His fear may infect me so that I myself am afraid. In the same way the complex of feelings which I call the happiness of another may flow into me, and thereby I myself become happy. This derived happiness will, of course, be enjoyed by me. Thus I can enjoy the happiness of another for itself. In other words I can, and often do, treat it as an end in itself. Thus an alternative definition of sympathy is that it is the capacity of a man to treat the feelings of others as ends in themselves.

It may be objected that if I seek the happiness of another because it yields me satisfaction or makes me happy, I am really treating his happiness as a means to my satisfaction and so not as an end in itself. This is a fallacy. I might equally say that when I eat a lobster salad simply to enjoy its taste, I am treating it as a means to my enjoyment and so not as an end in itself. By definition an end in itself is whatever *itself* produces satisfaction in me and is desired for that reason. And if I seek the happiness of another because this produces satisfaction or happiness in me, this is precisely what is meant by calling it an end in itself.

In the light of what has been said above we can see that the egoist, in saying that all human actions and motives are selfish, is either denying the possibility of sympathetic action or is at any rate guilty of an abuse of language. If he denies that the mother may be motivated by nothing but a desire for her child's happiness, because that may in itself yield the greatest possible happiness to her, he is denying plain facts. What he is denying is the psychological law of sympathy. But if he admits these facts, and yet argues that, since the mother seeks the child's happiness because it makes *her* happy, she is for that reason selfish, he is then guilty of a serious abuse of language. To see this we have only to ask what we *mean* by the words selfish and unselfish.

In what sort of cases should we ordinarily say that an action is unselfish? And in what sort of cases should we say that it is not unselfish? Let us take examples. The action of a father who, being himself in poor circumstances, works overtime, scrapes and pares, denies himself luxuries and even necessities, and possibly impairs his health, in order to give his son a good education, would—provided he expects no return from his son or anyone else—be universally called unselfish. Now suppose that he acted in exactly the same way, but that this time he did so because his son had been promised a lucrative post on reaching a certain standard of education, and had undertaken thereupon to make his father rich. No one would in this case call the father's action unselfish. It would not necessarily be described as selfish or bad. But we should say that the father's motives were self-interested and calculating. We should deny that they ought to be described as unselfish. What is the difference between the two cases?

In both cases what the father immediately desires and works for is the welfare and advancement of his son. But in the first case he desires this for its own sake, that is, as an end in itself. Of course this implies that the son's welfare yields him, the father, satisfaction. In the second case the father desires his son's welfare as a means to a further end, namely his own future enrichment. Thus what we *mean* by an unselfish act is one which is motivated by the desire for the happiness of another as an end in itself, and not as a means to any further end.

Of course it is true that when a man thus unselfishly desires the happiness of another, it is *his own* desire which causes him to act. And of course *he himself* achieves satisfaction through the fulfillment of this desire. How could it possibly be otherwise? An engine is only propelled into motion by its own steam, and not by the steam in another engine. And a man can only be propelled into action by his own desire, not by the desire of another man. And when his own desire is fulfilled, he necessarily feels satisfaction. It follows that we do not, and cannot, mean by an unselfish act one which does not aim at the satisfaction of any desire of the agent's. For no such action does or could exist. We mean by an unselfish act one in which the agent receives his satisfaction solely from the happiness of another person which the action produces, without aiming at any *other*, or *ulterior*, end. Thus the egoist's discovery, or rather tautology, that even so-called unselfish acts are done to satisfy the agent's own desire, does not make such acts selfish, and does not obliterate the distinction between selfishness and unselfishness.

The correct position is indicated in the diagram below.

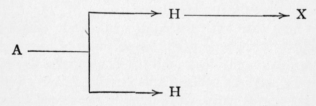

All actions which aim at the happiness of others are done to gratify the agent's own desires. But such actions divide into two kinds. *A* stands for the agent. *H* stands for the happiness of another person. The arrows from A to H in both lines indicate that the agent A is aiming at the happiness of this other person. X stands for some other end— which may be gold, or a reputation for kindness or anything else whatsoever—to the attainment of which A is treating H as a means. Thus in the action shown on the top line A aims at H, the happiness of another, but he desires it only as a means to some other end X. This action is self-interested. In the action shown on the lower line A also aims at H, the happiness of another. But the fact that the arrow stops at H, and that there is no further arrow to the right of H pointing to anything beyond, indicates that in this case H is sought as an end in itself. This is then an unselfish or disinterested act. And it is seen to be perfectly consistent with the fact that A does it, in a sense, for his own gratification.

But why does this act gratify A? The only possible psychological explanation is through the law of sympathy, the law that feelings tend to flow from one person to another. A's act produces H, which is a certain complex of feelings of happiness in another person. There is thereupon a backflow of the feelings H from this other person to A. This happens through the mechanism of sympathy. Thus we have the following:

The solid arrow represents the action of A which produces H, the happiness of the other person. The dotted arrow represents the sympathetic backflow of feelings from the other person to *A*. This backflow produces *A*'s satisfaction or sense of gratification. The expectation of it is his motive.

From this analysis we may now draw an important conclusion, namely, that *the psychological basis of every disinterestedly unselfish action is the principle of sympathy*. This may be used to throw light upon the question of the psychological basis of Christian ethics, the theory of human nature on which it is founded. I pointed out earlier that, since the founders of Christianity had not expounded the philosophical or psychological basis of their moral ideas, we had to divine it for ourselves. And I named sympathy as the basis of Christian ethics in the same way as reason was said to be the basis of Greek ethics. Since this suggestion admittedly finds no substantiation in the sacred writings of Christianity, it may well have appeared as an arbitrary guess. It should now be evident that this was not the case. The preceding analysis is in fact the proof of our thesis. For it shows that the psychological basis of every conceivable disinterestedly unselfish act is sympathy. But selflessness, which is the Christian moral ideal, is the same as disinterested unselfishness. Hence the Christian ideal is founded exclusively upon emphasis upon the principle of sympathy as a fact in human nature.

We have now to notice a marked difference between Greek and Christian ethics. From among the various elements of human personality the Greek ethics selects one for supreme emphasis, namely reason. Upon this it seeks to found the good life. From among the same elements Christianity selects another, namely sympathy, for supreme emphasis. And it seeks to build its idea of the good life upon that. But the Greek thinkers asserted the doctrine that reason is higher than the other psychic elements, and that for this reason it ought to govern them. And they attempted to justify this alleged superior status of reason by two definite arguments. The first was that man is higher than the other animals, that what makes him higher must be what he does not share with the other animals, and that this is reason. The second was that an examination of the structure of human personality shows that the proper function of reason is to control the other elements. Christianity, on the other hand, does not assert any definite doctrine of the primacy of sympathy; that is, it does not assert, in explicit terms at any rate, that sympathy is superior to, or higher than, reason, appetite, will, etc., and that it ought therefore to govern them. Nor does it offer any reason at all for selecting sympathy, rather than any other element of personality, as its basis for morals. It vaguely assigns to sympathy a leading rôle in the good life, without giving any reasons, and without explaining what is the relation between sympathy and the other psychic elements. On the surface at least the procedure of Christian ethics thus appears thoroughly arbitrary. It provides for itself no reasoned justification. Why should it select sympathy rather than will or hatred or aggressiveness or self-interest as the fountain of the good life? Its actual selection might be, for all one can tell to the contrary, a mere vagary or private preference of the founders of Christianity.

Of course this is not the real position. When the proper time comes I shall try to show that the Christian principle is capable of rational justification. But Christianity itself has never troubled to provide such a justification. This, of course, is just what one would expect. The founders were not philosophers, but common people. Their moral creed was an intuition, not a reasoned system of thought like the philosophies of Plato and Aristotle. This intuition was not the less true for being no more than an intuition. But the result of this procedure is that we who, amid the onslaught of hostile moral creeds, seek a rational basis for the faith which is in us, find ourselves without guidance. If there is a rational basis we shall have to discover it, dig it out, for ourselves.

Undoubtedly this has been one of the main weaknesses of Christianity. It offered the world its vague and noble intuitions, naïvely confident that men had only to turn their eyes to the light to see it. Christianity appealed to the world by its tender beauty, but left itself unarmed against the hostility of those who could not, or would not, perceive this beauty. The result has been that when it is attacked by enemies, by those for example who assert that sympathy is nothing but decadent weakness, it has no answer to make. It can only plaintively and ineffectually reiterate its moral vision. We who accept the ideal of selflessness, when we are offered instead the Nietzschean ideal of aggression and self-assertion, have no doubt which we prefer. But if we are challenged to show why the ideal which we reject is erroneous or ignoble, what answer can we give?

The rational justification which the Greek philosophers gave for their principle of the primacy of reason was not indeed free from elements of falsity. Of their two main arguments one, as we have seen, was fallacious. We have not yet examined the validity of the other. But the Greeks, if they did not provide a philosophical proof of their position which can withstand all criticism, did at least provide invaluable materials which can help towards the construction of such a justification. The Christian founders simply saw no necessity for a justification.

The Greeks asserted the doctrine of the primacy of reason. This meant that it is the proper function of reason to rule the other psychic elements. There is nothing to show that Christian ethics rests upon, or implies the view that, in any corresponding sense, it is the proper function of sympathy to rule the remainder of the personality. The most one can say is that in the Christian scheme sympathy is high-lighted. It is played up, while the other psychic elements are played down. It is credited with being the main-spring of moral action, while the part to be played by the other elements is minimized or even ignored. There is no objection to calling this a doctrine of the primacy of sympathy, and I shall sometimes use that phrase. But it must not be forgotten that it does not correspond, point for point, with the Greek theory of the primacy of reason.

In any case a problem is left on our hands. The Greeks assigned to reason the leading rôle in the psychological causation of the good life. The Christians assigned the same rôle to sympathy. The two positions do not appear to be consistent with one another. How can both reason and sympathy take the lead at once? Yet our Greco-Christian civilization owns allegiance both to the Greek principle of the primacy of reason and to the Christian principle of the primacy of sympathy. How is this possible? Is there an inner contradiction in the ethos of our civilization? Or has it somehow discovered a reconciliation? If so, it will have to be shown that, in spite of appearances to the contrary, the primacy of reason and the primacy of sympathy are not really inconsistent with one another. Sooner or later we shall have to face this problem.

CHAPTER VI

THE INFINITE VALUE OF THE INDIVIDUAL

A T THE end of the last chapter I mentioned the problem: How can Greek and Christian ideas of the good life have combined to form the ethos of our Greco-Christian civilization when the two sets of ideas do not seem to be compatible with one another? The problem may be said to arise at two distinct levels, the level of the superstructure of ethical ideals and the level of the psychological foundations. The arrows in the diagram indicate that in each case

the ethical ideal shown on the top line has arisen out of the psychological theory at the base. Our civilization has somehow contrived to fuse together the two types of thought in a single ethos. The resulting problem seems thus to be twofold. First, does the ethical ideal of moderation in any way contradict the ethical ideal of selflessness? Or can they exist harmoniously together in the same culture? Secondly, can the theory of the primacy of reason be combined with the theory of the primacy of sympathy? Has a harmonious combination of them actually been achieved by our civilization? And if so, how has this been done in view of the apparent impossibility of having two distinct elements of personality, reason and sympathy, each designated for the leading part in the ideal life? Can the soul have two captains?

The first of these problems presents no real difficulty. In the first place, as already pointed out, the characteristic note which our civilization has taken from Greek thought is not really the ideal of moderation but the theory of the primacy of reason. It is this which has somehow to be fitted into the Christian scheme. Of course we do as a rule think moderation a good thing, and aim at it in our lives. And no doubt in this we have been influenced by the Greek spirit, although it is also true that all reasonably civilized peoples, whether they owe anything to the Greeks or not, consider moderation in most things a virtue. In so far as this is the case, we have of course to ask whether Greek moderation is compatible with Christian selflessness.

The answer is that there is no insurmountable difficulty in combining the ideals of Greek and Christian ethics—provided we admit a certain amount of give and take, a certain spirit of reasonable compromise. There is indeed a difference of temper between the two. Christian morality tends towards extremism and even fanaticism. Self-sacrifice is itself an extreme idea. So is martyrdom, which is so characteristic of Christianity. The ideal of moderation is of course opposed to extremes. And though Greek history has its moral heroes and martyrs, yet the aim of the middle path is not one which of itself tends to produce heroes or heroic situations.

Yet this difference of temper does not prevent the best men from being both selfless and moderate. Moreover, the combination of the two virtues is rendered easier by the fact that they tend to cover different areas of a man's life, and so not to clash. On the whole, selflessness is an ideal of a man's conduct towards others, while moderation is an ideal of his conduct towards himself. Selflessness is a virtue which cannot be exercised except in a society. How can a man be unselfish, if there is no one to be unselfish towards? But a solitary man—supposing him to be provided with all the means of indulging his appetites to excess—might still be moderate.

The emphasis of Christianity is upon a man's love for his neighbors. Greek ethics is more self-centered. It is concerned mainly with how the man is to treat himself. He is within himself a city-state comprising his commanding part, reason; his executive part, spirit; and his mass of obedient or disobedient proletarians, the appetites. Morality is the proper relation of these parts with one another. It concerns the internal economy of the individual personality, not—except indirectly—its relations to others of its kind. And this picture is not fundamentally altered by the Greek belief that it is only in the state, in his civic relationships with others, that a man's personality can achieve its full development. And in the light of these considerations it is not difficult to see how moderation and selflessness can be combined.

Thus the only real difficulty to be faced is that of seeing how the primacy of reason and the primacy of sympathy—both of which are accepted by our civilization—can be combined, or have in fact been combined, without contradiction. But this cannot be understood without first examining the basic ideas of our civilization as they have actually developed in the world of modern Europe subsequent to the fall of the ancient civilizations. To this aspect of our subject I now turn.

Western civilization, especially as it appears in democratic countries and institutions, has for its inner soul or substance a special and peculiar cluster of ideas. I call them a cluster because they cling together. They imply one another. The chief members of this cluster are the ideas of (1) the infinite value of the individual; (2) the equality of all men (in some sense or other); (3) individualism; (4) liberty.

Of these ideas the first, that of the infinite value of the individual, is the *key* idea. This means that the other three ideas can be deduced from it; that they are in fact nothing more than corollaries of this one first and fundamental idea. Another way of expressing the situation would be to say that what we have here is in fact not four ideas, but only one single idea, that of the infinite value of the individual; and that the other three notions are really only aspects or facets of this one idea. I express all this by saying that the idea of the infinite value of the individual is the key idea of western civilization. It follows that if we can understand *it*, we shall have understood the inner essence, substance, or soul, of western civilization. It should then be easy to understand all the rest.

This cluster of ideas constitutes the ethos of western civilization. I am prepared for some objector to say that what we call western civilization has been in existence for some two millenia, but that some of the ideas of the cluster played very little part in it before late in the eighteenth century. Whether such a statement would be anywhere near historically correct I shall leave to historians to decide. For it may be that these ideas took nearly two thousand years to grow to full maturity, to become plain and explicit. But if so, then we shall have to say that they have been implicit in western civilization all that time. For the seeds from which they have grown are the Greek and Christian ideas which we have already studied, the idea of the primacy of reason and that of the primacy of sympathy. I may remind the reader of the fact that although the necessity of the abolition of slavery was certainly implicit in the Christian ethics from the beginning, this was not realized—that is to say, it did not become explicit in human consciousness—until the nineteenth century.

In this and the following chapter we shall have three main tasks. The first will be to understand the idea of the infinite value of the individual. What does it *mean?* For although it is a common phrase, although the statement that this idea is at the root of our democratic institutions is almost a commonplace, those who make use of this phrase seldom make any attempt to tell us what intelligible meaning can be attached to it. And I do not see how we can set about justifying it until we properly understand it.

Our second task will be to see how the other three ideas of the cluster of ideas flow from, are deductions from, this one fundamental idea.

Our third task will be to see how the idea of the infinite value of the individual, together with its connected ideas, necessarily grow out of the Greek theory of the primacy of reason and the Christian theory of the primacy of sympathy.

It will also be necessary, of course, to understand how this cluster of ideas has embodied itself in our institutions; to show, in fact, that it really does, as stated, constitute the inner soul or ethos of our civilization.

When we have performed the three tasks mentioned

above, we shall have the result which is expressed in the following diagram:

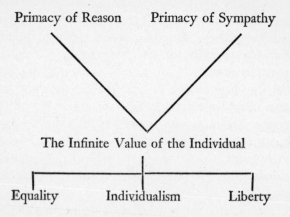

This shows that the theory of the infinite value of the individual flows from, or is deducible from, *both* the primacy of reason and the primacy of sympathy. It has its roots in both, and not merely in one. This is extremely important because it provides at least part of the solution to the problem of how the theory of the primacy of reason can be combined with the theory of the primacy of sympathy in our civilization without contradiction—a problem which was posed in the first paragraph of this chapter. If the relation expressed by the positions in the diagram can be established, it will show that the Greek theory and the Christian theory, though quite different from one another, both lead by different paths to the same conclusion, the same philosophy, namely that which is expressed in the words "the infinite value of the individual." Thus the two have been successfully combined, at least in actual history. This will be a kind of pragmatic solution of the problem. There will still remain, of course, the further problem whether there is any actual logical incompatibility between the Greek and the Christian theories. If there were, we could not finally justify our civilization, for we should have to admit that it contained in its essence a contradiction—a contradiction which would be sure to ruin it in the end, however successfully for the time being it might have pragmatically combined incompatibles. Meanwhile we may say that the diagram shows how the Greek spirit and the Christian spirit have actually become fused in our Greco-Christian civilization. This fusion has occurred through the Greek emphasis on reason and the Christian emphasis on sympathy having combined in the idea of the infinite value of the individual. We have now to see how this has been possible.

But first, what is the *meaning* of alleging that the human individual has infinite value? This, I think, is extremely difficult to understand. In particular it is difficult to understand what the word infinite means here. In what follows I shall give my own interpretation. If anyone objects to it, I can only say that I know of no other interpretation which gives any genuine sense or meaning to the idea.

We have, in my opinion, first to free the idea from theological and eschatological implications. Historically it has certainly *not* been free from such associations. It is connected in the first place with the conception of the infinite love of God. That a human soul has infinite value has certainly meant, among other things, that it is the object of God's infinite care and tenderness; that it has, in other words, infinite value *to God*. The idea has also no doubt been connected with the doctrine of the immortality of the soul. The soul's infinite duration of existence is in some way correlative to its infinite value. Perhaps it is thought that it ought to endure forever because it has in-

finite value; or perhaps the reverse is true, namely that it
has infinite value because it is to live forever. I do not profess to know which is the true theological doctrine.

My point is that we cannot make the philosophy of
democracy dependent upon any such particular theological
dogmas. If this were done, the very roots of democracy
would be destroyed as soon as the particular dogmas ceased
to be universally believed. It is essential to find in the key
idea of our civilization a meaning which is capable of justification independently of the truth of theological doctrines.

Moreover, even the theologian *ought* not to be satisfied
with saying that the infinite value of the soul means only
that God values it infinitely. For presumably this is not a
perfectly arbitrary valuation on God's part. God must
attach value to the soul because it *is* valuable. It cannot be
meant that it is valuable merely because God values it. It
must therefore have a value in itself independently of God's
valuation. Thus although the theologian may rightly assert
that God's infinite love of a soul is connected with its infinite value, he cannot assert that this is what its infinite
value *means*. Now what we are concerned to discover is
the meaning of its infinite value.

And here again we come to a parting of the ways which
always, in one form or another, keeps presenting itself to
us. When we speak of the value of a person—let alone his
infinite value—what kind of a scale of values do we have in
mind? Are we speaking of human values, or of absolute
cosmic values? *For whom* is it that a man is to have value?
Is it for himself? Or for other men? Or for the universe?

There are many who will crave for an interpretation of
democratic values in terms of an absolute scale. Without it
they will feel that their faith in things is rootless. This deep
craving is the price we pay for two thousand years of

oppression by the doctrine of value as imposed. All the profound and misty metaphysics of Teutonism has also this source. But we who have shaken ourselves free from this influence feel, in our return to humanism, that we have passed out of dark caverns into healthy air and pure sunlight. And there is nothing for it but for us and for those who differ from us in this matter to part company and go our separate ways. For our part we must interpret the meaning of the infinite value of man humanistically. Democracy cannot be for us the incarnation of the world-reason or of world-value. It is a human thing, made by human beings, for human purposes. If it serves human purposes, it is justified. If not, not. In accordance with these presuppositions I offer the following interpretation of the meaning of the infinite value of the individual.

Suppose we should strike out altogether from a human soul the psychological element of sympathy, leaving him the complete Hobbesian egoist, the completely selfish man —what would be the philosophy of value of such a man?

Certainly the very supposition of such a man is an abstraction. Probably none such ever did, or ever could exist —unless in an asylum for the insane. But it will nevertheless be profitable to make this supposition. Abstraction only means leaving out something. It is legitimate to simplify a problem by leaving something out temporarily, provided we do not forget to put it back again afterwards and take proper account of the difference it makes to our solution. This is a common method in science; and it will be our method here.

Let us call this abstract egoistical man, who is to be destitute of sympathy, the natural man or the animal man. The label will be something of a libel both upon nature and upon the animal world. For many animals do possess sym-

pathy. One has seen it in dogs and horses, even in birds.
I have never seen it in crocodiles—although I have watched
them for hours in tropical lakes and rivers—yet perhaps
they too evince it in some more or less negligible degree.
But let us adopt our label for what it is worth.

The value philosophy of the natural man will consist in
the attribution of various values to various things in his
environment—food, air, sunlight, water, his mate, and so
on. He will be able to establish some rough *scale* of values.
Thus an ox may be worth two pigs, a pig two cocks. Also
other persons, as being parts of his environment, will enter
into this scale of values on the same terms as horses, pigs,
trees, and inanimate things. In so far as the other person—
whether by his work or his play or even his qualifications
for becoming a dish at a cannibalistic feast—can serve the
purposes of the natural man, he will be valued by the natural man precisely as other things are, and he will have his
place in the scale of values which the natural man has set
up. This necessarily means that the value of the other person will be regarded as *finite*. For it will be measurable in
terms of other things. It may be the value of a hundred
oxen or two hundred pigs or ten thousand partridges. (It
is not, of course, meant that the natural man will be able
to specify *exact* numbers.) The value of the other person
will thus be specifiable in principle by a finite number. It
will therefore be a finite value.

There is also another important point to be noted here.
All these values which the natural man attributes either to
things or to other persons will be *instrumental* values. This
means that every one of these things or persons is valued
solely as a *means* to the gratification of the ends and desires
of the natural man. We must be careful not to fall into
verbal confusion here. If I eat a lobster salad for the sake of

its taste, it is, in one sense, an end in itself. This has already been explained. But I am now using the phrase "end in itself" in another sense. I am using it in the sense in which we should say that, in eating the lobster for its taste, I am treating it as a means to the satisfaction of my desires, and not as an end in itself. Whatever directly satisfies any desire of mine, and is not used as a means to obtaining something else which will directly satisfy my desire, is in one sense an end in itself. In this sense the lobster eaten for its taste is an end in itself. But in another sense, whatever directly satisfies my desire and is valued solely for this reason is being treated as a means to my ends. And in this sense the lobster eaten for its taste is a means to my ends.

It is in this latter sense that I say that the natural man treats all things, including other persons, as means to his ends. And still speaking in this sense, we may add that what alone is an end in itself for the natural man is the gratification of his own desires. All other things and persons are treated as means to this end. Moreover they all have a place in his scale of values owing to this fact. That one thing has for him twice the value of another means that it is twice as efficient an instrument for the satisfying of his desires. Hence nothing can be fitted into this scale of values unless it is, and can be treated as, a means to his ends. To say that anything is not a means to the fulfillment of his desires is to say that it has no place in his scale of values.

Now it is natural, if we attribute value to the means, to attribute it to the end also. To the end indeed above all. For surely the end must be more valuable than any mere means. And the means moreover seem to derive their value solely from the end. If A is the end and B the means, then B has value. But it would not have any value unless the end A were valued.

Suppose now, in the light of this, we ask what is the value to the natural man of his *ends?* So far we have spoken only of the values of his means. It is these alone which he arranged in a scale. And if we now ask what is the value to him of his ends—which, it must be remembered, are the satisfactions of his desires—we discover at once that they have no place at all in the scale of values which he has set up. For according to that scale all things are valued purely by their capacity to be means to his ends. The ends themselves therefore do not fall within the scale. Since all values are measured in terms of them, their value cannot be measured in terms of anything. It is incommensurable with the only scale of values which exists for the natural man. Thus the value of his ends is for him beyond all measure. That is to say, it is for him *infinite.* To all things other than his ends, other than the satisfactions of his own desires, he can attach values in a scale measurable by finite numbers. Since the value of the ends falls altogether outside this scale, exceeds all possible finite values within the scale, it is therefore, in this sense, infinite.

It is true that our man may set up a new scale of values in which ends are measured, not against means, but against each other. Thus he may think that the satisfaction of one desire is worth more to him than the satisfaction of some other desire. If he is very thirsty now but only slightly hungry, he will think it at the moment more valuable to satisfy his thirst than his hunger. But if we consider the sum total of all his desires at all times, and if we call the satisfaction of them all the satisfaction of his whole personality, we shall see at once that for him such satisfaction exceeds all possible or conceivable measures of value; and that its value is for him infinite. For nothing in the world could possibly exceed it in value.

The conclusion is as follows. The natural man can place everything in the world outside himself in a scale of values; and every such thing will have a finite value in that scale. But himself, the satisfaction of himself, the satisfaction of his personality, cannot be placed in that or any other scale. This end, the satisfaction of himself, exceeds beyond measure all finite values within the scale. It is for him infinite.

This analysis may appear difficult to follow. But the thought expressed in it is really extremely simple. It is no more than what is expressed in the question: "What shall it profit a man if he gain the whole world and lose his own soul?" This means that the value of his own soul to him is more than the value of the whole world. And this is another way of saying that its value for him is infinite. For it cannot be measured at all on the scale of values which he applies to all other things in the world.

Now it is precisely this meaning which we are to give, I think, to the phrase "the infinite value of the individual." But why did we, in that case, introduce the fiction, or abstraction, of the natural man? Because it is in the philosophy of the natural man that the conception appears in its simplest form. The point is that for him only *one* individual has infinite value, namely himself. All other individuals, as well as all the other things in his environment, have only finite value. We may thus express the contrast between finite and infinite value in the following way. By infinite value is meant the value which every man, even the purely selfish natural man, attributes to himself. By finite value is meant the value which the natural man attributes to all other things in the universe, including other persons.

If a tiger could conceptualize his implicit attitude to life and to the world, if he could state it in propositions, it would turn out to be, I think, just that of the natural man.

The tiger too would value all things outside himself in a scale of means to the satisfaction of his desires. But to himself he would attribute, I presume, an infinite value. He would rather lose the whole world than his own tigerish soul.

The conception of the infinite value of the individual as it appears in the philosophy of democracy differs from the natural man's conception only in one point. It says that each of us is to attribute infinite value not to himself only, as the natural man does, but to *all* human individuals whatever. It asserts that every individual has, and is to be treated as having, that same infinite value which the natural man attributes only to himself.

Thus we see that the conception of the infinite value of the individual is no mystery, but is inherent in the human situation. It was not invented by Christianity or by western civilization. It was, so to speak, always in the world. For every man must always have attributed infinite value implicitly to *himself*. The new principle which Christianity introduced into the world was not the idea of infinite value as such, but the idea that every man ought to attribute infinite value, not only to himself—as even the natural man did—but also to every other human being as well.

We have not yet discovered what grounds there are for this new and peculiar doctrine—to do this will be our next task. But we *have* discovered the *meaning* of the doctrine, which was the first problem we had to solve. We were puzzled by the question as to what meaning the word infinite could possibly have here. Our analysis has made the answer clear. The value which a man attributes to himself is infinite because it exceeds the value which he attributes to any conceivable possession or any conceivable thing in the world, or indeed to the whole world itself. It is not possible for him to place this value anywhere in the scale of values by which he measures all other things. The reason he cannot do so is that this scale measures only *means*, while himself—which is an elliptical expression meaning "the satisfaction of his personality, i.e., of all his desires and purposes"—is the *end*. All values save that of himself are finite because they can theoretically be given places on the scale. Since a man's own value is for him not measurable at all on the scale of finite values, it is accordingly immeasurable, i.e., infinite. Hence the meaning of the special Christian doctrine of the infinite value of the individual, or rather of all individuals, is that each man is to attribute the same infinite value to all other persons as he already naturally attributes to himself.

The next problem will be to discover the basis for the Christian extension of infinite value from "myself" to "every man." But before turning to this problem it will be helpful to mention another form in which the doctrine of the infinite value of the individual has sometimes been expressed. Kant supposed that what he called the "categorical imperative" is the fundamental law of all morals. The categorical imperative, according to him, could be formulated in several different ways. One of his formulations was as follows: "So act as to treat humanity, whether in thine own person or in that of another, in every case as an end withal, never as a means only." According to this, the essence of morality consists in treating all men as "ends in themselves" and not solely as means to our ends. The point which I wish to make is that this principle of Kant's is identical with the principle of the infinite value of the individual. It is simply a translation of that principle into Kant's peculiar philosophical language.

This follows from the analysis already given. According

to that analysis the reason why the value of my personality is for me infinite is that its satisfaction is the ultimate end of all my actions. The value of all mere means is finite. But the value of the end is infinite. Hence when the natural man thinks that the value of himself is infinite, the value of all other persons (and things) finite, what this means in effect is that he regards himself as the only end and all other persons (and things) as means. The special doctrine of western civilization and of Christianity may thus be expressed either in the form that we are to treat all men as having infinite value or in the form that we are to treat all men as ends. The two formulations mean the same thing. Hence Kant's doctrine that all men are ends in themselves is simply his version of the basic view of all western civilization that every individual has infinite value.

In what sense is it meant that all men are "ends in themselves"? We have seen that there are at least two possible meanings of this phrase. In one sense X is an end in itself to me if it directly satisfies a desire of mine. Thus I treat the lobster salad as an end in itself when I eat it simply for its pleasant taste. In the same way a cannibal who eats a man because he enjoys his flavor is treating his victim as an end in himself. But plainly this is *not* what Kant meant to advocate. What then did he mean?

According to the other meaning of "end in itself" which we have distinguished, the man who eats the lobster for its taste is treating it, not as an end in itself, but as a means to the satisfaction of his desire. In this sense what alone is an end in itself to me is the satisfaction of my desires. This is the sense in which Kant's doctrine is to be interpreted. In this sense the cannibal does not treat his victim as an end, but as a means to the satisfaction of his desire. Now the natural man treats only the satisfaction of *his own* desires as ends in this sense. The Kantian maxim means plainly that I am to treat the desires and purposes of other men as if they too were ends for me. I am to attribute the same value to the ends of other men as I attribute to my own ends. "Treat other men as ends in themselves" is therefore an elliptical phrase which means, "Treat the desires, purposes, and ends of other men in the same way as you treat your own." Or again it means, "Attribute to the satisfaction of other men's personalities the same infinite value which you attribute to your own."

The identification of Kant's teaching with the general doctrine of the infinite value of the individual which has here been made will become of importance when we come to discuss the basic differences between democracy and totalitarianism.

The next problem is to discover what basis Christianity has for extending the conception of the infinite value of a personality from "myself" to "all men."

We began by considering the abstraction of the natural man. To form the conception of him we simply took our conception of the normal or actual man and, by a sort of imaginary surgical operation, amputated from his soul the psychological element of sympathy. We found then that the value philosophy of this natural man consisted in attributing infinite value to himself as an end and finite value to all other persons as being only means to his ends. Let us now see what will happen if we put back again into his soul the factor of sympathy which we cut out.

The point of our proceedings, of course, lies in the fact that the psychological principle of sympathy has been established as being the basis of Christian ethics. Hence to ask what will happen to the natural man when we reinsert into him the factor of sympathy is to ask what difference will be made to the natural man's value philosophy by admitting the fundamental idea of Christian psychology.

Sympathy is defined as the infectious character of feeling. It means the flowing of feelings from one personality to another. By virtue of it the feelings of *A* pass over into *B* and become his feelings. (This of course is a metaphor. What actually happens is that feelings similar to *A*'s arise in *B*. There is not numerical identity, but only similarity. And there is no actual passage or flowing from one to another. Let all this be understood when I speak of the flowing of feelings from *A* to *B*.) Apart from sympathy, individuals are atoms, walled in and self-contained, private universes, monads without windows, wholly cut off from one another. Sympathy is the principle by virtue of which the walls are broken down and communication is established between atom and atom. Thereby the separate atoms cease to be atomic, overflow into one another, become continuous.

To the extent that this happens *society* becomes possible. And the different conceptions of society depend in large measure upon the extent in which the psychological principle of sympathy is admitted and realized. Thus it is significant that Hobbes, whose psychological egoism amounted to the total denial of the existence of sympathy, conceived society as wholly atomic. The individual atoms are for him merely accidentally joined together by wholly external relations. Democracy is accused by fascist philosophers of the same fault. If this were true—or perhaps we should say in so far as it is true—it is a great paradox and contradiction in democracy. For democracy is built upon Christian premises, of which the essential principle is sympathy. We shall have to examine this matter in its place.

At the moment we are concerned to discover what will

be the dialectical impact of the principle of sympathy upon the egocentric philosophy of the natural man. The general paradigm of this impact is as follows. Sympathy is the flow of feelings from one individual into another. The sum total of the individual's feelings is the core of his personality. By sympathy, therefore, personality flows into personality. Thus *A* discovers his own personality in *B*, and *B* discovers his personality in *A*. Now *A*, in virtue of his basic character as a natural man, knows that his own personality is of infinite value. And since he now finds his own personality in *B*, he is compelled to recognize that *B*'s personality also possesses infinite value. And since the interchange of sympathetic feeling is potentially universal as between all men, the necessary consequence is that each recognizes all other men as having, like himself, infinite value. Thus the theory of the infinite value of all individuals is completed.

The above statement is highly generalized. Let us see, therefore, what it means in concrete detail. What the theory of the infinite value of all individuals means in practical terms is that I am to treat the ends and purposes of another person as having the same value for me as my own ends and purposes. Now how is this possible? It is a psychological possibility only if his ends and purposes actually *become* my ends and purposes. I must "identify myself" with him, as the common phrase is. I must somehow make his ends my own. I can only do this if his feelings, purposes, and ends flow into me, and so become mine. And this is precisely what happens in cases where there is sympathy. For instance, a mother treats her child as having infinite value. This is possible solely because his pains hurt her, his joys delight her, his welfare *is* her welfare. In this case sympathy is at a maximum. But if a man bandages the wounds of a stranger, or feeds hungry people who are personally unknown to him, then—except in cases where he does it for self-advertisement or some other ulterior motive—it is rendered possible because he feels their hurts and hunger, because their feelings flow into him.

Of course, it is possible to perform such actions "from duty," as Kant said, without any sympathy at all. But this has only become possible to us now because other men before us have done them from sympathy. We can of course imitate their outward acts without possessing their inward feelings. And this outward aping of goodness was what poor Kant thought to be the essence of virtue. The aping would have been impossible if the original had not existed to be aped. And apart from such imitation, the fundamental source from which all disinterested altruism flows is sympathy.

Thus the maxim of the infinite value of the individual means that each is to treat the purposes of another as if they were his own. That this is a possibility for human nature arises from the fact that the purposes of the other may flow into me and so actually become my own.

In the light of these observations we may see how the theory of the infinite value of the individual is derived from, is in fact simply a logical deduction from, the Christian principle of the primacy of sympathy. That principle is, as we have seen, somewhat vague. It is much vaguer than the Greek doctrine of the primacy of reason. But it certainly means that the psychological element of sympathy is picked out from among all other psychological elements as that one which ought to be developed to the utmost, so that it can play the leading part in the control of our actions.

Now actually the sympathies of the best of us are extremely limited. We feel sympathy with a very narrow circle of people around us, and the further we go from the center of that circle the fainter our sympathy becomes. For this reason we actually *feel* only those souls who are extremely near to us to have infinite value; the mother feels it of her child, but not perhaps of someone else's child. Now if the doctrine of the primacy of sympathy were given effect to, if our sympathetic faculty were developed to the theoretical maximum so as to be extended to all men, we should actually feel all men to have for us the same value which the mother feels her child to have for her. But what the statement that "all men have infinite value" really means is, of course, that "we *ought* to feel all men to have infinite value, and we *ought* to treat them as if they had." It is in essence an ideal of action, rather than a statement of fact. But what now appears is that if we did put the theory of the primacy of sympathy into effect, that is, if we maximized our sympathy and allowed it to control us, then we should in fact treat all men as having infinite value. In this way the doctrine of the infinite value of all men is simply a deduction from the theory of the primacy of sympathy. It is thus based upon the fundamental principle of Christian ethics.

The diagram on page 126 shows the idea of the infinite value of the individual as being derived both from the Christian principle of the primacy of sympathy and the Greek principle of the primacy of reason. How it is derived from the former principle has just been shown. The next step will be to show that it also follows from the latter. That is, we have to prove that just as the theory of the primacy of sympathy implies the infinite value of the individual, so the theory of the primacy of reason also implies it.

That the theory of the infinite value of the individual follows from the Greek principle of the primacy of reason

is suggested to us at once by an examination of the philosophy of Kant. For Kant taught that the central principle
of morals is that all men should be treated as ends in themselves. And this, as we have seen, is equivalent to the theory
of the infinite value of the individual. Kant, however,
though one might expect otherwise, bases his conclusion
not upon Christian but upon Greek premises. It is deduced
by him from the rationality of man, not from his sympathetic nature. Kant, following the Greeks, takes reason to
be the supreme element in man. He then attaches to reason
a cosmic and absolute value. It is an end in itself, intrinsically and absolutely superior to the inclinations. Man therefore is an end in himself because he possesses reason. Thus
he deduces his moral theory from the doctrine of the
primacy of reason interpreted as meaning that reason has
an absolute value in the universe. This, of course, is in
accordance with his impositionism.

For this very reason we cannot follow Kant here. We
have rejected the notions of impositionism and of a cosmic
scale of values. We have accepted a humanistic interpretation of the primacy of reason, according to which it means
only that reason is supreme in human life because it is the
proper function of reason to control the other psychological elements. Thus Kant's proof that the infinite value of
man follows logically from the primacy of reason is not
available to us. We have to discover some other proof
based upon the humanistic interpretation of the primacy of
reason.

This is not difficult. In order to show the derivation of
the doctrine of the infinite value of man from the Christian premise of the primacy of sympathy, what we did was
to show that a man, if he allowed his life and actions to be
controlled by a maximized sympathy, would inevitably re-

gard all his fellow men as having the same infinite value
which he attributes to himself. And what we have now to
show is that a man, if he allowed his life and actions to be
controlled by reason, would also inevitably attribute to all
other men the same infinite value which he attributes to
himself.

We start, of course, from the position that the man already regards *himself* as having infinite value, but fails to
regard other men in this light. For even the natural man,
innocent of either Greek or Christian morals, does this.
This is inherent in the human situation from the start and
does not have to be deduced from the primacy of reason.
What has to be deduced is that the man who is guided by
reason will regard other men in this respect in the same
light as that in which he regards himself.

And this surely is very obvious. For other men are, in
the only respects which are relevant to the question, exactly *like* himself. And it will therefore be irrational to
treat them as being different. I will briefly elaborate this
argument.

When I say that *I* have infinite value, or that *I* am an
absolute end and not a mere means, what I mean, as already
shown, is that the satisfaction of my purposes, desires, and
ends has for me an absolute and infinite value. Therefore
it is the presence in me of *purposes, desires, and ends* which
gives me this infinite value. This, of course is the humanistic
interpretation as distinct from the Kantian interpretation,
according to which it is the presence of *reason* in me which
gives me infinite value. In the proposition "I have infinite value" the word "I" is an elliptical expression which
means "the satisfaction of my purposes, desires, and ends."
Now I know it to be a fact that other men also have purposes, desires, and ends. Pure reason alone, therefore, with-

out any aid from sympathy, will inform me that if I attribute infinite value to myself because I am a center of purposes and ends, I must in bare consistency attribute the same infinite value to other men, since they also are centers of purposes and ends. To think otherwise, or to act on any other basis, will be irrational and illogical. Therefore if I let myself be guided by reason I shall treat all men as having infinite value. And to prove this is to prove that the doctrine of the primacy of reason implies the theory of the infinite value of every individual.

We may put the same thing in another way. The primacy of reason means that our actions are to be controlled by rational considerations, and not by blind uncontrolled inclinations, appetites, and passions. Now to treat myself as an end and others merely as means is in fact to be guided solely by my own inclinations and desires. It means taking into account only my own ends and disregarding the ends of others. Reason forces me to admit that others too have ends which are on the same level and of the same kind as my own. But if A and A' are in fact identical in kind, it is irrational to treat them as if they were of different kinds. And this is what I do when I treat myself as an end and all others as means. Therefore to live the rational life—which is what is implied by the primacy of reason—means to treat all men as having the same infinite value which I inevitably attribute to myself.

What has now been established is that the belief in the infinite value of all men, which is the key idea of western civilization, is derived *both* from the Greek belief in the primacy of reason and the Christian belief in the primacy of sympathy. This is what was illustrated in the upper half of the diagram on page 126. Accordingly this diagram exhibits how Greek and Christian thought have mingled and coalesced to constitute the ethos of our Greco-Christian civilization. Also this enables us to give at least a pragmatic solution of the problem of how the doctrines of the primacy of reason and the primacy of sympathy, which seem incompatible with one another, can both be held at the same time by our civilization. The reason is that, even if they are incompatible as psychological theories, yet in their practical application they give rise to the same ideal of conduct, namely that ideal which is expressed in the view that we should treat all men as having infinite value. As being a mere pragmatic solution of the problem, this can only be regarded as an unsatisfactory makeshift. The final and complete solution is still to seek.

To our view that the theory of infinite value is derived both from Greek and Christian sources it may be objected that the theory was not in fact characteristic of Greek civilization. The idea was wholly absent from Greek consciousness. It came into existence only after the dawn of Christianity. It is peculiar to Christian civilizations. It has always been considered a characteristically Christian idea. Hence the derivation of it from Greek thought would seem to be artificial and misleading.

There is great force in this contention. But I think the solution of the puzzle lies in the fact that although the Greek principle of the primacy of reason logically implies the infinite value of the individual, it yet contained, in the absence of any emphasis upon the principle of sympathy, no emotional drive which could bring the idea to practical realization. We may often have in our minds abstract ideas which really imply certain practical conclusions. But in the absence of an incentive of some kind we do not draw the conclusions. Bergson has remarked that although the philosophy of Plato really implied the condemnation of slavery, yet actually to condemn slavery never occurred to Plato or to any other Greek of his time.[1] It required Christianity to bring the idea to fruition. It is the same here. Bare reason alone implies the infinite value of the individual. But reason, though it may in some sense control and direct men, does not contain in itself any actual impulse to action. Feeling, emotion, conation, are required for this. And this is what the Christian principle of sympathy supplied. Reason implied the infinite value of the individual. But, in the absence of some emotional incentive, the conclusion remained undrawn in the heaven of abstract logic. When Christianity came, the idea precipitated itself at once in human consciousness by reason of the emotional factor of sympathy.

We shall see in fact that the Christian principle of sympathy has supplied to western civilization precisely the emotional element which it required, and which Greek intellectualism lacked. Greece contributed the ideas, Christianity the feelings. Reason and sympathy both lead to the same result, the idea of the infinite value of men. In a practical application they may be regarded as two forms of one and the same force. Reason is the obverse of sympathy, and sympathy the obverse of reason. This one force, taking the form of cognition, is reason; taking the form of emotion, it is sympathy. Both were required if the idea of the infinite value of all men was to become effective in human affairs. Of course this statement that reason and sympathy may be regarded as two forms of one single force is not to be taken literally. They are in fact perfectly distinct psychological elements. But in their practical working they may—by a legitimate metaphor—be regarded *as if*

[1] Bergson, "The Two Sources of Morality and Religion," page 68.

they were two aspects of a single force which impels men to treat each other as having infinite value.

I shall close this chapter by giving some examples which illustrate how, even in small matters, the idea of the infinite value of the individual has permeated our feelings. That it is the basis of all our democratic ideals and institutions I shall leave to be demonstrated in the next chapter. But it will be useful to show also how it has influenced our feelings in many small ways in matters of daily life.

In Ceylon it is a common practice among poor Sinhalese peasants to sell their children as servants to wealthy families for a dollar or two. Now I think it is a fact that such a proceeding arouses in the western mind a peculiar feeling of disapproval and even horror. The Sinhalese, on the other hand, usually display no such feeling—unless perhaps they have been educated in Europe or otherwise subjected to powerful European influence. What is the reason for this difference?

The custom to which I refer is not slavery. The child remains free. Moreover the child may be most kindly treated, and may in fact benefit from the transaction. Of course such a system is plainly subject to grave abuses; and cases of the serious ill-treatment of the children are not uncommon. And no doubt for these reasons alone we should in any case disapprove of the system. But my point is that, quite apart from abuses, westerners feel a peculiar sense of repugnance to the idea of selling their children, while these orientals—who are mostly Buddhists—apparently do not. And the question is: What is the cause of this difference?

It certainly is not that the Sinhalese are not fond of their children. On the contrary, they tend to be almost absurdly fond of children. Nor are they by nature callous or cruel.

The explanation is that the Sinhalese, since theirs is not a Christian civilization, are without the idea of the infinite value of the individual. To westerners who possess this idea the sale of a child appears as a violation of its personality. And it is noticeable that what disgusts us is not the cheap price. If I were to sell my child and he in later years should reproach me, I could hardly excuse myself to him by saying: "I sold you for a million dollars. You see what a high value I set on you. And you ought to be greatly pleased." Perhaps I might claim some sympathy because of the greatness of my temptation. But the condemnation would not be lifted. For the amount paid is beside the point. Why? Because we feel that the value of the person is infinite, so that *any* price set upon him is an insult.

We saw earlier that the reason why we call the value of a person infinite is that it cannot be put anywhere in the scale of finite instrumental values. Hence his value is not an exchange value at all. The violation of personality when a child is sold consists therefore in the fact that he is placed in the scale of finite instrumental values. The amount for which he is exchanged is irrelevant. His worth, being infinite, exceeds any conceivable amount.

Many people experienced a feeling of revulsion when it was proposed to show the Dionne quintuplets as exhibits at the Chicago or New York expositions. I think that this feeling of revulsion may probably have had its source in the idea that such a transaction, since it would put a price upon the children, would be a violation of their infinite values. Whether such an application of the idea is reasonable or not is another question. Quite possibly it involves a logical muddle. Nevertheless it is an example of how deeply the idea of the infinite value of human beings has penetrated our consciousness.

It is obvious that the abolition of slavery arose out of the same idea. We do not object to slavery merely because slaves are often unhappy and badly treated. Of course, we *do* object on these grounds too. But we should object even if it were the case that all slaves were well treated. The reason is that slavery, even in the best conditions, is a violation of personality. The slave is bought and sold. He is treated as being solely a means to the ends of his masters. He is not treated as an end in himself. And as we have seen, the doctrine that men should be treated as ends in themselves is identical with the theory that they have infinite value.

It is notorious that western civilization sets—or used to set until recently—a higher value on human life than did oriental civilizations. Presumably this too is due to the influence of the theory of infinite value.

CHAPTER VII

EQUALITY: LIBERTY: INDIVIDUALISM

THE infinite value of the individual is the key idea in the cluster of ideas which constitute the ethos of western civilization. The other three ideas are those of equality, liberty, and individualism. These are also the fundamental conceptions on which is built the philosophy of democracy. Hence to show that they are simply deductions from, or alternative expressions of, the idea of the infinite value of the individual, will be to show that democracy is the final expression of the ethos of western civilization. We shall also by this means show that democracy is the political embodiment of combined Greek and Christian ethical ideals. For the derivation of the idea of the infinite value of the individual from the Greek and Christian conceptions has already been demonstrated.

I shall begin with the conception of the equality of all men. We have two questions to answer: (1) What does the conception of equality *mean*; in what *sense* are men alleged to be equal? (2) How is this idea derived from that of the infinite value of the individual? We shall find that to answer the first question is implicitly to answer the second; so that the two can be taken up together, and need hardly be kept separate.

It is quite obvious that, in one sense, men are hopelessly *un*equal. Some men are clever, some stupid. Some men are morally good, some bad. Some are powerful, some weak. Some are useful to society, some useless. Moreover, it is evident that there exist not only the extremes of cleverness and stupidity, goodness and badness, strength and weakness. All the intermediate degrees of these, and of all other qualities, are also to be found among men. There are, in general, superior and inferior men. There seems to be no particular quality or characteristic in regard to which it can be plausibly maintained that men are even roughly equal.

It is these facts which are constantly pointed out by those who tell us that the democratic theory of the equality of all men is inherently nonsensical and absurd. Nietzsche attacked democracy on the ground that it is based upon the doctrine of equality, whereas men are in fact obviously unequal. He had in mind the kind of inequalities which I have mentioned. Mussolini writes that fascism "asserts the immutable and fruitful and beneficent inequality of men, who cannot be levelled by any such mechanical and external device as universal suffrage." [1] And again: "In rejecting democracy fascism rejects the absurd conventional lie of political equalitarianism." [2] And it is obviously the same kind of inequalities which are referred to.

Now if the democratic theory did mean, as is suggested, that all men are equally clever, equally good (or bad), equally strong, equally useful to society, it *would* be precisely the sort of nonsense which its opponents represent

[1] Mussolini, *op. cit.*, page 28.
[2] *Ibid.*, page 30.

it as being. It *would* deserve the contempt which they pour upon it. The inference which ought to be made is that this is *not* what the doctrine of the equality of all men means. We may go further. I have mentioned certain particular characteristics or qualities of men, such as moral goodness or badness, usefulness to society, mental ability, in which men are plainly unequal. I will add that, so far as I know, *there is not a single human quality or characteristic in regard to which men could be said to be equal.* Clearly we have to seek the meaning of the doctrine of equality—if it has any meaning—along some entirely different line.

Let us begin by considering again Kant's formula of the moral law: "So act as to treat humanity, whether in thine own person or in that of another, in every case as an end withal, never as a means *only*." The italics are mine. The conception that every man is an end in himself is, as we have seen, identical with the conception of him as having infinite value. But now the italicized word *only* gives notice of the fact that a man, although he is an end, is *also* a means. It is important to realize that Kant does not deny this. What is immoral, according to Kant's formula, is not to treat men as means, but to treat them as *nothing but* means.

It is obvious that we have to treat each other as means to our ends. Life and society would be impossible if we did not do so. When I call in the doctor to treat my influenza, I am using him as a means to my ends—in this case to the end of recovering my health. When I employ a secretary to type my letters, I am using him as a means to various ends of mine. To generalize, all our duties and obligations to society or to other men are the ways in which society and other men use us as means to their ends. Kant's law means that, although we rightly and necessarily use men as means, we are never to forget that they are also ends in themselves. The doctor or the secretary, though employed by me for my own purposes, must all the while be treated as a being who is himself a center of consciousness, feelings, and purposes which are entitled to as much respect from me as I accord to my own.

From this it appears that each man has two values, or rather two kinds of value. He has his value as an end, which is an intrinsic, absolute, and infinite value. And he has his value as a means. For instance, he is a good or a bad doctor, a useful or a poor secretary. This value as a means is instrumental, relative, and finite. What is meant by the terms infinite and finite here has already been explained. A man's value as a means is finite because it can be placed in a scale of higher and lower. The good doctor is relatively higher in the scale, the bad doctor lower. But a man's value as an end is infinite because it is impossible to measure it in any scale. Finite values, as we saw, attach always and only to means; infinite values attach always and only to absolute ends. So that of the two kinds of value which every man has, his value as a means is always finite, his value as an end infinite.

We can now state the meaning of the doctrine of equality. *Men are equal in respect of their intrinsic values as ends, unequal in respect of their instrumental values.*

The inequality of their instrumental values refers to the differences of intelligence, strength of character, capacity for work, moral worth, etc., which are the familiar theme of those who keep insisting on the inequality of men. These differences make men more or less valuable members of society, better or worse workmen, physicians, lawyers, engineers. A man's value as a member of society means, of course, his value as a means to the ends of others (as well as of himself). His value as a lawyer also refers to the services he renders to others; that is, it is a value instrumental to their ends. Thus all the inequalities on which antidemocratic writers harp refer to the value which a man has as a means, and not to his value as an end.

Thus it is only in respect of their values as ends that men are equal. But we have still to explain in what sense there is equality. Evidently it has something to do with the infinity of the values. It would be natural to suggest that the intrinsic values of all men are equal because they are all infinite. To say this, however, might perhaps get us into trouble with the mathematicians. And I certainly do not want to involve this discussion in the mysteries of what mathematicians call infinite numbers. Perhaps it will be unobjectionable to state the doctrine in the following form. To treat the intrinsic values of men as unequal would be to contradict the essential nature of these values. For suppose that the intrinsic value of person A be treated as greater than that of person B. This means that the values of A and B now fall into some kind of scale, so that, for instance, the value of A may be twice the value of B. But the very essence of these intrinsic values is that they cannot be measured in any scale. This is what is meant by their infinity. We accordingly express this fact by declaring that the intrinsic values of all men are equal.

We may put the same thing in another way. The doctrine of infinite value means this: (1) that the satisfaction of my personality is *to me* of infinite value; that is, it exceeds any value which I can possibly attach to anything else in the world, or even to the whole world ("What shall it profit a man if he gain the whole world and lose his own soul?"); (2) that the satisfaction of another person's personality is *to him* of infinite value; and (3) that I ought to treat the satisfaction of his personality as having the same infinite value for me as has the satisfaction of my own personality. This is what is expressed by saying that the intrinsic value of all men as ends is equal.

We can now see, I think, that the exposition of the meaning of the doctrine of equality also shows how it is merely a deduction from the theory of the infinite value of the individual. For the exposition demonstrates that it is only when we treat men as ends that they can be regarded as equal. But the view that all men are ends, and should be treated as such, has been shown to be merely an alternative expression of the theory of the infinite value of the individual.

The doctrine of equality expresses itself, not only in formal laws and institutions, but in many of the instinctive reactions of human beings to one another. For instance, it is a commonplace that mothers often love and value their troublesome or even wicked children as much as—sometimes even more than—their good ones. But how is it possible to value equally two persons of entirely unequal merit? The reason is that the mother does not value her child as a means to some benefit to herself. She loves him for himself, that is, as an end. Thus it is the intrinsic value of the child as an end in himself, not his instrumental value, which is the object of her affection. For this reason she can love the bad child as much as the good. For their intrinsic values are equal. Thus her instinct, which is superficially irrational, expresses a profound intuitive rationality.

Wherever a human being, loving another, takes no account of his faults, steadfastly loves him in spite of cruelties, wrongs, crimes, and disasters caused by his ill-doing, without the love being crushed out or even lessened—if this ever happens outside novels—we have an intuitive realization of the intrinsic equality of bad men with good men. Indeed love, as distinguished from calculating and self-interested altruism, may be defined by the fact that its object is not the instrumental but the intrinsic value of the loved one.

If we turn from instinctive or emotional reactions to the field of social institutions, we find that the equality of men issues practically in such conceptions as equality of opportunity and equality before the law. And in all these we find that the distinction between men's unequal instrumental values and their equal intrinsic values is implicitly asserted. For instance, the notion of equality of opportunity implies that the inequality of men's abilities and powers is recognized. The more able and worthful are to be allowed to profit by their superior worth. But all are to be given the same start in the race. For if A were from the start handicapped as against B, this would have to be for some other reason than the superior instrumental values of B. It must accordingly arise from treating A as intrinsically inferior to B, that is, from denying the equality of their intrinsic values.

Equality before the law has the same implications. The inequalities of instrumental values are recognized. If B is a better man than A, he receives more at the hands of the law. He obtains his due reward. But what the law will not recognize is privilege. For privilege means that, apart from any question of their relative instrumental values, B is treated as intrinsically of higher worth than A. And this is to deny the doctrine of intrinsic equality.

The doctrine of equality has here been deduced from the infinite value of the individual. But it can be shown that it is directly implied both by the primacy of reason and by the primacy of sympathy.

It follows from the primacy of reason. For though it is rational to treat men differently on account of their differences, it is irrational to treat them differently in so far as they are the same. The opposite of the principle of equality is the principle of privilege. But privilege means treating men differently who are—so far as the relevant circumstances of the particular case are concerned—exactly on a par, and so deserving of similar treatment. It means inconsistency, and therefore unreason.

The doctrine of equality follows directly from the primacy of sympathy. For sympathy alone, if it were complete, if the flow of feelings from one to another were unobstructed, would lead us to place the feelings and ends of other men on the same level as our own. For they would then *be* our own. But to treat the ends of others as having the same value as our own is what is meant by the doctrine of equality.

The next idea that we have to discuss is that of liberty or freedom, which constitutes one of that cluster of ideas which is the ethos of our civilization. Very often the notion of freedom is thought to be *the* essence *par excellence* of democracy; and the doctrines of equality and individualism, while admitted to be marks of the democratic way of life, are tacitly treated as subordinate conceptions. This is a mistake. In the first place these three ideas stand all exactly on the same level, no one being any more important than the others, since all three are merely different facets of the one undivided idea of the infinite value of the individual. In the second place, the notion of freedom is not the real essence of democracy; that essence is the fundamental and underlying notion of the infinite value of the individual. Freedom is only one of the manifestations of this. The fact that, in the popular consciousness, freedom is given the leading place is due to merely historical causes. Those who in their own selfish interests refused to admit in practice the full implications of the theory of the infinite value of the individual—the denial of privilege for instance—have usually sought to gain their ends through the suppression of freedom. Hence the struggle against them has appeared in the guise of the struggle for freedom.

Freedom is not in itself an absolute end. What is really desirable is freedom *for* something, freedom to attain something, namely the leading of the good life. It is this which is the end. The setting up of freedom as the absolute end of democracy is an error which leads to the accusation that democracy is merely a system to enable everyone to do as he pleases without regard to others or to the common good. Freedom has appeared to men—and rightly—as an instrument of such paramount importance for the leading of the good life that they have come to think of it as an end in itself. But this is a mistake nevertheless.

Freedom is of two kinds. The first kind is *political* freedom, which means the democratic form of government, the rule of the people by the people themselves, or by their elected representatives. The second kind is what I may call *personal* freedom. It includes the special liberties of thought, speech, press, religious worship, assemblage, and so on. That these two kinds ought to be distinguished is shown by the fact that they may exist apart. Some British crown colonies combine autocratic government with freedom of speech, press, assemblage, etc., as completely established as they are in the United States. This is an instance of the second kind of liberty existing without the first. I am not aware of an instance of a genuinely democratic government which disallows the personal freedoms. But there is no logical reason why such a government should not exist. Of course both kinds of freedom spring from the same root. And we must accordingly declare a society in which one exists without the other to be a very imperfect example of a free society. Nevertheless the distinction is a real one.

What we have to show is that freedom of both kinds follows from the conception of the infinite value of the individual; that it is a corollary of this; and that it is therefore rooted in the fundamental ethos of our civilization and is not, as Mussolini has affirmed, an accidental excrescence of our civilization which happened to make its appearance in the eighteenth century.

I shall begin with the personal liberties. The simplest way of showing that they are a necessary consequence of the fundamental principles of western civilization is to exhibit them as following from the Greek principle of the primacy of reason; though they may equally well be derived from the theory of the infinite value of the individual. Their derivation from the primacy of reason is as follows.

Speech, press, and public meeting are merely different instruments which are used for one purpose, namely *discussion* or the expression of opinion. Hence the freedoms of speech, press, and assemblage are not really three freedoms. They are only three different forms of a single freedom, namely freedom of discussion. But discussion and deliberation are expressions of the human power of reason. It is solely because men are rational that they *can* discuss and deliberate. Speech is itself made possible only by the existence of reason in men—which is why man is the only animal which speaks. Hence freedom of discussion means nothing more than the right of men to use their reason to the full. But the Greek doctrine of the primacy of reason asserts that the good human life is above all the life controlled by reason. This obviously implies that in every individual reason must be allowed to have absolutely free play and complete expression. And this is impossible without freedom of discussion.

Personal freedom also follows from the theory of the infinite value of the individual. For what this above all implies is that the purposes and ends of the individual have an absolute value, subject of course to the proviso that they do not include the suppression of the absolute values of the ends and purposes of other individuals. This means that every individual has the right to develop his whole personality to the utmost. Now thought, deliberation, reasoning, and discussion are parts of human personality. Hence the right of discussion is merely part of the general right of the individual to develop his personality. And this right exists only if the intrinsic value of that personality is recognized. A man can claim the right of discussion on no ground other than that on which he claims the right to exercise his limbs, his artistic capacities, his religious feelings, or to give effect to any other of the normal and legitimate purposes of his life. The suppression of personal liberty is a violation of his personality just as the suppression of his artistic capacities would be. And unless the intrinsic value of his personality is granted, there is no reason why his personality should *not* be violated. Thus the rights of personal liberty depend upon, and flow from, the idea of the infinite value of personality. It is for this reason that where the infinite value of the individual is denied—as in the totalitarian states—personal liberties are denied also. This is perfectly logical.

Political liberty, though it has been distinguished for convenience of discussion, has the same roots and the same implications as personal liberty. But there is a very special sense in which the democratic form of government is an outgrowth of the Greek theory of the primacy of reason. This consists in the fact that its essence is government by discussion, i.e., by reason.

In a democratic state the relation between the rulers and the ruled is the relation of *persuasion*. The rulers, whether they be a congress, a president, or a parliament, have to persuade the people to accept the laws and the policies which they propose. If they cannot do so, they must either change their policies or make way for other rulers. The relation is similar to that between a chairman of a committee and its members. The chairman may, if he is a man of strong character, direct and control all actions and have his own way. Yet he does this only because the members consent, or because they trust him. He may not actually have to explain all his acts and persuade the others to them. But the theory is that he always could do so, and that his acts often pass unquestioned because they know that he could. In the last analysis he cannot act unless he can persuade the members of the rightness of his decisions, or unless they are already persuaded in advance by reason of their general knowledge of the agreement of his purposes and policies with their own.

Thus democratic government is government by persuasion. But government by persuasion is the same thing as government by reason. For persuasion, discussion, and deliberation are the forms which reason takes in its application to practical affairs. Democracy is therefore the direct expression of the Greek theory that reason should control human affairs. And it is accordingly natural that it should have been the Greeks who actually invented the democratic form of government. It is true that Plato—to whom more than to any other man we owe the elaboration of the doctrine of the primacy of reason—would not have agreed to this application of his doctrine. This was largely owing to the abuses of democracy in his own time. And I cannot, of course, discuss Plato's particular theories of politics here.

To the equation "persuasion = reason," there is likely to be, I anticipate, some objection on the part of the reader. But before I discuss objections to the view which I am stating, I should like to make it clearer by placing democracy in contrast with totalitarianism. We have yet to examine the philosophy of fascism. When we do so we shall find that one of its pillars is the Schopenhauerian theory of the primacy of the will, which is the direct contrary of the Platonic theory of the primacy of reason. In a totalitarian state the relation of the ruler to the ruled is not that of persuasion, but that of *compulsion*. The people may quite possibly acquiesce in his measures, even approve them enthusiastically. Nevertheless the relation is like that of a general to his troops, in contrast with the relation between the chairman of a committee and its members. The troops may enthusiastically follow the general, but this does not alter the fact that his relation to them is one of compulsion, not persuasion.

But compulsion is the expression of will, not reason. In its extreme form it is force. Force is the natural manifestation of will. Hence the totalitarian, or indeed any autocratic, form of government, has for its principle the primacy of the will. It is will which rules, not reason. Thus we have before us the simple antithesis—democracy as the rule of reason, totalitarianism as the rule of will.

I will now return to the objection that the identification of persuasion with reason is not justified. No doubt, it will be said, the rulers in a democracy have to "persuade" the ruled, but this is not as a rule done by reason, but rather by appeals to emotion, prejudice, interest, and even by unworthy tricks and lies. This is indeed one of the commonest charges made against democracy.

The charge may be true—at least in some degree. But it points, not to any fault in the theory of democracy, but to its abuse in practice. The democratic ideal is government by reason. That democracies do not live up to their own ideals is very true, and is due in very large measure to the exalted character of the ideals. But this is quite irrelevant to the question concerning what the ideals of democracy *are*. Our statement of the philosophy of democracy as embodying the principle of the primacy of reason is correct. To point to the fact that democratic rulers in fact more often appeal to emotions rather than to rational considerations has absolutely no bearing on the matter. We have said that the aim of democracy is the rule of reason. We have never said that democracies completely achieve their aim. Of course they fall short. The point may be made clear by a reference to the moral ideal of Christianity. This ideal is complete selflessness. It would be absurd to suppose that we disprove this by pointing out that Christians are in fact often very selfish.

In this connection there arises what some may think to be a debatable question in the theory of democracy. It is pointed out that in fact the rulers persuade the ruled by appeals to their self-interest. And it has been argued by some that this is not an abuse of democracy, but on the contrary correctly represents its nature and aims. For the essence of democracy is not, on this view, the rule of reason at all, but the rule of the *interests* of the majority.

If this view is taken, it becomes quite possible to defend the appeal which politicians make to selfish interests. For the government can only know where the interests of the majority lie if every individual voter votes for what is his own interest. The government can then know what the interest of the majority is by the simple process of counting noses. Hence the duty of the voter is, not to consider what will be best for the whole society, but to consider only what is best for himself. And if this is so, the politician who is seeking the votes of a particular set of people is quite right to appeal to their individual or sectional interests; and has in fact no business to bring in questions of the common good.

There is a corollary to this view of democracy. If this view is logically carried out, the people's representative becomes in the assembly their mere mouthpiece. He has no right, out of regard for the welfare of the society as a whole, to vote in the assembly in favor of any measure which seems contrary to the interests of the particular city, region, county, or state which selected him to represent its interests. It is not his business to consider the interests of society, but only the welfare of the narrow circle of his own constituents. He will therefore in the assembly merely carry out the commands of his constituents.

The contrary theory is, of course, that it is the duty of the representative in the assembly to consider the interests of the whole state. And in doing this he may sometimes have to vote against the regional interests of his own constituents. Similarly it will, at least in theory, be the duty of the individual voter to vote for the policy which he thinks best for the state, not for the interests of himself or his city or section of society. Thus farmers ought to take urban and industrial interests into account when they vote, and industrialists ought to take farm interests into account.

On the first of these interpretations of democracy—that which appeals solely to majority self-interest—the rule of reason is largely suppressed. Democracy then embodies rather a form of the theory of the primacy of the will. For interest is a manifestation of will, not reason.

In practice most democracies compromise between the two interpretations. Legislators do consider the public interest, and do not regard themselves as phonograph records merely reproducing mechanically the voices of their constituents. Yet the sectional interests which have elected them weigh with them far more heavily than interests which they do not directly represent. They would scarcely dare to vote, on the ground of the public good, consistently against the wishes of their own constituents.

Considered from the point of view of practical working there is much to be said for a compromise of this kind. It is probably inevitable. In a sense the essence of democracy is the capacity to compromise. And it is one of its virtues that it does not carry out any theory with too rigorous a logic. In human affairs the man, or the society, which starts from some clear-cut political premise and—come what may—carries it through with relentless logic to the bitter end, usually produces as consequence a huge agglomeration of misery. This is perhaps one of the faults of fascism.

Nevertheless we have to make up our minds between the two theories of democracy. It may well be possible to slip along pretty well most of the time on the basis of compromise, not knowing exactly what the ideal of democracy actually is. But there may come moments in history when a vital choice between the two theories has to be made, when we have to be clear-headed as to what is our goal. And there cannot, in my opinion, be any doubt as to the proper answer to the question. The interpretation which stresses only interest, ruling out reason, makes democracy merely a piece of machinery by means of which majorities may tyrannize over minorities. It is then simply the embodiment of mass selfishness. If democracy is to be in any sense a set of ideals, if it is to be the embodiment of a conception of the good life, these ideals and this conception must be those which arise from the Christian theory of sympathy and the Greek theory of reason. This is the heritage of our European civilization which is the ethical substance of democracy. To preach the theory that democracy in its essence is, and ought to be, nothing but a machine for registering majority and minority interests is to cut democracy loose from its roots in the ethos of western civilization.

It is precisely this fatal misunderstanding of democracy which renders it an easy victim of fascist criticism, according to which it is nothing but a battleground of contending egoisms, a gross materialism, unillumined by any spark of ethical and spiritual light.

The final member of our cluster of ideas is individualism. And individualism is a name for two distinct, though closely connected, things. First, it stands for a character which individuals in a democratic society are supposed to have; they are individualistic in their thoughts and actions. To be individualistic is thought to be a part of the democratic way of life. And since it is thus a character of private persons in their private lives I shall call it *personal individualism*. Secondly, individualism is the name of the democratic theory of the proper relation between the state and the individual. It is the theory that the state is composed of individuals and of nothing else, and that therefore the state exists solely as an instrument for the welfare of its component individuals. I shall call this *political individualism*.

There are two kinds of personal individualism which, although they are constantly confused, are in fact diametrical opposites. The first kind is simply the recognition of the infinite value of the individual. This is the only personal individualism which is a true and proper part of the philosophy of democracy. The other kind is egoism, the unbridled self-will of each individual, combined with a total disregard of the welfare of other individuals. Its motto is, "Every man for himself." It is the philosophy of the natural man. It is the denial of the genuine spirit of democracy. It is no part of the democratic faith. It may be called false, or bastard, individualism.

The true personal individualism is merely one of the aspects or facets of the theory of the infinite value of the individual. Its special flavor may be brought out by comparing it with the doctrine of equality, which is another such aspect. The notion of equality is the application of the theory of infinite value to human beings considered as *passive*. It concerns what they are to receive from others, namely equal treatment. But individualism emphasizes equality of opportunity. It is the application of the notion of infinite value to the human being considered as *active*. It concerns him as an agent carving out his personal destiny in the world. It means that each individual is to be free to use all his powers and capacities for the development of his own personality. He is not to be hampered and checked in the exercise of his individuality. He is to expand so far as it lies in him to expand. The theoretical basis of this right of each individual to expand his personality to the full is the belief that the personality of each individual has an intrinsic and absolute value, adding to the riches of the world. This expansion is to be treated as an absolute end, to be subordinated to nothing as mere means.

This conception carries with it as a matter of course the repudiation and annulment of its opposite, the false or bastard individualism. For the latter seeks at all costs to suppress the intrinsic values of others in order to make them into means for the ends of the one false individualist.

Confusion between the true and the false individualism is not only frequent, but deliberate. The egoist profits by the confusion, and encourages it. He names his greed and cruelty individualism purposely in order that he may pass them off as democratic virtues. He is the wolf in sheep's clothing. When ruthless and immoral business practices are recommended to us as being expressions of the individualism which is part of the faith of democracy, we have this intentional confusion. And the common phrase "rugged individualism" should be held under suspicion of aiming at a like deceit. It is true that there is a certain ruggedness which is a virtue. This is self-reliance, independence, and strength. And in so far as rugged individualism stresses these, it is consistent with democratic virtue. But ruggedness is also a name for absence of sympathy, for selfishness, disregard of the rights of others. And we may suspect that the egoist profits by this ambiguity too. Thus when men, not content with the plain word individualism, think it necessary to add the adjective rugged, we should be on our guard, should watch their actions to discover what they mean, whether they be sheep or wolves.

We saw in the last section that the failure to distinguish the true concept of representative government from its false interpretation as a mere machine for ensuring the dominance of majority selfishness is seized upon by fascists as a weapon against democracy. Just so, in the present case, the confusion between true and false individualism gives a handle to our enemies. It is easy for them to represent the spirit of individualism as merely that of universal egoism, because we ourselves often give it that false interpretation. Every greedy captain of industry, who, in the name of individualism, ruthlessly tramples on the rights of others, is handing ammunition to the enemies of democracy. It is therefore of paramount importance to distinguish the true from the false individualism.

I come now to a brief discussion of political individualism. This is the democratic theory of the nature and function of the state in its relation to the individual. The essence of the theory is that society is nothing but the sum of its component individual citizens plus their organization into a society or state. (It is not at present necessary to distinguish between society and the state, although the concepts of them are, of course, different.) There is nothing in society, or in the state, over and above the sum of the individuals. This is exactly as if one should say that a table is simply the sum of the pieces of wood which are its legs, sides, top, etc., plus their organization, that is, their arrangement in the particular spatial shape which constitutes them a table rather than a chair; and that there is nothing in the table over and above the pieces of wood plus their spatial arrangement.

The reader who is innocent of all metaphysical mystifications may well ask: What could there possibly be in a table over and above its parts and their spatial relations? And what could there possibly be in a state over and above its component individuals and their social and political relations?

The question about the table is perhaps unanswerable by anybody. But there are theorists who hold that a society, being a living organism, and not a mere inanimate thing like a table, does as a whole possess something which is not to be found in any of its parts or in the mere sum of them. A human being, or any organism, they say, is not merely the sum of his or its organs, such as stomach, legs, heart, liver, brain. Over and above all these things there is the life which pervades them all. This life is not a part of the organism. Nor does it belong to any one of the individual members. It is somehow possessed by the whole organism *as* a whole. Society, it is said, is like an organism. It has a life of its own which is distinct from the lives and souls of its individual members. And this life of the whole society is what there is in it over and above the lives of the individuals who are its component members. This, or something like it, is what is alleged by the philosophy of fascism.

The essential point of the contrast between the democratic and the fascist theories of the state is as follows. From the democratic view that there is nothing in the state except its individual members plus their social and political relations, it follows that the state can have no purpose and no interests which are not identical with the purposes and interests of all or some of its citizens. The interests of the state cannot in the end mean anything except the interests of a number of individuals. Likewise the welfare of the state cannot be anything except the welfare of individuals. It follows that the state as an organization only exists for the sake of advancing the welfare of the citizens. In other words the state is a means only. The individuals—their welfare, interests, and satisfactions—are the end. The state exists for the individuals, not the individuals for the state.

This is denied by fascist theory. For the fascist thinker, the state possesses a life and a personality distinct from, and superior to, the lives and personalities of its citizens. Therefore the state may have interests and purposes of its own which are not the interests and purposes of any individuals or sum of individuals, and which are superior to all individual interests. It follows that the state is not merely a means to the ends of individuals. Rather the individuals are means to the ends of the state. It is right to add that fascists generally maintain that in spite of this, the individual, in serving the state, does also always serve his own higher interests, and that his own supreme welfare will be found therein.

The democratic view of the state is nothing more than yet another manifestation of the theory of the infinite value of the individual. Since the value of the individual is infinite, the value of the state cannot be greater. To put the matter in another way, the theory of the infinite value of the individual means that the individual is an absolute end, and that he cannot be reduced to the level of a means to some other end. Therefore he cannot be treated as a means to the ends of the state, if these are considered as being something outside and beyond the ends of the individuals. The state must be a means to the ends of the individual, not the other way round.

The fascist theory, in making the individual a means to the ends of the state, is denying that the individual is an absolute end in himself. It is therefore denying the doctrine of the infinite value of the individual.

But here again democratic theory lends itself to easy attack from fascism unless we are careful to interpret it aright. We are familiar with the fascist criticism that, according to democracy, the individual need not sacrifice himself for the welfare of society or the state, and that democracy is therefore nothing but universal egoism. What are we to say of this?

According to the true democratic theory the individual certainly *can* be called upon to sacrifice his own interests to those of society. But the democratic theory is that this in the end means only that he is to sacrifice his own interests in certain cases *to those of other individuals*. The democratic theory will account the welfare of a thousand as of more importance than the welfare of one. And if the interests of the thousand and the one clash, the one must sacrifice his interests. But he does so for the sake of the thousand *individuals*, not for the sake of an abstract, imaginary, superentity called the state. Democracy and fascism alike hold that the individual must be prepared to sacrifice himself for society. But they give to the term society two different meanings. By the society for which the individual is to sacrifice himself democracy means the sum of the other individuals, or the majority of them, while fascism means something over and above all or any individuals.

If the reader will now turn again to the diagram on page 126, he will see that the theory of our civilization which it is intended to illustrate has been, in this chapter and the last, expounded and brought to completion. Chapter VI showed the derivation of the idea of the infinite value of the individual from the Greek theory of the primacy of reason, and also from the Christian theory of the primacy of sympathy. It showed how these two views of human personality were at least pragmatically reconciled in the theory of infinite value, which is the key idea of our civilization. Thus the upper half of the diagram was established. The present chapter has established the lower half by showing how the three fundamental ideas of democracy—equality, liberty, individualism—have been derived from the idea of the infinite value of the individual and are, in fact, nothing more than special aspects of it.

CHAPTER VIII

RATIONALISM AND ANTIRATIONALISM

Greek thought has dominated Europe in so far as Europe has remained true to the ideal of the primacy of reason. Emphasis upon human rationality as the guiding star in life has been, along with the Christian elements which have become fused with it, the lifeblood of western culture. We have now to trace the fortunes of the star of reason in a number of episodes in the Europe which intervened between the collapse of Greek civilization and the present day.

It seems to be almost a law of human affairs that great insights tend to destroy themselves by blinding or dazzling the men who achieve them. When men originate a great idea, they forthwith begin the process of its destruction by wildly overstating it, and thereby introducing falsehood into it—falsehood which may be destined one day to drag it down. It is a case of action provoking reaction. The great idea intoxicates its discoverers. It becomes with them an obsession. They apply it where it has no application. They see in it the solution of all manner of problems on which in fact it has no bearing. They oversimplify every-

173

thing in terms of it. They profess to see the imprint of its work in all creation. Thereupon begins the inevitable re-action. Men turn in anger or contempt against the manifest exaggerations of the idea. And since they cannot distinguish between the true idea itself and its exaggerations, they battle with equal fury against both. The original insight is endangered or destroyed in the process.

This is one reason why the history of human affairs tends to travel always in a zigzag path, to oscillate between extremes. It is this which causes the appearance of the dialectical movement in history, to which Marx, following Hegel, drew attention.

The history of the idea of the primacy of reason is a case in point. The Greeks achieved the insight. But they and their successors in the modern world exaggerated it into a fantastic rationalism. The overrationalization of life and of the world ran its course throughout the Middle Ages. Then came the Renaissance and that liberation of the human spirit which introduced the phase of world history in which we now live. It brought with it the beginnings of the reaction against reason. For four hundred years now the pendulum has swung backwards from its extreme point of rationalistic excess towards the extremes of antirationalism and irrationalism. We now live in an age of blind insurrection against the rule of reason in life—an insurrection which is at this moment threatening to overturn all civilization. Not reason now, but will (and its natural manifestation, force), is hailed as the ruler of life. And this is not merely a result of forces which were set going in the last decade or two by the wars and treaties of our own generation. It is the culmination of a movement of the human spirit which began at least four centuries ago. It is the fruit of a wild antirationalist reaction against an equally wild rationalism. Thus the swing of the pendulum began in Greek times, towards rationalism. The backward swing is still in progress. So that the whole movement, from left to right, and again from right to left, has occupied well over two thousand years and is not yet finished. So slowly does the pulse of history beat.

In this chapter our task is to study some aspects of this movement. But since our object is not history, but the truth about the good life, we shall have to discover exactly what the exaggerations of rationalism have been. Men in general, we said, cannot distinguish the original true insight from its subsequent distortions, and so in their blindness attack both. It is surely the task of the philosopher to do precisely this: to sift out the true from the false.

The whole affair began no doubt with the fundamental intellectualism of the Greek temperament. The Greeks were clever children, delighted with their own brilliance. They exulted in the exercise of intellect, in sheer play of mind, as a healthy animal exults in the play of its limbs. They loved clever sayings, paradoxes, casuistical distinctions, sophistries, repartee. They invented all manner of intellectual puzzles. The famous questions of Zeno the Eleatic are as much examples of sheer delight in riddles as they are of profound philosophizing. Reading Plato one gets the impression that men in those days sat rapt and intent, watching and listening to an argument between intellectual champions, as modern men might watch a skilled rapier encounter, appraising and applauding each point as connoisseurs.

Professor Dewey has told us that thinking arises when the human organism meets obstacles. Thinking is the effort to get around these obstacles. It is thus in its essence a practical activity, an instrument of successful action. So it is.

But the merit of the Greeks was that they were the first to break through the bonds of this dull and stupid truth; and in doing so to be the founders of civilization. They were the first to discover that thinking, besides being an instrument of successful living, can be a supreme source of immediate delight, that is to say, an end in itself. In this they are to be compared to that aboriginal genius who first found that eating, in addition to satisfying hunger and preserving life, can be made the foundation of the pleasures of the civilized palate. What matter that Professor Dewey, in the middle of the banquet, inappropriately propounds his solemn revelation that eating is nothing but an instrument of living? For culture, which consists in the adornments of life as distinguished from its mere necessities, rests upon man's capacity perpetually to discover new ends in what were originally nothing but means. The life lived on the level of bare necessity passes on from labor to labor, along the chain of instruments and means which extends itself forever, without finding anything which is a resting place and an end, never stopping in the ceaseless treading of the mill. Each thing leads to the next, but nothing leads to anything in the end.

Now life *is* this ceaseless treading of the mill. And there is no end to the bitter chain of instrumentalities till death brings final darkness on the apparently fruitless traveling along a road which leads nowhere. Nevertheless there is the possibility of joy and liberation. For man has made a supreme discovery, which is that he can turn what was originally a mere instrumentality into an end. Instead of going on, he can stand still for a moment in the sheer enjoyment of the stage at which he stands, and which he had previously taken to be a mere point of transition. That he must in the end pass on, tread the mill again. does not destroy the fact that he did in that moment achieve an absolute liberation from the wheel of things. These moments raise themselves like flowers along a dusty path. The richness of life is due to them, whatever joy there is in living. So perverse and stupid is that philosophy which keeps insisting that thinking, eating, singing, praying, drinking, making love, constructing philosophies, composing music and poems, are all merely instruments and means, instruments for making instruments for making instruments forever.

The Greek spirit made of thinking an adornment of life, a joy, instead of a tiresome tool for breaking the ground, keeping warm, capturing a mate, obtaining food. When the Egyptians geometrized the Nile mud, using mathematics merely to plow, of what account was it save to yield a sorrowful eating? But when Pythagoras discovered the theorem about the right-angled triangle he sacrificed an ox in jubilation. And since thinking seemed to the Greeks the highest joy, they naïvely conjectured that the life of God, which is pure happiness, must also be a life of pure thought. And therein perhaps the fatal exaggeration begins —the tendency to see in thinking the inner reality and secret of the whole universe.

But this was not the particular exaggeration to which the Greeks themselves were most prone. To make reason the essence of the universe, the stuff of everything, was reserved for certain choice spirits among the moderns. The Greeks indeed suggested that God was all thought. But then God was not for them all reality. According to Plato, He was the mere Architect, not the Creator of the world. There were pre-existent materials out of which He fashioned the world. These materials were neither thought, nor the product of thought. Thought was not the stuff of everything.

The Greek delight in reason caused them to conceive it as the crown of things. It existed in the first place for its own sake, an end in itself. This train of thought led to Aristotle's conception of intellectual virtue, by which he meant the philosopher's pure contemplation of truth. This was the highest achievement of man. And it had no end beyond itself. But the Greeks were also thus led to conceive reason as the ruler of human personality in practical affairs. This function is fulfilled by controlling the appetites and feelings. And this gave rise to the moral virtues, of which the principle is the golden mean. This idea that reason should control the other elements of personality was the pure unexaggerated doctrine of the primacy of reason. It was the great insight which was destined to be a guiding light of western civilization for upwards of two thousand years.

But now began the inevitable process of overstatement, of riding the idea to death. We may distinguish first of all two spheres in which the Greeks found reason to be supreme. First, it is supreme in practical affairs, in conduct. It achieves this supremacy by ruling the appetites. This is the true and genuine doctrine of the primacy of reason. But secondly, the Greeks found reason supreme in the theoretical sphere of truth, in the regions of science and philosophy. It became for them the great instrument for the discovery of truth. And the influence of their geometrical studies is evident here: geometry, it seemed to them, is a work of pure reason unaided by empirical investigation. For Plato also, pure science, pure truth, is knowledge of the "forms." And reason is the organ which knows the forms.

This led to the first overstatement of the claims of reason. The Greeks mistakenly supposed that mere reason alone could discover truths about the physical world. There are as a matter of fact two factors necessary for the discovery of physical truths. These are respectively reason and sense experience. By sense experience I mean whatever evidence comes to us through the physical senses of sight, hearing, touch, etc. The senses may be aided by instruments such as microscopes and telescopes, but what reaches us through these means is still sense experience. Also it makes no difference whether the evidence comes as a result of simple observation or as a result of controlled observation and experiment. Whatever we thus know through our senses constitutes the empirical element in knowledge. But the other factor, reason or the rational element, is also of course necessary. It makes possible the inferences, deductions, and inductive generalizations which are based upon sense experience, and without which it would be impossible to discern principles and laws in the flux of sensation.

It is perhaps hardly necessary to give examples of how reason and sense experience cooperate to yield knowledge. Astronomy is obviously the result of reason working upon materials originally supplied by the unaided eye, and more latterly through the telescope, spectroscope, and so on. Darwin discovered the principle of evolution by inductive reasoning based upon extended observations of the world's flora and fauna. Even our common-sense knowledge of things in the world about us results from simple reasonings upon the basis of what we see, hear, feel, etc.

The first exaggeration of the claims of reason to which we have to draw attention is the tendency to think that reason alone, without the aid of observation through the senses, can give us knowledge of things in the physical world. I say the *tendency* because perhaps no one ever went the length of supposing that sense experience could be dispensed with altogether. But men have leaned in that direction. They have minimized the importance of sense experience and maximized that of reason to such a degree that it amounted almost to the obliteration of the empirical element. Through this tendency there arose that exaggeration of the claims of reason which I propose to call the doctrine of *the epistemic primacy of reason*.

The theory that it is the proper function of reason to control the appetites, and so to guide human conduct, was the great and valuable insight of the Greeks; and it is this which has been the leading thought of western civilization. I call this the doctrine of *the psychological primacy of reason*. It is psychological because it means that reason is to rule the other psychological elements of personality. The epistemic primacy of reason means the view that reason alone, or almost alone, can yield knowledge of physical truths. The psychological primacy concerns man's *practical* life, his conduct of affairs. Epistemic primacy concerns his *theoretical* life, the life of intellect in science and philosophy.

The epistemic primacy of reason is the first distortion of the claims of reason which resulted from Greek rationalism and overemphasis on reason. It would not be true to say that the Greeks paid no attention to empirical evidence and relied solely upon reason in their science. There is plenty of evidence to the contrary. Aristotle was indefatigable in his collection of biological facts. He organized expeditions of discovery for the purposes of science. Greek astronomers deduced from observations of the heavenly bodies the spherical shape of the earth and made rough estimates of its circumference.

Nevertheless, the charge is in general true that they grossly overemphasized the part of reason in science and underestimated the part of observation. For instance, they supposed that the planets move in circular orbits. And the grounds of this opinion were that the circle is the perfect figure, and that the planets, being divine, must move in perfect orbits. Contrast this reliance on armchair reasoning with the patient observation and plotting of the actual movements of the planets which led modern astronomers to the discovery that the orbits of the planets are elliptical. As another instance, Zeno, finding that his abstract reasoning contradicted the empirical fact of motion, declared that motion is impossible and does not exist.

The false rationalism which tends to rely exclusively upon reason for *a priori* deduction of the facts of the world thus had its origin among the Greeks. It continued unabated through the Middle Ages. It sterilized and stultified science for upwards of fifteen hundred years. And it provoked the first violent reaction against reason in the antirationalist revolt of the scientists of the seventeenth century. Of this more later.

Epistemic rationalism reached its zenith in the philosophical system of Hegel in the late eighteenth century. According to Hegel the essence of the world is logic. It follows that if one can once grasp this inner logical essence of things, the main facts of the world can be deduced *a priori* without the aid of observation. What is real is rational, and what is not rational is not reality, but mere appearance. From the principles of pure logic, without relying at all on empirical evidence, Hegel seeks to deduce the nature of space and time, the existence of matter, the numbers of the planets, the facts of psychology, the characteristics of the state, the necessity of a police force, the varieties and outstanding features of poetry, painting, and sculpture, the truths of religion.

In addition to the theory of the epistemic primacy of reason there came into the modern world an even more fatal distortion and exaggeration of Greek intellectualism. I shall call it the doctrine of *the cosmic primacy of reason.* The original insight of the Greeks was the psychological view that reason must rule human personality. The epistemic primacy of reason held that knowledge of the facts of nature can be obtained through reason alone. The theory of the cosmic primacy of reason holds that reason is the ultimate reality which actually produces the world.

As the psychoanalyst tends to see the Oedipus complex in all culture, in all civilization, in art, religion, science; as the specialist in some rare type of disease tends to find this disease at the root of every human ill; so philosophers who exalt reason tend to see in it the secret of the entire universe. This movement of thought, secretly and silently incubating through the ages, suddenly burst into explicit statement in the famous philosophy of Hegel. The Absolute—which is the ultimate reality out of which the universe arises—is for Hegel a logical process of abstract categories, a cosmic and impersonal reason, an inner and immanent rationality of all things. This world-reason manifests itself in the world-process. Hegel calls the book in which he uncovers the final secret of the universe "The Science of Logic." Metaphysics, which is the study of the essence and nature of the world, and logic, which is the study of reason, are for him identical. The world is logic.

Hegel's followers in the nineteenth century did not imitate his extremism. But in greater or less degree the same spirit informs them. They held that, in one sense or another, mind or spirit is the essence of all things. Mind and

RATIONALISM AND ANTIRATIONALISM 183

spirit are terms more elastic than reason. They cover also will, feeling, and emotion. But as a rule, the core of spirit is conceived to be reason. For the Greek doctrine of the supremacy of reason over all other psychological elements exerts its influence here too.

It is of course impossible to include in this chapter anything like a detailed history of rationalism. But I may here sum up the main points which I have sought to make. Every kind of European rationalism has its origin in the Greek belief in the supreme value of reason. This began no doubt in a mere temperamental intellectualism, a love of mental exercise as an end in itself. It passed on to a definite belief that reason is in some sense the highest of all human faculties, and ought therefore to control the other elements of personality. This was the doctrine of the practical or psychological primacy of reason. But unfortunately the Greek love of reason led to wild exaggerations which have also infected the thought of the west. These exaggerations of the claims of reason are in general of two kinds. The first is the tendency to discount the importance of the evidence of the senses in the realm of knowledge, and to set up pure reason as the arbiter of empirical truths. This false type of rationalism I called the doctrine of the epistemic primacy of reason. The second is the tendency to find in reason the ultimate secret of the whole universe. And this I called the doctrine of the cosmic primacy of reason.

We have now to turn to a brief study of the insurrection against the overweening claims of reason which is a characteristic of the last few centuries.

The revolt began at least as early as the seventeenth century. Probably its beginnings can be discerned much earlier. But it is in the seventeenth century that it becomes explicit and avowed. And strangely enough it is modern science, in its beginnings in that century, which opened the attack. This is the opposite of what we should perhaps expect. For it is commonly supposed that scientific men are distinguished by their cold clear processes of reason, and that science itself is the supreme triumph of human reason. In a sense this is true. But there is another side to the picture.

That the contrast between the medieval period and the period of the rise of modern science is really a contrast between extreme rationalism and an antirationalistic rebellion is a point which has been made with profound insight by Professor Whitehead in his "Science and the Modern World." In the following remarks about seventeenth-century science I am largely indebted to him.

"Galileo," writes Professor Whitehead, "keeps harping on how things happen, while his adversaries had a complete theory as to why things happen. . . . Galileo insists upon 'irreducible and stubborn facts,' and Simplicius, his opponent, brings forward reasons, completely satisfactory, at least to himself. It is a great mistake to conceive this historical revolt as an appeal to reason. On the contrary it was through and through an anti-intellectualist movement. It was the return to the contemplation of brute fact; and it was based on a recoil from the inflexible rationality of medieval thought." [1] And on a later page Professor Whitehead writes: "Science has never shaken off the impress of its origin in the historical revolt of the later Renaissance. It has remained predominantly an antirationalist movement." [2]

[1] Alfred North Whitehead, "Science and the Modern World," page 12; Macmillan, New York, 1936.
[2] *Ibid.*, page 23.

The point is that medieval thought, following the Greek pattern, supposed that natural phenomena and events had reasons, and that if one could discern the reasons in nature one could predict the facts *a priori*. Thus the reason why the planets move in circles is that the circle is the perfect figure. Galileo and his friends declined to be persuaded that, because the facts were supposed to follow from certain reasons, therefore the facts *must* be so and so. They sternly rebuked the reasons, pointed at the facts, and insisted that the facts were final. If the facts showed that the planets move in ellipses, then they do move in ellipses, and no reasons why they must move in circles were to find a hearing. And there might be excellent reasons why heavy bodies should fall fast, light bodies slowly. But the reasons counted for nothing. The facts showed that in a vacuum both fall with equal accelerations.

The reasons to which the medievalists appealed were mostly of the teleological kind. It was assumed that God had a plan for the world, and that things in the world happened in the way they did *because* they were steps in this plan. This teleological outlook was one aspect of rationalism which the medieval world inherited from the Greeks. That the spirit is the same may be seen by reading the passage in Plato's "Phaedo" in which the following words are put into the mouth of Socrates: "I argued that if anyone desired to find out the cause of the generation or destruction or existence of anything, he must find out what state of being or doing or suffering was best for that thing. . . . I imagined that he [Anaxagoras] would tell me first whether the earth is flat or round; and whichever was true, he would proceed to explain the cause and the necessity of this being so, and then he would teach me the nature of the best and show that this was the best; and if he said that the earth was in the center, he would further explain that this position was the best, and I should be satisfied with the explanation given, and not want any other sort of cause. And I thought that I would then go on and ask him about the sun and moon and stars, and that he would explain to me their comparative swiftness, and their returnings and various states, active and passive, and how all of them were for the best." [1]

Against the whole conception of nature as governed by reasons and purposes the science of the seventeenth century appealed to the brute facts. Modern science was thus from the beginning antirationalist in the sense that, even if there are reasons for things in nature, the scientific picture of the world refuses to take them into account.

Our whole picture of the universe has changed. The turning point was the seventeenth century and the foundation of modern science by Galileo and Newton. The vision which confronted men's eyes from the time of Plato right up to that turning point was that of a world governed by reason and purpose, a world of which it could be said that events occurred either because it was good that they should occur, or because it was in some other way rational. The world was permeated by reason. But the picture after the seventeenth century has been that of a world of brute facts, destitute of reason, a phantasmagoria of moving shapes and colors and sounds without sense or rational coherence. Things follow one another, and the process of nature mechanically grinds itself out. There is no reason why things should be as they are. They simply are so. They might just as well have been utterly other. It is not that we do not know the reasons for things. There are no reasons.

[1] Plato, "Phaedo," in "The Dialogues of Plato," translated by B. Jowett, volume 1, page 482; Random House, New York, 1937.

Philosophy in the modern epoch has followed science in depicting a blind and reasonless world. When Hume in the eighteenth century pointed out that there is no logical connection between a cause and its effect, he was merely stating abstractly the view of the world which implicitly guided the practice of Galileo and Newton. He was giving formal expression to the antirationalism of the modern age which science had ushered in. He showed that an effect cannot be deduced rationally from its cause. There is no logical necessity binding particular cause to particular effect. Cold of a certain degree is followed by solidification of water. There is no resemblance, no affinity, no logical connection of any sort between the idea of cold and the idea of solidness. We merely find in experience that, as a matter of fact, cold is followed by solidification. So far as any rational or intelligible connection is concerned, it might as well have been followed by boiling, or by the turning of the water into oil, or by any other event whatsoever. Causality is nothing but an arbitrary set of sequences, devoid of reason. And this has been, roughly speaking, the creed of philosophers and men of science ever since. To be sure, there have been, and still are, philosophers who disagree with Hume. Whitehead has recently attempted to reintroduce the notion of reasons in nature. He is unlikely to succeed. The cast of the modern mind is too firmly set in the opposite doctrine.

Philosophies of the twentieth century do but on the whole restate in new terminologies the thesis of the blind meaninglessness of the universe. This is the practical upshot of the current fashionable positivism. And a recent book, characteristic of the time, is entitled "A World of Chance." [1] The point of it is that everything in the uni-

[1] E. G. Spaulding, "A World of Chance"; Macmillan, New York, 1936.

verse is "contingent"; that is, everything might just as well have been quite different, since there is no particular reason why things should be as they are. And even Whitehead, whose philosophy is in general a protest against this whole modern outlook, is compelled by the spirit of the age to characterize God, the final Reality, as being "the ultimate irrationality."

From this account it will be evident that the rationalistic orgy inaugurated by Hegel in Germany in the late eighteenth century was an anachronism, a movement born out of its time. It saw the world, not merely as rational in some of its aspects, but as through and through the very creation of reason. Hegel was born three hundred years too late. The world-vision which he sought to re-create and project into men's minds was already dead, long dead. It was only the tremendous power of his personal genius which succeeded in stamping his ideas on the philosophy of the nineteenth century, thereby destroying its contact with the modern scientific spirit. And though this lasted for a while, the vision faded out, and left philosophy once more with its picture of a reasonless world—the picture which it has today.

Modern science and modern philosophy are primarily reactions against the doctrines of the epistemic primacy of reason and the cosmic primacy of reason. Truths about the world are not to be discovered by *a priori* deductions or by armchair reasoning. Patient examination of the facts is what is required, or what is known as the empirical or historical method. This is the denial of the epistemic primacy of reason. Moreover, the scientific and Humean view of the world as reasonless, as an arena of blind mechanical laws and brute facts, is the denial of the doctrine of the cosmic primacy of reason, the doctrine that reason is the creator and ruler of the cosmos. What we have now to consider is the fate, in the modern world, of the doctrine of the psychological primacy of reason, the original Greek insight that it is reason which should rule in human affairs.

And here the outstanding fact is that the antirationalism engendered by science and philosophy from the seventeenth century onwards has overflowed into this region also. This is an example of the inevitable nemesis which great ideas bring upon themselves by the exaggeration of their claims. Men turn angrily against the exaggerations, and since they cannot distinguish the original true insight from its distortions, the insight itself is overthrown. The general character of our age is a blind attack upon reason all along the line. There has been engendered a wild irrationalism which does not discriminate between the legitimate and the illegitimate claims of reason. This is what has produced the crisis in our civilization, since our civilization is based upon the doctrine of the primacy of reason, at least in its psychological form. We have now to trace the origins of that modern irrationalism which denies, not only the epistemic and the cosmic claims of reason, but even its claim to rule in human affairs. We have to consider the modern denial of the doctrine of the psychological primacy of reason.

This particular type of antirationalism has no doubt its precursors in earlier ages. Something at least akin to it appears among the Greek Sophists, with such men as Thrasymachus and Callicles. The spirit of it is alive in the writings of Mandeville and Machiavelli. But in its peculiar modern form it begins with the German philosopher Schopenhauer.

Schopenhauer's great book, "The World as Will and Idea," was published near the end of 1818 with the date 1819. His philosophy is, in nearly all respects, the direct contradiction of that of his great rival and contemporary,

Hegel. Both philosophers teach that the world in space and time, the world as we know it, is an appearance only, an outward show, which bodies forth an inward essence, an ultimate reality. But for Hegel the ultimate reality is an impersonal world-reason; for Schopenhauer it is an impersonal world-*will*. This placing of will, instead of reason, at the heart of the universe, is of course in itself an anti-rationalist position. It is a denial of the doctrine of the cosmic primacy of reason. It led immediately, however, to a denial of the doctrine of the psychological primacy of reason.

The world-will which is, according to Schopenhauer, at the back of all things, which manifests itself in all things, is not conscious. It is blind. Above all it is irrational. It is probably misleading even to call it will. This is a mere metaphor, taken from human volition, which is its highest and most complete manifestation. One can use of it such words as urge, force, striving, even craving and hungering. But these too are metaphors for what is in itself dark and inscrutable.

The cosmic will individuates itself, becomes the world. Its essence is that it hungers to *be*. And it is this hungering for existence which causes existence, the existence of the world. The will manifests itself in all natural forces, such as gravitation, electricity, and magnetism, but above all in human volition.

As will is supreme in the universe, so, in its manifestation as volition, it is supreme in human life. It is at this point that we touch Schopenhauer's fundamental denial of the Greek doctrine of the psychological primacy of reason. The essence of man is not, as the Greeks thought, reason, but will. For will or craving is the essence of all life, indeed of the whole universe. Life in particular is simply the struggling and striving of the will.

It is will, then, not reason, which is the supreme ruler of man and of human life. What then is the place of reason in human affairs, according to Schopenhauer? The answer to this all-important question is brief and emphatic. *Reason is nothing but an instrument, a tool, of the will.* To be a subordinate servant, to do the behests of the will, this is its place and this its proper function.

Schopenhauer thinks that the truth of this can be seen by an examination of almost any example of human activity. For instance, man has the basic urge of hunger. This is an example of will; for Schopenhauer uses the word to cover man's whole desiring, conative, purposive nature. The will, in the form of desire for food, sets reason or intelligence to work. Its subordinate task is to discover the means for satisfying this demand of the will. It performs this task by discovering the arts of hunting, agriculture, and the like. Again, human volition demands warmth and protection from weather. Reason discovers the means to supply the need by inventing the art of building. Reason is everywhere the tool which the will uses to achieve its ends. It is the same in the life of the individual as in the life of the race. One man wishes to become rich, another to become famous. These are both ends set before the men by their wills. Both men excogitate means to achieve their ends; and this finding of the means is the work of intelligence. Thus will is everywhere the master, reason the obedient slave. This doctrine that will is the supreme ruler, that reason is nothing but its mere instrument, is the great modern doctrine of *the primacy of the will.* By its means Schopenhauer reversed at one stroke the belief which has been, since the time of Plato, one of the foundations of western civilization.

The ethical consequences of the new doctrine were not drawn by Schopenhauer himself, but by his disciple Friedrich Wilhelm Nietzsche. Schopenhauer's own ethics were a curious mixture of Christian and Buddhist principles. Nietzsche combined the Schopenhauerian doctrine of the primacy of the will with the Darwinian theory of evolution. Schopenhauer's will to live becomes in his hands the will to *power*, and this combines admirably with the evolutionary concept of the perpetual struggle of life against life. The essence of life, says Nietzsche, is the will to power. This means that the one supreme end which life sets before itself is the acquisition of power. The evolutionary struggle for existence is now interpreted as the struggle for power.

Moreover, evolution, which Nietzsche uncritically identifies with progress towards the ethically nobler, demands that the struggle should continue unmitigated. For on it depends further evolution, further progress. Whatever is *good* has been the result of the evolutionary struggle for power. Hence the struggle must go on, for any mitigation of it will slow down or stop the process of evolution; and so put an end to the production of what is noble and good.

Nietzsche draws the inevitable consequences. The strong, hard, brave, ruthless, fighting man is the ethical ideal. And he consciously contrasts this ideal with that of Christianity which sets before us the example of the gentle, kind, merciful, sympathetic, selfless man as that which we are to follow. There results an ethics which is the diametrical opposite of the Christian.

That Schopenhauer's doctrine of the primacy of will would lead to an ethical ideal the very opposite of the

Christian was of course to be expected—even if Schopenhauer himself failed to foresee this consequence. For sympathy and reason have an affinity to one another. They hang together. As we have seen, the primacy of reason and the primacy of sympathy lead to the same practical results, however different they may be as theories. Hence a psychological doctrine which is the reverse of the doctrine of the primacy of reason is certain to end in an ethical ideal which is the reverse of the Christian. The inherent affinity between the theories of the primacy of reason and of sympathy respectively is shown by the fact that Nietzsche, starting from a denial of the primacy of reason, deduces from this premise a denial of the value of sympathy. For a contempt for sympathy is one of his leading characteristics.

I shall not at the moment pursue further the Schopenhauerian-Nietzschean theory of the primacy of the will, though it will have to figure largely in the remainder of this story. It will be plain to the reader that it is the direct repudiation of the fundamental tradition of our Greco-Christian civilization. I turn now to a brief account of certain other manifestations of the contemporary attack upon the doctrine of the primacy of reason.

The influence of religion in the western world has been in the main, as one would expect, on the side of rationalism. It was indeed against the extreme rationalism of the medieval world under the Roman Church that modern science was in rebellion. And the position since the Reformation has not in this respect undergone any fundamental change. Protestantism has on the whole continued in the civilized tradition of the primacy of reason. This could scarcely have been otherwise if we are right in asserting a deep-seated affinity between the psychological principles of reason and sympathy. The Protestant "right of private judgment" is itself a corollary of the Greco-Christian conception of the infinite value of the individual. It is the religious counterpart of the individualism which is a prominent feature of the theory of democracy.

But it was hardly to be expected that in the post-Renaissance period the ever-growing spirit of antirationalism would fail completely to penetrate the religious consciousness. Such penetration as has occurred has usually taken the form of an attempt to replace reason, as the organ of the inner life, by some form of nonrational intuition, feeling, inspiration, or direct mystic vision. Calvin, Luther, Pascal, Schleiermacher, the Quakers, and many other individuals and sects exhibit this tendency.

But it is in a philosopher, rather than in any of the great religious teachers, that the intuitionist form of antirationalism has reached its high-water mark. The most radical of all attacks ever made upon reason is that of the French philosopher Bergson. According to him the intellect does not give us truth about the world. On the contrary, it falsifies whatever it touches. Truth is known only through intuition.

It matters not whether the emphasis be placed upon feeling, as by Schleiermacher, or upon will, as by Schopenhauer, or upon intuition, as by Bergson. All these philosophers extol what Aristotle would have called "the irrational parts of the soul" at the expense of reason. All alike belong to one and the same movement of the European mind, the violent reaction against the age-old and dominant tradition of Europe, the tradition of the supremacy of reason.

According to Bergson reality is a peculiar kind of flux, in which nothing ever *is*, but everything always *becomes*. It is a continuous flow. The intellect does not perceive it in this way, however, but cuts the flow up into a series of discrete parts, each of which is static. Only in this way can the intellect find any foothold for its operations. Bergson compares it to a cinematograph which can only picture movement by slicing it into a long series of static sections. In doing this the intellect completely misrepresents reality.

But man possesses another faculty besides intellect. This is intuition. By using intuition he can perceive reality as it is. And Bergson's own theory of reality, one is given to understand, is the product of his intuition, not of his intellect—although he is admittedly compelled to use the methods and language of the intellect to explain it to us.

Intuition has been developed, according to Bergson, out of animal instinct. Instinct in the animal is practical in its function. It teaches the bee to hive, the bird to nest. It enables certain of the wasps to sting in their nervous centers, and so to paralyze without killing, the insects which are to be the future food of the wasp young. But instinct can be unhooked, so to speak, from its practical ends, and used theoretically as a means to pure knowledge. It then becomes intuition, which is capable of yielding us the truth about the universe.

Intuition is for Bergson definitely higher than reason. It is the source of all pure truth. All that reason can do is to arrange the truths of intuition into tidy and ordered systems.

Before closing this account I will give one more example of contemporary philosophic antirationalism. This is found in the American philosophy variously known as pragmatism and instrumentalism. It is above all things surprising that this philosophy should have been brought to birth and should flourish in the land which is *par excellence* the home of democracy; and that it should be fervently preached by men noted and rightly honored for their liberal thought. For it is in essence allied with precisely those forces of unreason which today repudiate democracy. It belongs in the camp of the upholders of the primacy of the will. I do not profess to be able to explain how this has happened. But there are crosscurrents in the world of ideas. Strange confusions are possible. It is not uncommon for men of thought to force together tendencies the most contrary and irreconcilable. One must be content to remark that instrumentalism and liberal democracy are strange bedfellows.

But if anyone doubts the essential connection between instrumentalism and the antirationalist revolt of the modern world, he need only reflect on one or two obvious facts. The very name instrumentalism proclaims the connection. It means that reason or intellect is reduced by this philosophy to the status of a mere instrument of something else—whether it be will, desire, appetite, action, or what not. Reason is dethroned, and one or another of the "irrational parts of the soul" put in its place. Whether in the hands of James or Dewey, this philosophy has constantly proclaimed itself anti-intellectualist. Lastly, one has only to look in the writings of Nietzsche to find a theory of knowledge which is practically indistinguishable from pragmatism, and which is there plainly deduced from the Schopenhauerian theory of the primacy of the will. And this has been adopted by the intellectual leaders of modern Germany, who use it to justify the prostitution of science, history, and all learning to the practical ends of the Nazi state.

It is difficult, if not impossible, for any nonpragmatist to give an account of pragmatism which will be accepted as a correct interpretation by pragmatists themselves. The reason for this appears to the present writer to be that they prefer to express their ideas in loose, unprecise, and ambiguous language. Any attempt to pin them down to precise statements is at once repudiated as a "misunderstanding" of their meaning. In these circumstances I shall not attempt to give any account of the details of their theories.

Suffice it to say that pragmatism began its career as a theory of the nature of truth. And it has continued to be in essence such a theory, although its ramifications have passed over into many other problems. It had hitherto been generally supposed that by the truth of an idea was meant its correspondence with the facts. But this, we were now told, is a mistake. An idea is true, not because it corresponds with facts, but because it is advantageous to us in our lives, helps us to adjust ourselves to our environment, surmounts obstacles for us, leads in some way or other to successful living and successful action. An idea is not something true or valuable in itself. It is true or valuable only as an instrument of human purposes.

It thus seems clear that pragmatism stresses the purposive, conative side of man, rather than the rational side. It makes truth and knowledge functions of conation. That thought is good and valuable and true which serves human purposes. The thought which thwarts them is bad and untrue. It is clear that the tendency of all this is to subordinate thought, reason, and intellect to human purposes; and thus to set purpose, or will, in the supreme place. Pragmatist writers have been glad to acknowledge the affinity of their thought with that of Bergson. I do not remember a similar acknowledgment of their close relationship to Schopenhauer and Nietzsche. But I do not see how this can be disputed. Their complete subordination of reason to purpose is but a special version of the doctrine of the primacy of the will.

We have traced in brief outline something of the story of the adventures of reason in the world during the last two thousand four hundred years. The essential outline is that the Greeks, being the first to make the life of thought an end in itself, perceived further that reason, not emotion or appetite or will, ought to govern human action and human affairs. This was the great doctrine of the psychological primacy of reason which, combining with Christian ideas, issued in the achievements of western civilization. It was, and is, the lifeblood of our European culture. But owing to the inevitable impulse of men to overestimate the value and importance of an idea, it underwent distortion through monstrous exaggerations. It turned on the one hand into the belief that reason, without empirical evidence, could discover the whole nature of the universe —the doctrine of the epistemic primacy of reason. On the other hand it transformed itself into the metaphysical theory that the ultimate reality which produces the universe out of itself is reason—the doctrine of the cosmic primacy of reason. In the course of ages these exaggerations produced the inevitable reaction, the violent swing of the pendulum to antirationalism.

One of the tragic facts about history is that human reactions are undiscriminating. The storms of human feeling beat blindly. They destroy the good along with the evil. So it has been here in the history of reason. Absurd and fantastic claims in favor of reason have engendered absurd and fantastic recriminations against it. There has now grown up a climate of opinion of which the main characteristic is a hatred of reason. If the reaction against rationalism had condemned the epistemic and the cosmic varieties of it, and *stopped short there*, all would have been well. But this is not the way of reactions. The downswinging of the pendulum does not suddenly stop at the middle point. The tragedy is that the reaction against reason has included the psychological primacy of reason also. Reason is dethroned, not only in the wide universe, but in human life. Unreason takes its place, an evil usurper. But this doctrine of the psychological primacy of reason was necessary to our life. Without it civilization totters.

Philosophers, like other people, tend to be violent partisans. They vote blindly, either for rationalism and intellectualism, or for antirationalism and anti-intellectualism. Surely we can now, in the light of our researches in this chapter, be more discriminating. There are good and bad rationalisms, good and bad anti-intellectualisms. And the core of the matter is this: the doctrine of the epistemic primacy of reason was false. We cannot deduce the characteristics of the world by armchair reasoning. We have to examine its features empirically. The revolt of science against the overweening claims of reason in this respect, the inauguration of the empirical and historical methods, were wholly justified.

As to the doctrine of the cosmic primacy of reason, this looks on the face of it like the fantastic magnification of a personal obsession into the secret of the universe. But it is not necessary for us to take sides here, or to condemn the theory out of hand. Let us admit that we do not know the ultimate secret of the universe, and that therefore any theory about it *might* be true. The point that we ought to lay hold of is that it is of no importance for the maintenance of our civilization whether the doctrine of the cosmic primacy of reason is true or not. The only form of the theory of the primacy of reason which civilization needs is the psychological form. It is the belief that reason is the guiding star of human life, that it is the crown of human personality, that its function is to govern the other elements of personality—it is this, and this alone, which has been the inspiration of our civilization.

We have seen some of the forces of the human spirit which are now working against this theory of the psychological primacy of reason. We have seen that the theory is necessary to our civilization. What we have not yet examined is whether the theory is in itself actually *true*. We have taken it for granted because it was shown as a necessity of our life. But it might for all that be false. It is difficult to believe that a civilization which has lasted two thousand years, overtopping in its achievements all civilizations of the past, is founded on a lie. Yet if we are to believe Schopenhauer and those who think with him, this must be the case. And we cannot in the end avoid the issue. Was Plato right, or was Schopenhauer? Is reason the master of human personality, or is it the mere slave of the will? This ultimate question looms up in the path before us. On the answer to it depends—or at least in large measure depends—the question of the evaluation and justification of the civilization which we now seek to defend. If Plato was wrong, if Schopenhauer was right, then not only must our civilization perish because it is rooted in a falsehood, but moreover it ought to perish.

All that has so far been said in this second part of our book is merely descriptive. It has described the ethos of our civilization. It has shown it to consist in the fundamental idea of the infinite value of the individual. It has exhibited the various facets of this idea—equality, liberty, individualism. And this whole cluster of ideas it has traced to their sources in the Greek doctrine of the primacy of reason and the Christian doctrine of the primacy of sympathy. And now in the present chapter it has explained how an opposite set of ideas has arisen, based upon the theory of the primacy of will. But none of this mere description can answer the fundamental question, first forced upon us by Schopenhauer, whether the root ideas of our civilization, the primacy of reason and the primacy of sympathy, are in fact true. And without a decision of this question, democratic ideals, though they can be described, cannot be *justified*. But this issue must be left to the last part of our book.

CHAPTER IX

TOTALITARIANISM

D URING the last two decades there has suddenly sprung into being a set of moral and political ideals, a way of life, which is profoundly hostile to democracy. It declares itself the enemy of democracy. And the democratic peoples, both of Europe and America, recognize in it a mortal foe of their cherished way of life.

In the preceding chapters I have attempted to describe the root ideas and ideals which constitute the ethos of western civilization and the foundations of democracy. In the present chapter I shall try to provide a brief answer to the question: What is the ethos of totalitarianism?

It is important to realize at the outset that the policies of the totalitarian states are not mere alternative methods for achieving the same set of ends and ideals, the same conception of the good life, which we ourselves seek to achieve by democratic means. They represent a wholly different conception of the good life, a completely different set of ends and ideals. Totalitarianism and democracy are not two different ways of doing the same thing. Not only do they go by different routes, but they seek to arrive at different destinations.

This is what is meant by the claims of the dictator states that they are seeking to found a new kind of civilization, a "new order." This implies that they dispute the validity of the basic ideas and ideals, the ethos, of the old civilization which we represent. In the present crisis of the world what we have is not a civil dispute between two branches of a single civilization, but a clash between civilizations. What distinguishes one branch of a civilization from another branch of it is that, although the two branches aim at the same ultimate ends—have the same philosophy of life—they seek to achieve them by different means. For instance, Britain and the United States, though having the same democratic ideals, have very different political constitutions and modes of government. What distinguishes two civilizations is that they seek to embody in their institutions divergent conceptions of the good life. This is the situation as between democracy and totalitarianism.

It is the failure to recognize this which makes most contemporary criticism of totalitarianism so futile. It is inept, for instance, to keep reiterating that the totalitarian state destroys the happiness of individuals by suppressing liberty. For the totalitarian state does not regard either the happiness of individuals or their liberty as ultimate ideals. And it is of little value to compare democracy with totalitarianism in respect of efficiency. For efficiency concerns means only. It is the capacity of a person or an institution to realize his or its ends. And means which are efficient for one set of ends may be utterly inefficient for another. Totalitarian methods may be efficient in achieving totalitarian ends. But they are inefficient for all the ends of democracy. Thus any criticism of the totalitarian state which proceeds upon the basis that it fails to achieve for its citizens the sort of life which *we* think good is beside the mark.

A genuine criticism of totalitarianism must do two things. First, it must isolate and expose to our view the ends and ideals, the conception of the good life, the philosophy, which is implicit in totalitarianism. Secondly, it must seek to show—if this is possible—that this conception of the good life is inherently inferior to the conception of the good life which is entertained by democracy. In the present chapter I shall be concerned only with the first of these two tasks. The second part of the program is only possible if we have at our disposal definite criteria for judging between rival sets of moral ideas. The discovery of such criteria was attempted in the first part of this book. Their application to the problem of democracy versus totalitarianism will be the subject of the last part.

It follows from this that neither the economic nor the purely historical aspects of totalitarianism fall within the scope of our inquiries. I shall make no attempt to discuss the historical facts which may be considered the cause, or a part of the cause, of the rise of totalitarianism. Nor shall I consider its economic policies or background. My aim is solely to discuss its philosophy, its ethos, its ideals, its conception of the good life.

Italian Fascism and German Nazism certainly have much in common. But they are also extremely different. We are not concerned, of course, with superficial details. But the differences extend even to fundamental ethical attitudes. For instance, Nazism has been much more deeply infected with the doctrines of Nietzsche than has the Italian form of totalitarianism—though the difference, it must be confessed, is one of degree only. Perhaps what most clearly and closely binds them together is their view of society and the state.[1] And I shall begin with this.

It is sometimes suggested that totalitarian philosophy derives from two sources, the so-called idealistic theory of the state, which was founded by Hegel, and the ethical teaching of Nietzsche. Both these statements are somewhat unguarded. Italian Fascism has affinities with the philosophy of Nietzsche, but is hardly derived from it, though Nazism, in some of its aspects, certainly is. The relationship with the idealistic theory of the state is also a matter of some doubt. Fascist writers, for instance the Italian Rocco [2] and the British Major Barnes,[3] repudiate it. It is true, however, that the totalitarian view of the state bears a strong family resemblance to the idealist theory, whether there has been actual inheritance of ideas or not.

It is also often said that whereas democracy regards the state as a means, the individual as the end, totalitarian theories reverse this order in that they make the individual merely a means to the ends of the state. I believe that in substance this is true. Yet here too one should be on one's guard against oversimplification. Otherwise one will be unduly surprised to find written in "*Mein Kampf*," "There can be no authority of the state as an end in itself; as in that case all tyranny on earth would be unassailable and sacred. If a people is led to destruction by the instrument

---

[1] Failure to distinguish between these two very different conceptions, *society* and *the state*, is one of the errors of totalitarian philosophy. But it is not one of the errors which I wished to emphasize in this book. I have accordingly allowed myself to speak almost indifferently of society or the state since the distinction between them is not one which anywhere enters into the substance of my argument.

[2] Rocco, "The Political Doctrine of Fascism." All the quotations from Rocco in this chapter are from the same pamphlet.

[3] J. S. Barnes, "Fascism," page 39; Butterworth, Home University Library, London, 1931.

of governmental power, then the rebellion on the part of each and every member of such a nation is not only a right but a duty." [1] And elsewhere Hitler says, "Human rights break State rights." [2] Nor are these isolated or exceptional utterances. Similar remarks are scattered through the book. It is true that Hitler is not in any sense a systematic or consistent thinker. But his statements can hardly on that account be entirely ignored.

The truth is that it is doubtful whether totalitarianism has any clear and consistent set of doctrines at all. Fascist writers keep insisting on the "intuitive" character of fascist thought, and have a tendency to depreciate reasoned statements of theory. The fascist view of life, says Barnes, "is eminently synthetic, arising from the habit of thinking intuitively rather than in terms of abstract propositions." [3] Fascism, according to its advocates, expresses itself in action, rather than in thought. Certainly its statements of doctrine are vague and ambiguous, and it is difficult to avoid the suspicion that the constant appeals to action and intuition are used as a smoke screen to conceal its absence of clear thinking. In regard to the relation between theory and action fascism is the very opposite of communism. Communism began with an elaborate theory, worked out to the last detail. Action came afterwards with the Russian Revolution, which was an attempt to realize the preconceived theory. But Fascism began in Italy with action, and only afterwards attempted to construct a theory to justify the action. Referring to the period of the march on Rome, Mussolini writes: "I had in mind no specific theoretical program." And he adds: "Fascism did not arise out of a

[1] Adolf Hitler, "*Mein Kampf*," published by Reynal and Hitchcock, page 122.
[2] *Ibid.*, page 123.
[3] Barnes, "Fascism," page 63.

doctrine previously drafted at a desk; it was born of the need for action and consisted in action." [1]

The lesson of this is that statements like those quoted from Hitler above do not at all prove that totalitarianism does not in fact completely subordinate the rights of the individual to those of the state, if this is what appears from an examination of the *actions* of the totalitarian states. Their own appeal is to action, rather than to expressed statements of doctrine. They can hardly complain therefore if the theoretical basis of their actions is inferred from the actions themselves.

As regards the question of the relations between the individual and the state, the position appears to be as follows. Totalitarianism enormously magnifies the importance of the state, and minimizes the importance of the individual. It definitely subordinates the individual to the state in a degree utterly incompatible with democratic ideas. The total lack of respect with which the totalitarian state treats the rights of individuals does in fact justify the statement that it considers the individual as a mere means to the ends of the state.

Respect, of course, is a feeling, not a thought. And the absence of respect is the absence of a feeling. And what the totalitarian attitude evinces is an absence of the feeling of the *sacredness* of the individual's rights. Now sacredness is a peculiar note of feeling which is appropriate to the infinite. Finite things may have great value, but they are secular, never sacred. Only the infinite is sacred. The word comes definitely from the vocabulary of religion, which is the feeling of the infinite. Hence where the feeling of the sacredness of the individual's rights and liberties appears, this signifies always the presence of the idea of the

[1] Mussolini, *op. cit.*, pages 19 and 20.

infinite value of the individual. And where the feeling of sacredness is absent, we can be certain of the absence of the idea of the infinite value of the individual. Accordingly, the essential characteristic of totalitarianism is its repudiation of, or perhaps we should rather say its blindness to the existence of, the key concept of western civilization, the belief in the individual's infinite value. And since this belief is identical with Kant's conception of man as an end in himself, the individual in the totalitarian state is treated as a means and not as an end.

It is time to turn, however, to the positive exposition of the totalitarian conception of the state. And although it is doubtful whether this can be regarded as a direct descendant of the idealist theory founded by Hegel, it will be helpful to set down a few facts about the latter. For the two theories have at least a close resemblance which it will be useful to exhibit.

According to Hegel the Absolute, or the ultimate reality of the world, is a dialectical process of logical categories. The details of this do not concern us. As a rough statement it is true to say that this means that the Absolute is reason. But this ultimate cosmic reason is not a conscious or personal being. It is rather the immanent rationality, or logicality, of the world.

This Absolute, or world-reason, according to Hegel, produces, or manifests itself in, the world, in a series of rising stages, the details of which Hegel attempts to elaborate. At the bottom come space, time, matter, motion. Higher up come organic phenomena, and then man. The human world rises in a succession of stages, somewhere among which is the state. The state, therefore, is a manifestation of the Absolute, and it is a higher stage or manifestation than the individual man. And since the world-reason is identified by Hegel with "spirit," the state is a manifestation of spirit. From one point of view it is one and the same world-reason, or spirit, which manifests itself in all things, from the lowest clod of matter to the most sublime creations of the human mind. But since we have here successive rising stages of manifestation, it may be said in another sense that each stage has its own special spirit, and hence that the state has a spirit of its own. Moreover, since the state is a higher stage of the Absolute than the individual man, so is the spirit of the state a higher being than the spirit of the individual man.

If the reader should at this stage express a doubt whether all this tall talk has any very definite meaning, I for one should sympathize with him. I can at any rate make the meaning no clearer. Nor, I believe, can anyone else. And whether the ideas here expressed are clear or hazy, true or false, intelligible or unintelligible, they are important and cannot be ignored for the reason that they have exerted an enormous amount of influence in the world.

It should be noticed that in the Hegelian theory, although the state is credited with possessing a spirit of its own, this does not mean a *conscious* personality. This spirit of the state is no more conscious than the reason or immanent logic of the world which is the Absolute.

Nevertheless such a theory as Hegel's lends itself fatally to that kind of interpretation, or misinterpretation. Moreover, it contains implications which, whether or not they have directly influenced totalitarianism, are extremely consonant with its attitude. In the first place the state is a higher manifestation of the world spirit than the individual man is. Thus at once the individual and his liberties and rights are belittled before the majesty of the state. And since the state is a manifestation of the Absolute (which is Hegel's substitute for God), it is thought of as something divine. It tends to become deified. Hegel himself speaks of it as "this actual God."

Whatever may be the historical connection, or lack of connection, between the Hegelian and totalitarian theories of the state, there can be no doubt that they both belong to the same general type of theory, and that this type of thinking about political matters was first introduced by Hegel. I now turn to a brief exposition of the main characters of the totalitarian theory itself, so far as it can be gathered from the writings of Fascist philosophers.

It is sometimes suggested that, according to the totalitarian theory, the state possesses a soul, a personality, a consciousness of its own, distinct from the consciousnesses of the individual citizens who compose it. It is true that Fascist writers speak of the spirit, and the personality, of the state. Such language might well have been used by Hegel without meaning to imply that the state has a separate consciousness. And I do not think we are intended to draw this inference from the language of Fascist philosophers.

But the central doctrine of totalitarianism—according to its own proponents—is that *society has an organic character*. This is invariably contrasted with the supposed 'atomistic' character of democratic theory. Democratic theory is supposed to deny the organic character of society. And the totalitarian or organic view is said to imply that a society has a life and a spirit which continues through the ages and is not simply the sum of the lives and spirits of particular individuals or even particular generations.

It is best at this critical point to let Fascism speak for itself. And I cannot do better than quote from Rocco's "The Political Doctrine of Fascism," which was in some sense an official pronouncement of Fascist doctrine issued under the imprimatur of Mussolini himself. Speaking of democratic theory, Rocco writes: "Society according to this concept is merely a sum total of individuals, a plurality which breaks up into its simple components. Therefore the ends of a society, so considered, are nothing more than the ends of the individuals who compose it and for whose sake it exists. An atomistic view of this kind is also necessarily antihistorical, inasmuch as it considers society in its spatial attributes and not in its temporal ones; and because it reduces social life to the existence of a single generation. Society thus becomes a sum of determined individuals, *viz.*, the generation living at a given moment. This doctrine, which I call atomistic and which appears to be antihistorical, reveals from under a concealing cloak a strong materialistic nature. For it endeavors to isolate the present from the past and the future, it rejects the spiritual inheritance of ideas and sentiments which each generation receives from those preceding and hands down to the following generation, thus destroying the unity and the spiritual life of human society."

The doctrine that society is merely a sum of individuals is, Rocco believes, the assumption of all European political theory, from liberalism to socialism, prior to the advent of the Fascist revolution. "All of them," he says, "consider the happiness and welfare of individuals to be the goal of society."

Thus far Rocco is merely criticizing democratic philosophy before going on to the positive exposition of the Fascist theory. But there are already important points to be noted.

It is correct that democratic theory regards society as simply a sum total of individuals, provided of course that it is understood that there is also the fact of social organization. It is also correct that the ends of a society, so considered, are nothing but the ends of the individuals who compose it, and for whose sake it exists. This is the democratic doctrine that the state is a means to the ends of the individual, and not *vice versa*.

It is incorrect that democratic theory confines the concept of society to the sum of the individuals *of a single generation*, or that it regards their ends, their happiness and welfare, as the sole ends of the society at a given moment. I shall comment on this later. I shall also reserve for later discussion the charge of atomism.

It is to be noted that Rocco's remark that all democratic doctrines "consider the happiness and welfare of individuals to be the goal of society" clearly implies that Fascism does not share this opinion.

It is also clearly implied that Fascist theory, in contradistinction from democracy, does not regard the life of society as merely a sum of the lives of the individuals who compose it. Society as a whole has its own life, just as a human body as a whole has a life distinct from the lives of the cells which compose it—if this is the case. This life of society continues uninterrupted through generation after generation. It follows, or is supposed to follow, that the ends of society are not the same as the ends of the individuals. And the implication, though it is not stated here, is that since the life of society is greater, and larger, and of higher order than that of any individual, therefore the ends of society take precedence of the ends of any or all individuals.

We may proceed with Rocco's exposition of the positive doctrine of Fascism. After remarking that social groups "are fractions of the human species," he adds that for this reason "they must possess the same fundamental traits of the human species, which means that they must be considered as a succession of generations and not as a collection of individuals. It is evident therefore that as the human species is not the total of the living human beings of the world, so the various social groups which compose it are not the sum of the several individuals which at a given moment belong to it, but rather the infinite series of the past, present, and future generations constituting it. And as the ends of the human species are not those of the several individuals living at a certain moment, being occasionally in direct opposition to them, so the ends of the various social groups are not necessarily those of the individuals that belong to the groups but may even possibly be in conflict with such ends."

This gives us the central idea of Fascism and its essential difference from democracy. According to democratic theory a society is no more than the sum of its individuals, and therefore the ends of the society are simply the ends of the individuals. Consequently the state is an instrument for carrying out the purposes of the individuals. According to Fascism a society has a life which is not the sum of the lives of the individuals. It is a life over and above all individual lives. Hence the ends of society are not necessarily the same as the ends of any or all of the individuals. The society has ends and purposes of its own. And the inference, though not stated in the passage quoted, is that individuals must be regarded as instrumental to the ends of society. And this of course involves a break with the ancient doctrine of western civilization that the individual is—in Kantian phraseology—an end in himself.

But now, if one attempts to inquire more precisely what it is in the life of a society which is *something more* than the sum of the lives of individuals, one notices in Rocco a curious vacillation and hesitancy. There seem to me to be two quite distinct suggestions, between which he hesitates. First of all, Rocco clearly means to dispute what he thinks (wrongly) to be the democratic doctrine that a society is nothing but the sum of its individual members "at a given moment." This is what he says is "antihistorical." As against it he emphasizes that a society is a succession of generations extending from the past, through the present, to the future. He insists that the individuals of the past and the future must be included in the concept of a society as well as the individuals of the present. And the inference would be that in the present actions of the state the interests of future generations must be taken into account as well as the interests of those now alive. Rocco's own language, and that of other Fascist writers, often seems to suggest that this is *all* that is meant by the "organic" concept of society, and that the *something more* which a society is supposed to include over and above the lives of the individuals as envisaged in the democratic theory is simply the lives of past and future individuals.

But if this is all that the Fascist theory means, every democrat may, so far as I can see, heartily agree with it. It is quite false to say that the democratic theory believes society to consist only of the individuals now alive. It is just as much part of the democratic view that men now should work for their children, and their children's children, and should be prepared to sacrifice themselves for the benefit of future generations, as it is part of the Fascist theory. For instance, Britons at the present moment (April, 1941) believe that they are fighting and dying to preserve their own free way of life both for themselves and for future generations of Britons. And even in the question of finance we see regard for future generations. When a democratic government insists that as large a part of some vast necessary expenditure (say the costs of a war) as possible should be raised from taxation and not borrowed, what is this but insisting that we should now pay as much as we can for future generations, and not make them pay everything for us?

Moreover, if the definition of political atomism is any view of society which regards it as no more than a sum of individuals, then the Fascist theory, interpreted in this fashion, is just as atomistic as the democratic theory. For on this view a society is, not indeed the sum of now living individuals, but the sum of all past, present, and future individuals. But this is still simply a sum of individuals. And that a society *is* nothing more than the sum of its past, present, and future individuals, and that therefore the state is simply an instrument for securing the welfare of all these individuals—a means to their ends—is precisely the theory of democracy.

One is therefore forced to suspect that the Fascist theory does intend something more than this. For Rocco insists that the Fascist concept of society is not atomistic but organic. What is there more, then, in the organic view of society beyond the bare insistence that it covers the past and the future as well as the present? Reflecting on this question, one does not see what this more can be unless it is the assertion that society as a whole has a soul, or at least a life, which is numerically distinct from the lives and souls of any or all of its individuals. And this is the second suggestion which seems to be contained in Rocco's discussion.

One turns to him to discover whether this is what is meant, and one reads: "When I say organic I do not wish to convey the impression that I consider society as an organism after the manner of the so-called organic theories of the state; but rather to indicate that the social groups as fractions of the species receive thereby a life and scope which transcend the life and scope of the individuals identifying themselves with the history and finalities of the uninterrupted series of generations. It is irrelevant in this connection to determine whether social groups, considered as fractions of the species, constitute organisms. The important thing is to ascertain that this organic concept of the state gives to society a continuous life over and beyond the existence of the several individuals."

This is a quite extraordinary passage. It begins by suggesting to the reader's mind the idea that society is an organism, a sort of huge animal, in which case it might be thought to have a soul or life of its own distinct from the lives of the component cells. But the idea is only *suggested*, not asserted. Indeed, as soon as it has been implanted as a suggestion in the reader's mind, it is hastily withdrawn and apologized for. It is declared to be irrelevant. And the last sentence of the passage seems to return to the interpretation that organic simply means that society includes the individuals of the past and future as well as those of the present.

It is evident that Rocco is here performing a conjuring trick. By a rapid manipulation of the hands he first waves before our eyes a certain astonishing idea—that a society is actually, and not merely metaphorically, an organism. He then makes this idea disappear and declares that it was never there at all.

What is the object of this strange procedure—quite a novel method in philosophy, so far as I know? The aim is quite clear. It enables him both to eat his cake and have it. He wishes us to draw from the idea that a society is actually an organism certain inferences which are favorable to Fascist methods of government—such as that the interests of the individual may be ignored and treated as mere means to the ends of the state considered as a supersoul or superlife. And he wishes to do this without actually asserting the idea from which these inferences are to be drawn —since that idea is, if not openly absurd, at least open to obvious criticism and attack. The method consists in first suggesting a certain doubtful premise, then drawing from it the conclusions you want, then getting rid of ("liquidating") the doubtful premise before anyone has time to attack it. The conclusions, it is hoped, will then remain firmly established in our minds.

I have quoted and analyzed Rocco's statements, at tedious length I fear, because his presentation is authoritative. I do not believe that a similar treatment of other Fascist philosophers would throw any further light on our problems. And I have not, in any case, the space for such treatment here. The conclusions I would suggest are these: that a clear and consistent theory of the nature and function of the state is not to be found in Fascism; that it emphasizes the unity and continuity of the social group over long periods; that it insists (quite rightly) that the state is not a mere device for securing the interests of the individuals of the present to the disregard of the interests of the citizens of the future; that it frequently uses language which seems to imply that society has a life, purposes, and ends which are distinct from those of all or any individuals whether of the present, past, or future; that when pressed as to this last point it is hesitant and doubtful and inclined to retreat to the position that its meaning is only that society must be regarded as including the individuals of the past and the future as well as those of the present.

From the theory of the state thus understood, or not understood, we may now see what deductions of a practical nature are drawn by Rocco as to how the state should act. He writes: "Instead of the liberal democratic formula 'society for the individual,' we have 'individuals for society' with this difference however: that while the liberal doctrine eliminated society, Fascism does not submerge the individual in the social group. It subordinates him, but does not eliminate him. . . . For liberalism, the individual is the end and society the means; nor is it conceivable that the individual, considered in the dignity of an ultimate finality, be lowered to mere instrumentality. For Fascism society is the end, individuals the means."

This passage at any rate dispels any lingering doubts we may have had as a result of the expressions quoted from Hitler earlier in this chapter. Here it is at last unequivocally stated that in Fascism individuals are regarded, not as ends, but as means to the ends of the state. It is true that there is a weak attempt to water this down by saying that the individual, though "subordinated," is not "submerged" or "eliminated." But these phrases are not further explained. And they appear to be no more than phrases, having little, if any, definite meaning. No one is likely to suggest that Hitler's statements show that the German form of totalitarianism is more moderate, more solicitous of the individual, than the Italian form represented by Rocco. And if the statements of Hitler and Rocco seem to contradict one another, we may unhesitatingly conclude—in the light of all the facts and the evidence—that it is Rocco's which more accurately represent the real spirit of the totalitarian theory. And that theory can be summed up in a phrase—

the repudiation of the entire Greco-Christian philosophy which centers around the idea of the infinite value of the individual. It follows as a mere matter of course that the three aspects of that idea which we earlier distinguished—equality, liberty, and individualism—are also repudiated.

As regards equality and individualism, their rejection is explicitly admitted by Fascist writers. "Fascism," writes Mussolini, "denies in democracy the absurd conventional untruth of political equality . . . it affirms the immutable, beneficial, and fruitful inequality of mankind." [1] And again, the same authority contrasts democratic and liberal "individualism" with Fascist "collectivism." [2]

It is true that the individualism which Fascists reject is understood as that bastard individualism which is identical with egoism. But Fascism does not replace it by the genuine doctrine of individualism which I have already explained. It merely repudiates individualism altogether. Similar remarks apply to the doctrine of equality. What is explicitly rejected by Fascists is the admittedly false doctrine of the *instrumental* equality of men. But this is not replaced by the genuine theory of their *intrinsic* equality. Equalitarianism is simply thrown overboard altogether.

What has been written thus far is mostly a description of Italian Fascism. This is the original and milder form of the totalitarian philosophy. If we now turn to Nazism, what we find is essentially the same philosophy, the same assertions and denials, but also the addition of important new features. This, after all, is what we should expect. Totalitarianism was born in Italy, and passed from thence to Germany. It attains there its full stature, together with a coloring in keeping with the genius of the German people.

[1] Mussolini, *op. cit.*, pages 28 and 30.
[2] *Ibid.*, page 39.

I think it is not unfair to say that Nazism is the fully developed form of Fascism. We must now examine the German additions.

The first is the concept of race. Italian Fascism practically identifies society with the state and the state with the nation as organized under Fascist control. In Germany both the state and the nation are dominant concepts, but the vague concept of race is superadded. We need not, however, waste any time on this. The "pure Aryan race" is, of course, a myth without the slightest ethnological justification. And it makes little difference to the fundamentals of the totalitarian philosophy of the state. Nor shall I, in this chapter, say anything of Nazi anti-Semitism. No one would wish to deny the enormous human importance of this. But it has little importance for the theoretical side of totalitarianism which I am here discussing. Its only importance philosophically is that it is a prime example of the rejection of the fundamental ideas of western civilization, the intrinsic value of individuals, their status as absolute ends, and their right to equal treatment. It thus envisages no new philosophical or political principle, but only an exemplification of principles already discussed in the earlier pages of this chapter.

The main philosophically important modification of totalitarianism which we find in Germany is the definite adoption of a Nietzschean ethical ideal. It is true that this is applied primarily in the sphere of international relations; that its application in private life is not so clear. There are signs of a similar tendency in Italian Fascism, for instance its denial of human equality, its tendency to glorify struggle and war, its aggressive foreign policy, its appeal to force rather than to reason. But it is not clear that Nietzsche's work had any direct influence on the Italian theory.

It is in Germany that Nietzschean tendencies become explicit.

The derivation of Nietzsche's ethics from the Schopenhauerian doctrine of the primacy of the will has already been noticed. But Nietzsche was also profoundly influenced by the Darwinian theory of the survival of the fittest, which had not been published when Schopenhauer constructed his philosophy. These two ideas, derived from Schopenhauer and Darwin respectively, are the sources of Nietzsche's system.

The theory of evolution is supposed to show—though it is extremely doubtful whether it actually does show—that the ceaseless struggle of all against all is the eternal law of all life; and further that the evolution of species has wholly depended upon it. According to Darwin, the struggle is for existence. But Nietzsche substituted for this the idea of the struggle for power. Schopenhauer had written that the will, manifesting itself in living beings, causes each being to seek its own uttermost self-gratification, and so to strive against all the others. He thus recognized the perpetual struggle for existence before the discoveries of Darwin. He explained it as the product of the will. But he did not, of course, associate it with the upward trend of an evolutionary process.

Nietzsche takes over and transforms these ideas. The will to power is the essential character of living beings. It leads to the struggle of life. And this in turn leads to evolution. Nietzsche's next step is forthwith to identify evolution with advance, progress, movement towards the higher and nobler. This *ethical* addition to the theory of evolution is no part of the scientific view. But it is the crucial point in Nietzsche's philosophy.

In taking this fateful step Nietzsche failed to see that the suggestion that man is higher than the ape—without which his philosophy falls to the ground—and his suggestion that his imaginary superman will be higher than man, require for their justification a cosmic, nonhuman, and absolute scale of values which is entirely out of accord with the naturalistic presuppositions of his own philosophy. This is a fatal contradiction in his system. He also failed to note that the science of biology as such gives no countenance to the identification of evolution with ethical progress. But he nevertheless drew the conclusion that, since the struggle for life and power is what has produced the advance to higher and nobler types, it is therefore the very condition of the production of further and still higher nobleness in the world. Hence a true ethical teaching must glorify struggle. It is right that the weak, the poor, the feeble, the lowly, should be crushed out of existence by the strong and powerful. For this is the very nerve of the evolutionary process.

Any ethic which proceeds on the opposite principle is therefore false and bad. The Christian ethics does this. It is founded upon sympathy for the weak and humble. It preaches that they should be protected and helped. The strong should succor the weak. This is the very opposite of the truth. It is counter-evolutionary. It points man in a backward and downward direction.

Nietzsche therefore develops an ethics which is in every point the diametrical opposite of the Christian. Its principle is not selflessness, but self-assertion. It is based not upon the primacy of sympathy but on the rejection of sympathy as a ruling psychological element. Its ideal is not the gentle, humble, loving, charitable, selfless, sympathetic man; but the powerful and power-loving man, aggressive, self-assertive, ambitious, ruthless, hard, brave, merciless. The weak are not to be helped, but wiped out. Sympathy is despised as softness and feebleness.

Thus Nietzsche's ethics repudiates the whole principle of sympathy on which Christianity is based. And it also repudiates the doctrine of the primacy of the reason. For Nietzsche teaches, with Schopenhauer, that reason is merely a tool of the will. The will is supreme. Nietzsche's philosophy accordingly attacks the twin bases on which western civilization has been built.

It should be added that, according to Nietzsche, the powerful and ruthless men in the world constitute a master race, the rest being a slave race. The Christian ethics is called a slave morality, while Nietzsche's new ethical principles are called a master morality. Further, Nietzsche decries democracy on the ground that it is based upon the false principle of equality. He rightly recognizes it as an outgrowth of Christian ideas, and condemns it on that very ground.

Nietzsche's ideas evoked interest throughout the world, and made some disciples in most countries. But in America, France, England—indeed in all countries outside his homeland—his followers were no more than a handful of eccentrics. Only in the German consciousness has the Nietzschean philosophy taken vital hold. And this happened not only after the Nazi revolution. Even before 1914 the strong working of Nietzsche's thought in Germany was evident in the publications of many influential writers. But after the Nazi revolution Nietzscheanism came to be tacitly incorporated in the *Weltanschauung* of the German rulers. Thereafter it multiplied and proliferated. The Nazi revolution may be regarded, from one point of view, as the triumph of the Nietzschean element in Germany.

It is true that Nietzsche himself was no nationalist. He

called himself a "good European." And in his ethical teaching he was not thinking of the struggle of nations. But thus to apply the spirit of his doctrine to the international scene has been precisely the work of Nazism. It is also true that Nazism stresses the idea of self-sacrifice in the sphere of the relations of the individual to the state. And of course self-sacrifice is a Christian, not a Nietzschean, ideal. But this is a mere corollary of the transfer of the Nietzschean ideology from the sphere of the relations of individuals to the sphere of the relations between states.

If one asks wherein this Nietzschean character of the German form of totalitarianism appears, the answer is twofold. First, it appears plainly in contemporary German political literature. There is, for instance, in Hitler's *"Mein Kampf"* a great deal of rather crude biological talk. The purport of it always is that, because of the eternal law of struggle in nature nations must continually struggle for power against nations. War is not only inevitable, but glorious, because it is the apotheosis of struggle, and struggle is what leads upward to higher levels of nobleness. There can be no talk of humanitarian ideals as between nations. Such ideas are mere softness, or worse, treachery to one's own nation. The sole consideration must be the self-interest, greatness, glory, and indefinite expansion of one's own race. This is all simply Nietzsche's philosophy extended from the sphere of individual relations to that of international politics. The very phrase "power politics," which is commonly used of that technique in international affairs of which the Nazis are past masters, is eloquent of the influence of Nietzsche.

Secondly, the same character appears more plainly still in the overt behavior of the German state. The whole of German foreign policy is simply a point-by-point application of Nietzsche's ideas. There is one great race, the Aryan, especially the German branch of it, superior to all others. It is to be the master race. (It is true that Nietzsche, in talking of the master race, did not refer to the Germans. The Nazis, of course, give their own peculiar twist to his ideas.) Other inferior races are to be its servants. The method of international politics is not to be reason, but force. This is a most significant point, for throughout the history of western civilization there has appeared, waveringly and dimly, the ideal that not only internal but also international affairs ought to be controlled by reason. The existence of a body of international law is a product of this feeling. And the feeling itself is an instance of the principle of the primacy of reason. The international tribunal at The Hague was another instance. Certainly in a great war it is not only one side which takes liberties with international law; both sides may try to find loopholes for doing what they want. But it is only German policy which embodies a complete and total disregard of it both in the spirit and in the letter. This is because they have no belief in the ideal of the supremacy of reason as between nations; but accept rather the ideal of the supremacy of will, or force.

Of late years the democratic nations have persistently urged that international disputes should be settled at the council table. This is, of course, an attempt to apply the principles of persuasion and reason. These efforts have met with no response.

The methods of war advocated and used by the Germans are Nietzschean. Small and weak nations are to be ruthlessly crushed. The mass bombings of civilians, the complete disregard of treaties, promises, and guarantees are but the application to the life of nations of the Nietzschean precept that the strong man will, without the least scruple, use any and every means to destroy his rivals. German apologists are fond of pointing to the fact that the democratic countries have in the past used force to master weak peoples. This is of course true. Nor is there any reason for us to seek to excuse our own crimes. But the point is that, according to the philosophy of life which we democratic peoples follow, they *are* crimes; whereas according to Nazi philosophy they are not. The sins of the democratic peoples have been breaches of their own Christian ideals. Those of the totalitarian powers are deliberate and logically consistent applications of their philosophy. And what I am of course concerned with here is, not the question of how far the nations have carried their ideals into practice, but the ideals themselves.

Thus a change from the Greco-Christian philosophy of life, with its principle of the supremacy of reason, to a Schopenhauerian-Nietzschean philosophy, with its principle of the supremacy of will, is evident in the external relations of the totalitarian states. But it is equally evident in their internal policies. To see this we have only to recall what was pointed out in Chapter VII—that in a democracy the relation of the ruler to the ruled is a relation of persuasion, while in a totalitarian state it is a relation of compulsion; and that persuasion is an expression of reason, compulsion an expression of will. Hence the internal political ideal of democracy is government by reason, while that of totalitarianism is government by will.

There is one more characteristic of Nazi activities which, though in itself less striking and sensational than their international policies, is perhaps to the careful observer even clearer evidence of their abandonment of the Greco-Christian tradition of reason and their adoption of the philosophy of will. This is the Nazi attitude to truth, knowledge, science, and education.

Nietzsche developed a theory of knowledge which is practically indistinguishable from pragmatism. He did not, of course, use that name, which is of later American origin. But since he held that the will is supreme, reason and intelligence being merely its instruments, it followed for him that the characteristic products of the intelligence, namely ideas, have merely instrumental value. They are nothing but instruments which the will uses in its struggle for power. Hence truth and knowledge are not, as the Greeks supposed, ends in themselves. And their value is relative to the ends of the will. Hence ideas are to be embraced, not on account of their correspondence to the objective facts, but on account of their utility in forwarding human purposes.

Now this is the opposite of the whole tradition of science. It is true that instrumentalists, like Professor Dewey, tell us otherwise. It is indeed above all to science that Professor Dewey goes to prove his instrumentalism. This is not the place for a technical discussion in epistemology. And I shall only say that Professor Dewey's conception of the basis of science is, in my opinion, grossly superficial. The ideal of the scientific mind has been, throughout the history of the west from Greek times to the present day, not to appraise theories by their capacity for helping human beings, but by their correspondence with the facts of the objective world. Of course science has sought, among other things, to discover truths which shall be of service to men. But it is a monstrous perversion to suggest that the quality of being serviceable to men is what, in the opinion of science, has rendered its discoveries true.

The long struggle of scientific truth against ideas to

which men clung on no good grounds except that they suited human purposes clearly shows this. Men fought against the Copernican theory precisely because it took away from them a set of ideas which, by making man the center of the universe and magnifying his importance in the scheme of things, enormously encouraged and helped him in the battle of life. Science replaced this set of ideas by another which was true to the facts but which undoubtedly served to damp down man's courage and enterprise. Exactly the same thing may be said of the long ecclesiastical struggle against the theory of evolution. Both controversies are examples of battles in which science fought on behalf of ideas which corresponded with facts against views of things which men desired to perpetuate because of their human utility.

It is a commonplace that science refuses to allow its conclusions to be dictated by emotion, feeling, or any kind of human purpose save the pure purpose to discover the truth. Science is, and always has been, rationalistic in the sense that, once given the bare facts which have been observed, it insists that reason alone—not feeling, emotion, or human purpose—must interpret them. It specifically seeks to exclude human purposes from having any say in its conclusions. From this angle, pragmatism, urging as it does that science and truth generally are merely instruments of human purpose, is seen as a relapse to a prescientific mentality.

This rationalism of science is not inconsistent with the kind of antirationalism which, as I have already pointed out, it also possesses. Science is antirationalistic in the sense that it rejects the doctrine of the epistemic primacy of reason, the idea that armchair reasoning alone, without facts, can discover the truth. Science is rationalistic in the sense that it accepts the doctrine of the psychological primacy of reason in so far as that principle applies to its procedure.

Science accepts this principle in the sense that it holds that will, emotion, and purpose are to be excluded from the mental processes of the scientific discoverer, and that reason alone is to guide the constructions he puts upon the observed facts.

It is precisely because western science is based upon the notion of the primacy of reason that its birthplace was Greece. It is for the same reason that Europe is the only continent in which science has ever truly flourished. China and India had great civilizations. But their science has been negligible. And the reason is plain. They have not the tradition of subordinating personal ends, emotions, and feelings to the control of reason. And without that tradition there can be no science. And the pragmatic theory of knowledge, which repudiates that tradition and bases itself on the primacy of the will, is antagonistic to science, and it will—if it obtains the mastery in Europe and America—ultimately extinguish the torch of human knowledge.

Now the Nazis have adopted from Nietzsche the pragmatic view. It coheres, of course, with their entire philosophy of life. And this explains their policies toward the universities and toward education as well as their attitude toward science. Education is, like everything else, a mere instrument of state purposes. Science is directed to teach alleged truths which, whether they fit the facts or not, make men amenable to Nazi control. Learned men in the German universities now teach ideas about race which every competent ethnologist outside Germany knows to be pure myth. Truth, as meaning a correspondence of ideas with the objective facts of the world, is not honored. And this explains the wholesale expulsion from Germany of many of its most illustrious scientists.

Thus in one way or another—in its deliberate creed, in

its "intuitions," in its practical actions—totalitarianism is a denial of the entire tradition of the civilization of the European peoples. It rejects every one of their fundamental insights, beliefs, and principles. It repudiates the infinite value of the individual and the whole of the connected cluster of ideas including the ideals of human equality, liberty, and individualism. It does this because it has taken as the founders of its new civilization Schopenhauer and Nietzsche, instead of Plato and Christ. It seeks to wipe out the civilization of Europe, based upon the principles of reason and sympathy, and to found instead a new civilization based upon the doctrine of the primacy of the will.

PART THREE

Ultimate Questions

CHAPTER X

THE STATE AND THE INDIVIDUAL

THE two founders of western civilization were Plato
and Christ. We stand now at the parting of the ways.
A new order is arising, or seeking to arise, which repudiates
the visions of these men, which seeks to destroy their work
and to found a wholly new type of civilization. And the
prophets of the new order are Schopenhauer and Nietzsche.

In the preceding chapters I have placed over against one
another the two rival philosophies, that of democracy and
that of totalitarianism. But nothing which has so far been
said in this book can decide for us—at any rate on purely
rational grounds—which of these two philosophies we
ought to accept as true. For instance, we have seen that
democracy is based upon the theory that every individual
has infinite value. We have endeavored to understand the
meaning of this idea. And we have discovered its sources in
Greece and Palestine. It is thus no doubt a very *old* idea.
But is it true? We have so far made no attempt whatever
to show that it is. And if we believe it to be true, what
reasons can we give for our belief in it?

Again, this idea of the infinite value of the individual is

rooted in the Greek idea of the primacy of reason and the Christian idea of the primacy of sympathy. Doubtless it follows from them, so that if they are true it is true. But are they true? The doctrine of the primacy of reason is now disputed, and a contrary doctrine, that of the primacy of will, is set in its place. Have we any good reason, then, to assert that our view, the view on which our western civilization has been built, is actually true and that the opposite view is false?

It seems to me that there are three questions with which we are now brought face to face in our attempt to discover whether our democratic civilization is capable of rational justification. These are the three ultimate issues between democratic philosophy on the one hand and totalitarian philosophy on the other. They are as follows:

(1) Is it true that the welfare of the individuals in a society or state is the sole end of the society or state? Or is it the case that the individuals ought to be treated as means to some higher end said to inhere in the society as a whole? This is the problem of the relation between the state and the individual.

(2) Is the doctrine of the primacy of reason true? Or the doctrine of the primacy of will? Was Plato right or was Schopenhauer?

(3) Is the doctrine of the primacy of sympathy true or false? Was Christ right or was Nietzsche?

If we decide in favor of democratic theory, then a subsidiary question will arise, namely: Are not the theories of the primacy of reason and the primacy of sympathy incompatible with one another, since it may be said that the two psychological elements, reason and sympathy, cannot both be in control of personality at the same time? How can both doctrines be true together?

The present chapter will be concerned only with the first of the three questions.

The democratic theory of the relation of society to the individual is that the state—as well as all the other institutions of society—exists solely as means towards the welfare of the individual citizens. This view, which is disputed by the totalitarian philosophy, rests upon two grounds:

(1) Society and the state are wholly composed of individuals organized in a certain way. Society is completely analyzable into its component individuals plus the relations which exist between them, so that when the analysis has been performed there is nothing left over unaccounted for. It follows that the only ends and purposes which can possibly exist at all in a society are the ends and purposes of individuals. Consequently all the activities of the society, in so far as they are directed to the achievement of purposes at all, must necessarily be directed to the achievement of the purposes of individuals, since these are the only purposes which have any existence. Hence the state can have no end except the welfare of individuals, and the state and its institutions are to be regarded as means to the ends of individuals.

(2) The individual has infinite worth. Hence his welfare is an absolute end. He cannot, therefore, be treated merely as a means to the alleged ends of the state. To treat him as mere means to the ends of the state is to deny his intrinsic and infinite value.

The second of these two arguments cannot be discussed in this chapter. For the infinite value of the individual, which is its premise, is based upon the Greek doctrine of the primacy of reason and the Christian doctrine of the primacy of sympathy. Hence these two doctrines have first to be validated, and to do this will be the work of our last two chapters. In this chapter I shall discuss only the first argument.

The first argument is based, it would appear, not on any special ethical theory which is peculiar to the democratic, or the Christian, or the Greek view of life, but on mere common sense. What can there possibly be in a table except the pieces of wood which compose the table plus their arrangement in a certain spatial pattern? And what can there possibly be in a society except the individuals who compose it plus their arrangement in a certain social pattern? That there cannot possibly exist in a society any purposes except those which exist in the minds of individual men and women seems so plain and obvious a truth that the burden of proof is certainly upon anyone who disputes it. Totalitarian philosophers do dispute it. Hence it is reasonable to ask them to bring forward their arguments. And if we find on examination that these arguments are based upon fallacies and so fail to convince us, we shall be entitled to return to the common-sense view that a society or a state has no purposes except the purposes of the individuals who compose the society.

The ground upon which totalitarian philosophers put their case is the alleged organic character of society. The democratic view they label atomistic. They oppose the atomistic and the organic theories of society to one another. And they say that the atomistic theory is false.

This, it will be said, is precisely what makes the difference between a table and a society. The table is not an organic being, but a mere dead thing. Hence the view of it which finds it to be composed of nothing but certain pieces of wood in a certain spatial arrangement may be substantially correct. But a society is a wholly different kind of thing because it is an organic being. And in the case of an organic being it is *not* true that it consists merely of a number of parts mechanically conjoined in a certain way. There is in such a being something over and above its mere parts and their conjunction, namely the life of the organic being as a whole. And this is as true of a society as it is of any other organic being.

Now there is no doubt that the totalitarian philosophers are right in saying that there is a great difference between a society and a dead thing like a table. And I see no objection to expressing the difference by saying that the society is, in some sense or other, organic. It is organic at least in the sense that it is composed of organic beings, namely men and women, while a table is not. And *perhaps* it is organic in some other way or ways yet to be specified. But obviously the important question will be: Exactly *in what sense, or senses,* is it organic; and does the fact that it is organic—in whatever sense or senses we decide that this is true—justify the conclusion which totalitarian philosophers seek to draw from it, namely that a society as a whole has a life and purposes which are not the same as the lives and purposes of all or any of its individual citizens?

When totalitarian philosophers say that society is organic, they do not make this statement for its own sake because of its mere intellectual interest or abstract truth. They make it solely in order to draw from it certain inferences as regards practical action. They wish to infer that the individual may legitimately be sacrificed for the purposes of the state in a manner, and to a degree, which is not considered legitimate in democracies. They wish to infer that the individual is not an end in himself, but that the state is the end to which the individuals are means. Therefore it is not enough to say simply, "Society is organic"—a vague statement which may no doubt, in some sense or other, be true. We have to discover what sense of the word organic will bear the weight of the desired inferences, and whether society is organic *in that sense*.

I have already admitted that a society may be called organic if all that is meant by this is that its component parts are human and therefore organic beings. But this, of course, would be admitted by everybody, whatever his social philosophy might be; and it plainly will not bear the weight of the desired inferences. It will not follow from this that individuals are not ends in themselves or that society as a whole has a life and purposes for which the ends of individuals may legitimately be sacrificed. Hence this cannot by itself be the sole meaning of the totalitarian doctrine that a society is organic. We have to find some additional meaning.

The following may quite reasonably be suggested. Not only are the individuals who constitute the smallest parts of a society organic beings; but the relations which exist between them are also organic relations. Thus a society is a collection of organic beings bound together by organic relations. And this idea, it may be said, is the meaning of the statement that society is organic.

This raises the question: What is an organic relation? And how does it differ from a relation which is not organic?

Now whether there really are, in the last analysis, two distinct kinds of relations, one of which may be called organic, the other nonorganic, I do not know. This involves extremely difficult and abstruse questions in what may be called the philosophy of relations. But it certainly is the case that philosophers have often made such a distinction. And in what follows I shall merely repeat what has often been said without raising the technical question of its correct analysis. For there is no doubt that the distinction is a useful one which has some real foundation in the facts of the world.

Philosophers, then, have often distinguished between what they called internal and external relations. And I think that an internal relation is the same as an organic relation, while an external relation is the same as a nonorganic relation. External relations are also sometimes called mechanical or accidental relations. And internal relations are also sometimes called essential relations. The following definitions will suffice for our purpose, although I do not pretend that they are at all accurate or precise.

Any two things, X and Y, are said to stand in an external, or mechanical, or accidental, or nonorganic relation, if the removal of the relation between them would not substantially alter the natures or characters of X and Y. They are said to stand in an organic or internal or essential relation if the removal of this relation would substantially alter their natures or characters, so as to make them different kinds of things from what they were when they stood in the relationship. To state the same distinction in another way: X stands in an organic relation if, outside that relation, it would not be X but something different such as X'. And it stands in an accidental or nonorganic relation if, outside that relation, it would still be X. Or to put it in still another way: a relation is organic if it changes the nature of the things which enter into it; it is nonorganic if it does not change them. I will now try to give a few examples.

On my table at this moment there is an ink bottle and a tobacco jar. The ink bottle is *to the left of* the tobacco jar. This relation of being "to the left of" the tobacco jar is an accidental or nonorganic relation. For if I took the ink bottle out of this relation, if I put it on the *right* of the tobacco jar, or took it out of the room altogether, this change of relations would not in any way affect the natures either of the ink bottle or the tobacco jar. We can feel sure that if we examined them before and after the change of position—even if our examination were made with a powerful microscope—we should not find that any change had occurred in their characters.

So far as I know all purely spatial relations are non-organic. Suppose we have a pile of stones. Now remove one of the stones out of the pile and take it to the other side of the world. You have entirely altered its relations to the other stones of the pile. It has ceased to be a part of the pile at all. But this will not in any way alter the nature of that stone. It will be exactly the same stone, having the same weight, shape, color, and mineral composition, whether it is in the pile or out of it. We should then say that its relation to the pile was a purely mechanical or accidental or nonorganic relation.

Examples of so-called organic relations are, I think, much more doubtful. But I will try to give some. Consider the relations between the parts of an organism and the whole organism. They seem to be quite different from the relations between a single stone and the whole pile of which it is a part. For if you remove a part of an organism, say a hand, from the whole organism, it ceases to be the sort of thing it was while it was attached to the organism. Aristotle was perhaps the first person who ever made this sort of distinction. For he remarked that if a hand is cut off from the body, *it ceases to be a hand*.

This kind of relation, which has the peculiarity that it seems to alter the natures of the things which enter into the relation, has been called organic because its most conspicuous examples are to be found in the relations between parts of living bodies to one another. But there are also supposed to be examples in certain parts of the nonliving world, for example in the sphere of art. For instance, the notes in a melody are not the same, taken each by itself, as they are when they are combined in the melody. Middle C, if it is struck as a single isolated note, has a certain sound. Its sound in the middle of a tune is not the same, for its relations with the other notes alter it. Or a blob of paint has quite a different character in its place in a picture from the character it would have if it were the only piece of paint on the canvas. For reasons of this kind works of art have often been compared to organisms, and have even been supposed to be in some sense or other alive, although I suppose this is not meant to be more than a metaphor.

Now suppose we apply this distinction between the two kinds of relations to a society, and ask whether what we usually call social relations are organic or mechanical—what answer ought to be given to this question? As a matter of fact different answers have been given by different social philosophers. Consider, for example, the political theories of Hobbes. According to Hobbes men in the natural state existed without any social or political organization at all. Humanity was pictured as consisting of nothing but isolated individuals uncombined into societies. Since these individuals were wholly selfish, each trying to grab everything for himself, they lived in a state of continual war of all against all. Finding that this state of affairs reduced all alike to absolute poverty and misery, men agreed by a mutual contract of all with all to give up each the rights which he had against all the others, and hand over all such rights to a single sovereign authority, whom all would thenceforth obey as a ruler. This was the origin of society.

The point to notice is that, according to this account, society and the state are not natural growths but artificial arrangements. They arise through a mere mechanical and external device. It follows that social relations are not an inevitable part of human nature; they have been created, or adopted, as a result of an agreement which, if circumstances had been different, might never have been made. Thus social relations are not essential to man as man. They are merely accidental. For a man, according to this view, is a man whether he stands within social relations or entirely outside them. Social relations are nonorganic.

This view of Hobbes is the extreme atomistic view of society. For it regards men as mere social atoms, mechanically combined in a society just as atoms are mechanically conjoined in a stone, or as stones are mechanically conjoined in a pile.

It is now generally recognized that any such view is false. It is not merely that, historically speaking, there never was such a contract as Hobbes suggests. It is not even true that society can be understood by saying that it is *as if* it had been based upon such a contract. For whatever the actual historical origin of societies, this atomistic picture wholly misrepresents their now existing nature and the nature of the relations which subsist between the individuals who compose them.

Social relations are not merely artificial and accidental. They are essential to the nature of man. Aristotle observed in a famous phrase that man is a "political animal by nature." In saying this he anticipated and put his finger on the essential falsity of the Hobbesian view. He was suggesting, as against it, a version of the organic view of society.

To show that social relations are organic one may point to considerations of the following kind. A solitary human being—if one can be imagined—would be so utterly different from a human being in society that he could scarcely be described as human at all. For it is only in society that the most important *human* characteristics can be developed. The solitary man might be physically and biologically much the same as other men. He might be the same on his purely animal side. But his spiritual character would be utterly different. Indeed it could hardly exist at all. For man's spiritual nature consists largely in such things as his capacity for family affection, for being a father, a husband, a brother, a son; for being a friend or an enemy; for co-operating with other men for a common purpose; for subordinating his personal interests, at least sometimes, to those of the community at large, or at least to those of his club, his firm, his trade union, his party; for becoming along with other men a member of various associations, business corporations, institutions; and finally for being a member of the political institution which is called the state. Thus standing in social relations to other men is an essential part of human personality. Without them human personality could not develop, could scarcely exist. This means that a man outside social relations would be utterly different from what he is within such relations. The social relations alter his nature. They are therefore, by definition, organic relations. All this would, I think, be almost universally admitted at the present day.

Hence when totalitarian philosophers say that society is organic, they probably mean at least two things: (1) A society is composed of parts which are organisms, namely human beings. (2) The relations which subsist between the parts of the society, i.e., between its component individuals, are organic relations. And that society is organic in both these senses I shall admit to be true.

But now comes the crucial question. Totalitarianism, as we saw, does not assert the organic view of society for its mere abstract truth value, but in order to draw from it the conclusion that the individual is not an end in himself, but rather a means to the higher ends of society. Hence the question is: Does the organic view of society, interpreted as meaning only the above two propositions, logically imply this conclusion? If it does *not*, then either the totalitarian theory is false, or at least groundless, or else the totalitarian philosophers must mean to include in what they call the organic view of society some meaning in addition to what is contained in the above two propositions; and it must be from this additional content of the theory that their conclusion that the individual is a mere means to the higher ends of the state is to be drawn.

We have already seen that the first proposition which we have admitted to be true, namely that a society is composed of organic beings, does not in any way imply the totalitarian conclusion. So what we have now to see is whether the addition of the second proposition, namely that the relations between these beings are organic relations, implies it. And I think it will be at once clear, as soon as the question is understood, that it does not.

For in the first place the statement that social relations are organic is perfectly consistent with the theory of democracy—which could not be the case if it implied the totalitarian conclusion. The fact is that the assertion of Rocco that democratic theory is necessarily atomistic is quite untrue. For no democratic philosopher at the present day adopts a position like that of Hobbes, or denies that social relations are organic.

The democratic theory is that apart from the ends and purposes of individuals there do not exist any other ends or purposes which have to be considered. This means that when we speak of the ends of society, or of the state, we cannot really mean anything except the ends of a number of individuals; or in other words that the ends of society are completely analyzable into the ends of a number of individuals.

But the truth that social relations are organic has no tendency whatever to show that this is false. It has no tendency to show that, over and above the ends and purposes of individuals, there exist in a society any other ends and purposes. If a society consists of the individuals X, Y, and Z, the fact that X's ends and purposes and personality are largely influenced and even constituted by his social relations with Y and Z does not in any way establish, or even suggest, that the community consisting of X, Y, and Z has a set of ends and purposes which are distinct from any of the ends and purposes of X, Y, and Z. My family consists of myself, my wife, and my two children. Certainly my personality is vitally affected by the fact that I am a father and a husband. Similar remarks apply to the other members of the family. This is what is meant by saying that the relations between the members of the family are organic. But the interests of my family are nevertheless simply the interests of myself, my wife, and my two children—this and nothing more. There are no family interests over and above these. And what is true of a community of four persons will surely be true of a community of forty millions, such as we may have in a society or nation or state. The mere size of the community cannot possibly affect this conclusion.

Hence it is clear that the conclusion regarding the relations of society and the individual which the totalitarian philosophers wish to draw from the organic character of society does not follow if this organic character is held to mean nothing except that a society is composed of organic beings related by organic relations. There must therefore be some additional meaning of the organic theory of society if the totalitarian conclusion is to be drawn. What can this additional meaning be?

The illustration of the interests of my family, which I gave above, immediately suggests at least one addition to the theory. For when I said that the interests of my family are simply those of myself, my wife, and my two children, it might have been objected that I certainly ought to have included the interests of the yet unborn generations of Staces. They certainly ought to be remembered in the family councils. I gladly accede to this addition. If I in some way acquire a large fortune, I shall consider it my duty to try to conserve it for my descendants. In just the same way the totalitarian philosopher may well insist that a society has interests over and above those of its now living members, namely those of future generations. And as a matter of fact this is, as we have seen, one of the points upon which totalitarian philosophers do most strongly insist as a part of their organic theory of society. So that we may frame, as a third proposition of that theory (to accompany the two stated on pages 243 and 244) the following: (3) A society has interests over and above those of its presently living individuals, namely those of future generations, and the satisfaction of these ought to be included among the ends and purposes of the state now; and further, individuals now living ought to be prepared to sacrifice themselves at least to some extent for the welfare of future generations.

But clearly from this additional premise the totalitarian philosopher still cannot draw the conclusion which he wishes, namely that there are in a society ends and purposes over and above the ends and purposes of any individuals; and that all individuals ought to be regarded as means to these higher social ends. For future generations too will consist simply of individuals. The society, thus interpreted as including the men and women of the future, is still nothing but a sum of individuals. The addition of future generations only means the addition of more individuals. Thus all the three propositions which we have now accepted as parts of the meaning of the organic theory of society are entirely consistent with the philosophy of democracy. They ought indeed to be welcomed by democratic thinkers. And they do not in any way imply the totalitarian view that society is not a means to the ends of individuals, but that individuals are means to the ends of society.

Accordingly it becomes clear that if the organic theory is to imply the totalitarian conclusion about the relations between society and the individual, there must be a still further element, a fourth proposition of some kind, which will have to be included in the theory. What can this fourth proposition possibly be?

I cannot myself see any alternative but for the totalitarian thinker to assert at this point that the additional proposition is: (4) A society actually *is* an organism. For from this it may perhaps follow that the society has purposes which are numerically distinct from the purposes of any individual; and that the purposes of individuals ought to be subordinated to the supposedly higher purposes of the whole society. I do not myself think it is clear that even then the conclusion which he wants does necessarily follow. For it does not seem at all certain that all organisms can be said to have purposes. A plant is an organism, and it seems to me to be exceedingly doubtful whether it can be said to have a purpose except in a purely metaphorical sense. But it is possible that this fourth proposition might be thought, in certain special cases, to give some grounds for the totalitarian conclusion.

I pass over that point for the moment. What I wish now to point out is that the totalitarian philosopher has been forced to assert something which he was plainly very reluctant to assert. For we have seen that totalitarian thinkers never do actually say that a society *is* an organism. They suggest the idea in vague terms, but carefully refrain from committing themselves to it. Rocco says that it is "irrelevant . . . to determine whether social groups . . . constitute organisms." It is now clear that so far is it from being irrelevant that it is rather absolutely essential for him to show that social groups are organisms. For without this assertion the totalitarian conclusion will not follow. It will not follow merely from the organic character of society understood as meaning anything less than this.

It is also quite clear why Fascist thinkers recoil from the statement that a society actually is an organism. The reason is that the statement is a palpable absurdity. There is no objection to speaking of the organic character of a society. For certainly there is some analogy between social relations and the relations between the parts of an organism. And it is useful to point this out. But to say that a society is an organism would be to talk absurd nonsense. What sort of an organism could it be? A huge animal? Or a huge plant?

Or a bacillus? Or an organism of some entirely new kind at present unknown to biology?

The proposition that a society is an organism surely does not need to be taken so seriously that formal arguments have to be offered against it. Yet in case there should be any reader who thinks that it deserves serious discussion, the case may be very briefly put as follows.

The onus is clearly upon those who assert that a society is an organism. For no one would say that its being an organism is self-evident. What evidence, then, can be brought forward for thinking that it is? Only, so far as I know, certain vague and metaphorical statements. It is said, for instance, that the individuals in a society arise and pass away, while the society itself continues to live on; just as the cells in a living body arise and pass away without the organism dying.

But the statement that the society "continues to *live on*" begs the question. It assumes from the start that the society is a *living thing*, that is, an organism. If we get rid of this question-begging phrase, and say instead merely that the society "continues to *exist*"—which is, of course, true—we see at once that the argument is worthless. For the same might be said of a collection of animals in a zoo. The collection, of course, continues to exist, although the individual animals die. Indeed the same may be said of any collection of merely inanimate things, such as coins or stamps. The collection continues to exist even though individual stamps or coins are destroyed and replaced by others. But no one would argue that, for this reason, the collection of animals in the zoo, or the collection of coins or stamps, is an organism.

Next it is said that a society, like an organism, comes to birth, grows, matures, and dies. But all this is pure metaphor. Or if taken literally, it is untrue. A society is not born in any literal sense. It does not proceed from a womb as a result of a sexual act, nor come into existence through any other process of organic origination known to biologists. Nor does it undergo anything remotely resembling physical death. A society or a state or a nation comes to an end because its individuals become scattered or conquered or absorbed into other nations or societies.

Nor does a society carry through any of the other activities which are the common marks of organic beings. For instance, it does not reproduce itself. Nor does it take nutriment, as both animals and plants do.

Finally, in every known multicellular organism the various parts are physically conjoined, so that the whole organism forms a single physical object. But the individuals in a society are not all joined together like Siamese twins. And in all organisms the several parts keep relatively to one another the same spatial positions. They do not wander about within the contour of the organism. The head does not change places with the tail, nor the toe with the eye. But the individuals in a society move freely about from place to place.

If then a society is not an organism—although it may be called organic in the senses already explained and admitted —what possible reason can there be for supposing that there exists in it a life or a purpose or a set of purposes which are numerically distinct from the lives and purposes of the individual men and women who are its members? The entire suggestion of such a superlife or superpurpose is a farrago of nonsense. And if there is no life or purpose in a society except those of individuals, it is plainly false to say that individuals are, or should be treated as, means to such a life or purpose. And with this conclusion the central doctrine of the totalitarian theory of the state falls to the ground.

We may now ask what is the upshot of the whole matter in regard to the question of the proper relation of the individual to the state.

There are only two theories with which we are concerned. One is that a society consists of individuals standing in certain relations, and of nothing else. There are no purposes in the society except the purposes of individuals. And the welfare of a society cannot mean anything except the welfare of the sum of its individuals. From this it follows of necessity that the state and all the institutions of the society cannot possibly be anything except means for achieving the ends of individuals. This is the view of democratic philosophy.

It is perfectly consistent with this philosophy to hold that it may be the duty of individuals to sacrifice themselves and their narrow personal interests for the welfare of society or for the state. But society or the state only means a sum of individuals. Therefore, that an individual should sacrifice himself for the welfare of society can only mean that he should, in certain circumstances, sacrifice himself for other individuals. And this is, of course, perfectly in accord with ordinary moral views.

Thus it is nonsense to say that the sacrifice of the individual for society is a concept peculiar to totalitarianism, and that it is absent from the philosophy of democracy. According to both the totalitarian and the democratic views it may often be the duty of individuals to forego their personal interests for those of the whole society. But the expression 'society' has different meanings for the two philosophies. For one it means the sum of individuals. For the other it means a wholly nonexistent and fabulous super-being.

According to the totalitarian view the life of a society consists of (1) the lives of individuals, plus (2) a distinct life which is supposed to be associated with the society as a whole. This second life is supposed to be higher and more important than the lives of individuals. And from these premises it is supposed to follow that the state is not a means to the ends of individuals, but on the contrary that the individuals are means to the ends of the state.

The totalitarian view is based, according to its own assertion, upon the theory that society is organic. We have examined the various possible meanings of this conception. We found that it certainly includes the following tenets:

(1) That the members of a society are organisms, to wit, human beings.

(2) That the relations between them, commonly called social relations, are organic relations.

(3) That a society must be regarded as including individuals of the past and future as well as of the present; and that the interests of future generations of individuals ought to be considered by the state in its present actions.

We admitted that all these three statements are true. We also pointed out that they are entirely consistent with the philosophy of democracy; and that it therefore is not true that democratic philosophy is atomistic, since it admits the organic theory of society so far as it is contained in these three statements. We also made it plain that from the organic theory of society as thus understood the totalitarian view of the relation between the state and the individual—namely that the individual is a means to the ends of the state, and not *vice versa*—does not follow.

Therefore if the totalitarian conclusion is to be drawn,

some further meaning must be given to the organic concept of society. This meaning we found in the statement:

(4) That a society actually *is* an organism, not in any metaphorical, but in a strictly literal, sense.

This fourth proposition is not asserted by totalitarian philosophers, who face it, in fact, with extreme reluctance. But they are now forced into a corner. They *must* hold it if the conclusion regarding the relation between society and the individual which they wish to draw from the organic concept of society is to follow, or to have the slightest ground. If they do not hold it, their philosophy falls to the ground as a simple *non sequitur*. But if they do hold it, their philosophy is based upon a falsehood. For a society is not an organism.

We may therefore conclude that the democratic theory is true which says that a society is nothing but a sum of individuals plus their social organization; and that therefore the state cannot be anything except a means to the ends of individuals.

This, however, is only a part of the theory of democracy; and it is on the whole the least important part. It is only this part which has so far been validated. Whatever else there is in the philosophy of democracy will have to be justified by quite other arguments than those found in this chapter.

CHAPTER XI

PLATO OR SCHOPENHAUER?

THE considerations which were developed in the last chapter do not justify our western civilization. Nor do they justify democracy. They merely show that one particular antidemocratic argument is ill-founded. And this result is merely negative. It dissipates fanciful conceptions of the state as a superindividual. It tells us that the ultimate human unit is the individual—as indeed anyone possessed of clear common sense would know without any argument. That a society is composed of individuals and nothing else, that it is an assemblage of men working for their individual though common purposes, and that its political machinery is justified only in so far as it achieves these individual purposes—could any truths be plainer than these?

But that this is only a part of the philosophy of democracy, and by no means a distinctive part, will be evident from the fact that it would be accepted not only by the democrat but by every political philosophy in the world except totalitarianism. An oriental despot who ruled his subjects by force and with no object save to enrich himself would entirely agree that society is composed of individuals only, and that the institutions of the state are not ends but mere means for the ends of individuals. But he would limit the individuals to whose ends the state is a means to one, namely himself. The members of an aristocratic ruling class, governing a society and making laws exclusively in their own interests, would also agree to the same abstract propositions. But they would limit the individuals whose purposes were to be regarded as the ends of the state to themselves.

The positive and distinctive characters of a democratic civilization are that it believes in the infinite value of the individual, and in the ideals of equality, liberty, and individualism. It is these which have still to be validated. They are themselves the expression of two fundamental philosophical ideas, the Greek theory of the primacy of reason and the Christian theory of the primacy of sympathy. Therefore what remains to be done is to provide a rational justification for these two ideas. I shall not in detail discuss again the concepts of equality, liberty, individualism, and the infinite value of the individual. I shall assume that it has already been satisfactorily shown that they are deductions from these two philosophical ideas; so that their truth will be proved by discovering proofs of these two ideas. In this chapter I shall discuss the doctrine of the primacy of reason; and in the next the doctrine of the primacy of sympathy. And if these root ideas can be validated, I shall consider that the ethos of our civilization has been justified, and that my task is complete.

That reason should be the ruler of the individual human soul, and ultimately of all human affairs, was the thought of Plato. It passed into the stream of history. It became the inspiration of the western world. It produced democracy. But an exaggerated rationalism gave rise in time to an exaggerated antirationalism. In the course of this reaction there arose the assertion that not reason, but will, is the proper ruler of man, reason being a mere slave of the will. Schopenhauer's doctrine of the primacy of the will was set up as against the ancient teaching of Plato. It passed from the philosopher's study to the market place. It has become the guiding idea of what claims to be a new and superior civilization. Thus the issue—or at least one of the two issues—which the modern world has to face is this: Was Plato right, or was Schopenhauer?

What are the criteria to which we have to appeal? We are setting one civilization against another and asking which is superior. Ultimately we are setting one ethical ideal against another, the ideal of the life of reason against the ideal of a life uncontrolled by reason, dominated by will, and using reason only as a means for achieving its ends. How are we to compare these ideals so as to say which is the better, which the worse?

Does not the question, it may be asked, necessarily involve us in a vicious circle? For by what standard are we to judge which is the better? It must be a standard of better and worse, that is, an ethical standard. What ethical standard can we possibly employ except one of the very two to be judged? And of course a Platonic ideal will be judged better by the Platonic standard, a Schopenhauerian ideal by the Schopenhauerian standard. Either this, or we must find a superstandard by which to judge both. But to do this would be to admit that neither of the two standards being compared is the ultimately true standard. And so we seem to move in a maze from which there can be no outlet.

The solution of the puzzle lies in this: that every morality is a set of rules which aims at enabling men to live the good life, that is, the healthy, happy, harmonious, satisfactory life. Therefore this conception of *the satisfactory life* is the ultimate standard by reference to which all moral ideals are to be judged. Moral ideals are better or worse, higher or lower, according to their success in helping men to lead satisfactory lives. But this ultimate end, the satisfactory life, is not itself a *moral* end or a *moral ideal* at all. For it is not something which we *ought* to aim at. There is no sort of obligation, or sense of obligation, connected with it. It is simply something which, as a matter of fact, we all do aim at. And if anyone asks for a proof of this proposition that "all men wish for a satisfactory life" I am inclined to think the answer is that it is simply a tautology, and therefore necessarily true.

There is thus no circle involved in our procedure. We are not judging between the Platonic and the Schopenhauerian ideals of living by using one of them as the standard. We are assuming that both of them are attempts to tell us what we all want to know—how to live a satisfactory life. We therefore judge between them by trying to discover which of them succeeds best in the attempt, which of them does in fact yield the most satisfactory life. Nor are we guilty of setting up a standard of supermorality by which to judge between moral standards, thus admitting that neither of the two which are being judged is the real moral standard. For the standard by which they are to be judged is not itself a *moral* standard at all. It is not a moral ideal.

But how are we to judge which of two sets of moral rules will yield the most satisfactory human life? Here I can only repeat the considerations which I urged in the first part of this book. A set of moral rules, I tried to show, is like a set of rules for treating dogs, except that moral rules aim at a healthy personality whereas rules for the good dog life aim merely at a healthy physical body. The rules for a good dog life grow out of and express dog nature. The nature of the dog requires plenty of exercise, while that of the cat does not. Likewise the rules of a good human life will grow out of and express human nature. They will differ from the rules of a good dog life inasmuch as human nature differs from dog nature. They will take account of human personality. This means that the best moral ideals for men will be those which best express human personality, which give proper scope for the development of all its parts and elements in their natural order and proportions.

These considerations led us to develop definite criteria for judging between moral ideals, which the reader will find, if he wishes to refer to them, at page 64. The three criteria there given may be combined into a single statement by saying that of two moralities the one is truer and better which more adequately expresses human nature; which assigns to each element in human personality its proper function, place, and importance in human activity; and which, because it does these things, leads to a more satisfactory human life.

The criteria assume that an element or factor of human nature, by virtue of the mere fact that it is such an element or factor, is entitled to its due expression in human action. Hence any moral ideal which seeks wholly to suppress any element of human nature whatever must be to that extent a false ideal. For instance, if there is any type of asceticism—and I do not say there is—which aims at the total suppression of the physical passions and appetites, this type of asceticism must be a false ideal. For the physical appetites are a part of human nature. And if it were true that the moral ideal of Nietzsche sought completely to suppress the psychological fact of sympathy—and I do not say this would be a fair account of Nietzsche's morality —this would alone be sufficient to condemn it in this respect.

It may be thought that this principle, that every element in human nature is entitled to its due expression in action, will lead to difficulties of the following kind. It implies that everything in human nature is, if given only its due weight and place, good; or in other words that no element of human nature is in itself bad. And this may be thought to be extreme. For instance, cruelty, it may be said, is a part of human nature. And it is surely in itself a bad principle. And would not our criteria imply that even cruelty must be allowed a place in action? And is not this a conclusion from which we should recoil?

I think that the answer to this is quite clear. For the purpose of explaining it I will take first another example of the same kind, and then return to the case of cruelty. Supposing the objection had been that cowardice is a part of human nature, but that nevertheless cowardice is in itself bad, and not entitled to a place in the good life. I should answer that cowardice is *not* a psychological element in man in the sense here meant. But *fear* is such an element. Fear is a basic emotion. Fear as such *has* its proper place in life. It has a function to fulfill. It is therefore entitled to expression in action in its proper place. Cowardice, however, is the improper functioning of fear; or it is fear in the wrong place; or it is an undue amount of fear. Now the very definition of moral evil which is implied by our humanistic principle is that it consists in the improper functioning of psychological elements which, if they function properly, are good. Hence we can say, quite consistently with our principle, that cowardice is everywhere evil and has no right to a place in life at all.

The solution of the puzzle about cruelty is quite similar. The fundamental psychological element with which we are here concerned is not cruelty, but a tendency to feel satisfaction at the pain of others. I cannot doubt that this, like any other feeling, has its proper function in life. There are occasions in which we *ought* to feel satisfaction at the pain of others. Resentment is a part of our nature, and a necessary part; and it certainly includes a desire to give pain. Westermarck even makes resentment of a certain kind one of the springs of our moral ideas. Now when we say of a man that he is cruel, what we mean is that the desire to give pain and to find satisfaction in it has in him achieved an improper ascendancy over other tendencies and feelings, that it has got out of control, run riot, dominated the man. Thus cruelty is the improper functioning of an element of human nature. The element itself is not evil, and it has its proper place in the good life.

The question before us is the issue between the primacy of reason and the primacy of will. But I fear that even now I am not quite ready to come to grips with it. For the question of procedure and method is all-important here. We have to be quite clear that the method we propose to use is legitimate.

That method will consist in attempting to discover what is the proper function of reason and what is the proper function of will. If we know this, we shall certainly also know what are the proper relations between the two; and whether the reason ought to be master of the will, or the will master of the reason. Is this a justifiable procedure? And can this sort of question be answered?

I can only answer that this is a common method in the medical and biological sciences, and that I cannot see the slightest reason why it should not be used in psychology.

We know for certain that it is the proper function of the heart to pump blood, of the lungs to purify it, of the stomach to digest food, of the eyes to see, of the ears to hear, of the afferent nerves to convey sensory impulses to the brain, etc.

How do men of science know these facts? Simply by observing that these are the things which these various organs actually do in the bodies of normal and healthy persons; and that if any of these organs fails to do these things there results a state of the body which is felt to be unsatisfactory, and which is therefore called by such names as disease, ill-health, and the like.

There is a common belief among philosophers that science has never anything to say about what *ought* to be the case, but can only tell us what *is* the case. This appears to be nothing but a prejudice. For it is quite obvious that when the physician says that it is the *proper* function of the heart to pump blood, he is *ipso facto* saying that it *ought* to pump blood.

The elements or parts of the mind are not indeed so clearly defined or separated as the organs or parts of the body. And in consequence of this, no doubt, any conclusions we may draw about the proper functions of the elements of personality will be vaguer, less precise, than corresponding conclusions about the proper functions of the organs of the body. But this does not at all affect the principle of the method. If the method as such is valid in the one case, it is valid in the other.

Objection may be made that to speak of the proper function of either a physical organ or a psychological element involves the idea that it has a purpose. And this introduces teleology. And teleological views of things are now very much out of fashion because it is thought that we can-

not attribute purpose to nature. At any rate, even if a teleological view of the world might find justification in some
ultimately omniscient philosophy of things, it has been by
common consent excluded from science ever since the seventeenth century. And therefore to introduce into our
thinking the notion of the purposiveness of either bodily
organs or psychological elements is contrary to the recognized procedures of science. It is frankly unscientific.

Now the mere fact that the biological sciences *do* make
use of the notion of proper function in regard to the bodily
organs ought to warn us that there is some mistake in this
criticism. And on reflection we see quite clearly that the
concept of proper function, as used in biology, is *not* a
teleological conception and has nothing at all to do with
the idea of purpose. The notion of proper function and the
notion of purposiveness are quite distinct and have nothing
whatsoever to do with one another. And the criticism we
are considering simply muddles the two together.

The proposition "it is the proper function of the heart
to pump blood" is, I should say, scientifically true. But the
question now is what it *means*. It does *not* mean that there
is, or was, a purpose in nature, or in the mind of God, or
in the universe, to pump blood; and that the heart is being
used by nature, or by God, as a means to achieve this purpose. It has no purposive implications of any kind. What
it means is (1) that in normal human beings the heart actually does pump blood; and (2) that if in any human being
the heart ceases to pump blood in the normal way, there
ensues a condition of the body which may be disease or
may be death; and that therefore (3) the pumping of blood
by the heart is one of the conditions of health, that is, of a
satisfactory bodily life. These are all plain statements of
fact which can be verified by ordinary processes of obser-

vation. There is nothing teleological about them. And they do not entail any sort of "metaphysical" theory about the world.

Exactly the same remarks can be made about such statements as "the proper function of reason is to rule the appetites" or "the proper function of reason is to be an instrument of the will." No doubt in this sort of case various problems are raised which do not occur in the physical application of the notion of function. For instance, what is meant by ruling the appetites? And in what way can reason be said to rule them? These are special difficulties which beset the attempt to apply the notion of proper function to reason, will, appetite, and so on. But none of these difficulties have anything to do with the question now raised—whether statements about the proper functions of the parts or elements of personality imply the concept of purpose. And the answer to this question is that they do not. The conception of proper function which I am applying in the field of psychology is identical with the conception of proper function as used in biological science. And in neither case is there any question of teleology.

The method which I am advocating is, of course, the method of Plato himself. In the "Republic" he relies, I think, upon two arguments to establish the doctrine of the primacy of reason. One is that reason is intrinsically higher, nobler, than the appetites, and therefore ought to rule them. I have already rejected this argument on the ground that it implies an absolute or cosmic scale of values. The other is that it is the proper function of reason to rule the appetites, as we see in the case of the man whose appetite urges him to drink while his reason warns him not to.

This fact, that the method I propose to use is derived from Plato, may possibly be thought to weight the scales in favor of Plato and against Schopenhauer. Naturally, it will be said, if we use Plato's method, we are likely to come to his conclusion and not that of his opponent. But if this method is, as I have tried to show, a good and correct scientific procedure, this objection can surely not be raised. However, the really decisive answer to the objection is that this very same method is precisely the method on which Schopenhauer himself relies to prove the doctrine of the primacy of will. I shall show this when I come to examine Schopenhauer's argument.

Having decided the question of method, we may now pass to the consideration of the problem itself. What are the proper functions of reason and will in the practical life of man, and how are they related to one another? I will begin by trying to state a little more clearly in what senses the terms reason and will are being used.

Reason, as the word is here used, includes, I think, three kinds of mental operation. The first is the power of abstract thinking, the capacity to form general ideas. The second is the capacity for what is ordinarily called reason*ing*, whether this be inductive or deductive. The third is the ability to deliberate, to discuss any matter. This last is the sense of reason in which it is written in the scriptures, "Come let us reason together, saith the Lord."

Perhaps the question might be raised: What justification is there for bringing together under one head what might appear to be three distinct mental capacities? The question is a highly technical one. But the general answer, in my opinion, is that both reasoning and deliberating depend entirely upon, and are in fact developments of, the ability to form abstract ideas. The fundamental nature of reason is the power to frame concepts, or to think conceptually.

Reasoning and deliberating are but special ways in which this power is being used.

The word will has been used in many different senses by different writers. I shall use it here in Schopenhauer's sense, since it is his doctrine which is under discussion and which has so deeply influenced the world. Any kind of desire, appetite, impulse, drive, urge, instinct, emotion, or feeling which tends to issue in action is by him included under the general heading will. We may be inclined to say, therefore, that a great many quite different things are here bundled together. What they have in common, however, is that they are all, in some sense or other, impulses to action. They all belong to what psychologists sometimes call the conative side of the mind as distinguished from its cognitive, or contemplative, side.

We can now place side by side the respective arguments of Plato and Schopenhauer. A thirsty man, says Plato, may be drawn by the appetite of thirst to drink. But his reason may counsel him to refrain. We are to suppose that there is some good reason why, in the particular case, he should not drink. For instance, the water may be polluted or poisonous. In the well-adjusted man, in such a case, reason will win the day. It will thus rule over appetite. It is only in the ill-adjusted man, the abnormal man, the man whose life either is or will become unsatisfactory to himself, and probably to others, that appetite will overrule reason. Plato simply generalizes from examples of this kind. In mentally healthy men, reason rules the appetites, and it is only these men who live satisfactory lives. Therefore the proper function of reason is to rule the appetites.

It will be seen that the method here consists in observing what Plato conceives to be the normal working of the elements of personality; and in seeing in such cases what reason actually does. This is parallel to the observation of the fact that in normal and healthy men, the heart does actually pump blood. Plato has also observed that in ill-balanced or bad men the appetites have their own way and are not restrained by reason. For instance, men thieve because the rational part of them is overcome by the lust for gold, which is an appetite. This is parallel to the observation that in certain diseased bodies the heart fails to pump in the normal way.

If now we turn to Schopenhauer we find in the first place that he purports to deduce the primacy of the will from his ultimate metaphysical principle, the view that the reality behind the world of appearance is a kind of impersonal cosmic will. But we need not attach any importance to this metaphysical argument, which is not, I think, the real basis of his opinion. The view that will is the master of life, and reason merely its instrument, is based upon what Schopenhauer believes he has observed regarding their actual relations. For it is quite plain that, at least in many cases, reason does act as an instrument of the will. Man desires food. This is an example of will, according to Schopenhauer's usage. Reason or intelligence finds the means for satisfying the desire by discovering the arts of agriculture, hunting, the breeding of livestock. The will drives men to seek shelter from wind and cold and rain. Reason discovers the means in the art of building houses. A man's will impels him to seek riches or fame. Intellect plans the means for the attainment of these ends. In general will determines the ends we seek, reason discovers or invents the means. Thus will is the captain, reason the steersman.

Quite evidently the method here is the same as Plato's. It consists in observing what reason actually does in normal men. What it does, says Schopenhauer, is always to discover the means for carrying out the behests of the will. To be the instrument of the will is therefore its proper function. It will be noticed, however, that the second part of the method—which should consist in observing what bad effects follow if reason fails to perform its proper function—is missing in Schopenhauer's procedure. And this is a serious defect which makes his argument practically worthless.

How are we to account for the fact that Plato and Schopenhauer, using identical methods, reached diametrically opposite results? Consideration of their respective arguments will lead us to suspect, I think, that each has got hold of a part of the truth, and mistaken it for the whole. If so, our task will not consist in entirely agreeing with one and contradicting the other; but rather in attempting to reach a more adequate analysis of the facts. And it is, I think, quite evident that there are many cases, like those imagined by Plato, in which thought, or reason, or intelligence, determines us not to do things which we want to do. And it is not unnatural to say in such cases that our desires are governed by our reason. Likewise there are numerous cases in which the intellect acts precisely as Schopenhauer says it does, as a discoverer, namely, of the means of satisfying our desires.

Let us look again at the arguments of both Plato and Schopenhauer in order to discover, if possible, what each has left out. First of all Plato. He represents the desire to drink as pulling in one direction, and reason as pulling in the other. There is a sort of tug of war. Reason, in the well-adjusted man, pulls appetite over the line; and this is called an example of reason ruling the appetites. But in the ill-adjusted man appetite pulls reason over the line; and this is called an example of appetite ruling reason.

But this is a greatly oversimplified version of what actually happens. It overlooks an essential point, which is that *mere reason exerts no force*. Reason alone is never a motive to any action. It does not push or pull. The actual propulsion to act comes always from our conative nature, from what Schopenhauer calls the will, from some desire, impulse, instinct, feeling, or emotion. We eat because we are hungry, walk because of a desire to reach our destination, or perhaps merely because of a desire to exercise our limbs; we run away because of an emotion of fear, or stand our ground because of a desire to kill our enemy. We refrain from drinking polluted water because we desire to retain our health. Of course it is not meant that there is always one and only one desire or impulse or feeling for each act. Most of our actions are due to a number of motives acting together. But all such motives are conations, never pure acts of the reason.

There is therefore a sense in which Schopenhauer is right. It is in every case what he calls will which impels to action. Conation is the steam which causes the wheels of life to move. It is the *sole* motive power in our lives. It is what alone *drives us on*. Indeed, Schopenhauer's statement that will alone is the driving force of our lives is to all intents and purposes a tautology. For he includes by definition under the term will all those parts of our nature —all impulses, feelings, desires, instincts—which tend to issue in action. Hence his statement could not possibly be false.

In the light of this we can now return to an examination of what actually happens in the case which Plato represents as a tug of war between reason and the appetite of thirst. What happens is that the desire to drink pulls in one direction, while the desire of the man to retain his health pulls in the other. The victory of the latter desire is what Plato calls the rule of reason over appetite. We can hardly help feeling that in some sense or other he is right. But where exactly does reason come in?

It comes in, I suggest, in the following way. The man who, for reasons of health, refrains from drinking, does so because he knows that the misery of ill-health which may result from drinking will far outweigh the momentary satisfaction of slaking his thirst. How has he gained this knowledge? The answer is quite clear. It is the result of inductive reasoning performed either by himself or by others from whom he has obtained the knowledge. It is through reason alone, used inductively, that men have been able to rise to generalizations of the type, "This sort of action generally leads to this sort of result." In the present case the relevant generalization is, of course, "Drinking polluted water often leads to ill-health or bodily ailment or discomfort of some kind."

These considerations lead to the following tentative conclusions. The function of the will is to produce action, to be the steam in the human engine. At least *one* of the functions of reason is to provide the man with data, in the way of information, on the basis of which the will can act. In this respect we might compare the human being to an insurance company. The moving power in all the actions of the insurance company is the desire to make a profit. (There may be other desires, of a more benevolent or social character, but they can be ignored for the purposes of our illustration.) This desire to make a profit corresponds to the will. But the company acts on the basis of an enormous mass of information regarding such matters as mortality rates which it has obtained from its actuaries. This information has been obtained by inductive and mathematical reasoning. And the function of supplying this information to the company corresponds to the function which reason performs in the life of the individual man by supplying him with such information as that drinking polluted water leads to certain undesirable results.

Thus, though Plato erred if he supposed that reason can exert a direct pull on men's actions, he was yet in a sense right. For reason does *indirectly* influence action by giving important information on the basis of which men decide between alternative possibilities of action. The man who blindly follows his immediate impulses, for instance the man who satisfies his thirst in disregard of the rules of health, is like an insurance company which should refuse to avail itself of the information supplied by its actuaries.

We may now glance again at Schopenhauer's argument to discover, if possible, something of what he has left out. He is right in his general contention that it is the will alone which is the driving force of action. Indeed this is, as we have seen, a mere tautology. But from this he concludes that the will alone determines the ends which a man will set before himself, and that therefore reason cannot have any function except to discover the means by which the will is to reach these predetermined ends. But in this he is quite wrong. For this is to assume that reason cannot *alter* our decisions to perform certain actions which the will demands to be done. It can only advise as to *how* these actions are best to be performed. Will, in his view, first decides irrevocably, and without allowing reason any voice in the matter, what objectives the man will aim at. Reason is then consulted as to the best means of reaching these objectives. But our analysis already shows that this is false. Reason can and does, in normal cases, profoundly alter the actual decisions of the will. It does so by the indirect methods to which we have already drawn attention. It may show that the objectives which the blind will is setting before itself are undesirable because they will lead to evil results which only it, and not will, can foresee.

I now propose to leave the arguments of both Plato and Schopenhauer behind, and to embark upon a new analysis of the functions of reason in the practical life. The brief discussion of their views which has here been possible was designed merely to show that both were inadequate and left out important factors of the situation. And I do not think we can advance any further by sticking too closely to an examination of their doctrines.

It should be remembered in what follows that what we are concerned to discover is the *practical* functions of reason; that is, the way in which it works in influencing our actions. We are not directly concerned with its function in the theoretical spheres of science and knowledge. On the other hand we shall find that we cannot really keep these two separate. For in the last analysis it is through its theoretical action as a producer of knowledge that reason influences what we do. It is, of course, a complete mistake to suppose that we have one faculty which we call theoretical reason and another faculty which we call practical reason.

The practical functions of reason are, I believe, at least three in number.

First: Reason is, as Schopenhauer rightly pointed out, an instrument of the will in that it discovers the means for carrying our desires into effect. The examples already given are sufficient to prove this. We desire to eat, and reason discovers ways of procuring food. We desire wealth, and reason plans the means of acquiring it. I want to go to

New York. My intelligence sets me consulting maps or railway timetables.

Originally, I daresay, this was the only function of reason. The evolution of human intelligence out of the animal mind must have occurred through the development in some individuals of a capacity to discern quicker, better, and more intelligent ways of satisfying the original crude animal desires. And for some time after the emergence of the human stock men had before them perhaps no ends save these crude animal satisfactions. And the further, though still primitive, development of intelligence may have consisted solely in the gradual discovery of better means for their achievement. Thus it must have been that flint implements came into use. And the men who wanted to kill animals for food invented the bow and arrow. Thus it may have been true in the dawn of human life that will, in the form of animal desire, was the sole determinant of ends, while the dimly emerging reason was nothing but its instrument. The perception of this truth is perhaps one of the things which tend to make philosophers like Schopenhauer declare that reason still is, in its essence, *nothing but* an instrument of the will. But in this they commit a gross fallacy. For the nature of a thing is not to be restricted to what it was in its crude origins. It is to be gathered from what the fully developed thing is *now*.

Second: The second function of reason is to be, in effect, *the creator of new ends*. Both the meaning of this and its enormous importance require some considerable explanation.

Let us begin by comparing the life of an animal, or even of the most primitive and brutish man, on the one hand, with the life of any highly civilized man on the other. They differ, of course, in innumerable ways, some of which are scarcely relevant to our inquiry. But I wish to draw attention to one tremendous difference. The ends, or purposes, or desires of the animal or the animal-like man are extremely few in number. They are confined to the satisfaction of some two or three fundamental kinds of immediate urges or impulses. The cravings of hunger, thirst, and sex press upon him; the desires for warmth and coolness; possibly the desires to retain before consciousness certain pleasant sensations of color, sound, or touch. With these few the list seems almost to come to an end. Some half a dozen kinds of end seem open to him and no more.

Moreover, these few elementary desires are all created by immediately present stimuli. This means that the life of the animal or the animal-like man is confined to the present time and the present place. It is anchored to the here and now. Fleeting memory images may indeed make for him occasional brief excursions into a ghostlike past, excursions which must be, it would seem, almost wholly unrelated either to the present or to each other. And vague premonitions of the immediately oncoming moments may sometimes intrude themselves into the vivid present. But to all intents and purposes the statement is true that such a being is prisoned within the present.

Now compare this with the life of a civilized man. The first thing we notice is the enormous elaboration of ends and purposes. Instead of some half dozen, there are open for his choice literally hundreds and thousands of possible purposes. And these purposes are no longer confined to the satisfaction of immediate urges. They extend indefinitely into a far future. It is not merely for warmth or food *now* that such a man plans and works, but it may be for an end which he knows will not be achieved for ten, twenty, or thirty years.

This vast enrichment of man's life thus consists in two essential facts: first, the tremendously increased *number* of his ends; and secondly, their extension into an indefinitely long future. How has this enrichment come about? How have the multitude of new ends been created? This, I answer, has been the work of reason.

The nerve of the process has lain in the power of what is technically called induction or inductive reasoning. This means the capacity to generalize from experience. By generalizing we learn that phenomenon *A* is usually followed by phenomenon *B*. For instance, we learn in this way that solidification of water follows extreme cold; that the striking together of flints produces fire; that to cook food makes it soft, pleasant, and digestible. In science this process of induction is what gives us knowledge of what are known as laws of nature. But men reasoned inductively long before the dawn of science. Practically all the knowledge which men have about the world around them is the product of inductive reasoning. It is in this way that we know that the winter will be followed by the spring, that in the spring the trees will bud and blossom, that tomorrow morning the sun will rise, that certain foods will nourish us, that some substances will poison us, that our parents will probably feed us when we are young, that men who are starving will probably rob us, that our friends may be expected to help us, that if we immerse ourselves in the sea we shall drown, that wooden boats of a certain shape will float.

It will easily be seen that all knowledge about the future, and also all reasonable opinion about the probable future, is entirely the work of inductive reason. I do not know whether any animal can properly be said to expect the sun to rise tomorrow. Perhaps some animals do have a vague expectation of this, though I think the question is at least doubtful. There can, however, be no doubt that the animal is, as I said before, almost wholly confined within the present. And what we learn from these considerations is that it is reason alone which has liberated man from imprisonment within the present. *Reason is an eye into the future.*

The next point to notice is that the multiplication of human purposes to which we have already drawn attention is a consequence of this liberation of man's life from the bonds of the present and the opening of the future to his vision. If I, at this moment, could not look at all into the future, I could frame for myself, at this moment, no possible purposes except those which are dependent upon immediately present stimuli. If I happen to be now hungry, I could form the purpose of getting food. If I happen to be cold, I could form the purpose of making myself warm, provided the means were immediately at hand. If I am neither too cold, nor too hot, nor hungry, nor thirsty, nor uncomfortable, nor tired, nor otherwise pressed by some immediate want or need, I should be able to form in my mind no purpose at all. I should sit doing nothing, or perhaps go to sleep. This indeed is what the animal in such circumstances actually does. But because I can look into the future I can, though at the moment suffering from no special want, frame to myself any one of a thousand purposes. I can purpose to finish this book, to enjoy a vacation at the seashore in the summer, to teach my students better next term, to read certain books which have long lain unread on my desk, to make better preparation for my family after I die, to become a saint or a criminal or an artist or even a world conqueror. Doubtless I could not achieve all these ends. But the point is that the possibility of at least trying to achieve any or all of them is now open to me. And this fact depends entirely upon my capacity for inductive reasoning.

It will now be understood in what sense it was said that reason is a creator of new ends. Of course it is true that nothing could be an end to me unless I desired it. And as desire is, by definition, part of the will, the will is necessary in order that anything should be an end. But the function of reason here is to reveal to men new possibilities which may, if he desires them, become ends to him. Perhaps it would be more accurate to say that reason is a revealer or discoverer of new ends, rather than their creator. But since these ends could not come into existence for us but for the operation of reason, it seems fair to speak of reason as their creator. At any rate the word matters little so long as the idea is understood.

The relation of reason—in its second function—to will in the practical life seems to me to bear a close resemblance to the relation of reason to sensation or sense perception in the theoretical life. Our entire knowledge of things in the material world is the result of the co-operation of two factors, reason and sense perception. We see, hear, touch, taste and smell things. This is the factor of sense perception. Reason takes these crude materials of sense, and upon the basis of them builds up our entire knowledge. Now animals, or some of them, have senses at least as acute as ours. They can see, hear, or touch all that we can. Yet they have scarcely anything which could reasonably be described as knowledge. Hence the whole of the enormous elaboration of human knowledge, its entire advance upon the blank ignorance of the animal mind, has to be attributed to the other factor, reason.

Now it seems to me that bare will has to be compared, in this respect, to bare sense experience. It yields nothing but the wretchedly poverty-stricken purposive or conative life of the animal. Man would have remained in that condition forever but for the function of reason in revealing to him many thousands of new purposes for which to live. The enormous enrichment of human life by the discovery and elaboration of new purposes has been wholly the work of reason. And reason therefore is superior to, or higher than, will in the practical life in much the same sort of sense in which it may be said to be superior to, or higher than, bare sensation in the theoretical life of knowledge. This does not mean that it is intrinsically superior in some mystical or cosmic sense, but only that it is superior in what it has contributed to the enrichment of life.

Perhaps a few examples of the work of reason in the creation of new purposes may be in place here. The fundamental human impulse upon which man's social life is based is no doubt a species of nonrational feeling. We may call it gregarious feeling, though it is really a variety of sympathy. This feeling, as being conative, belongs to the will—in Schopenhauer's wide sense. But by itself it can lead to nothing but the crude herding of animals. It has been through the work of reason alone that genuine social and political purposes in the human sense have become possible. For all co-operation is possible only through intelligent action. It may perhaps be said that, since the original social urge is nonrational, what we have here is an example of that very subordination of reason to will which Schopenhauer pointed out. But this is absurd. Perhaps reason *began* its society-building work as the mere instrument of the gregarious instinct. But in the course of doing so, it opened up countless new roads leading to what in fact became entirely new purposes of which the crude will, without its aid, could never even have dreamed.

All deep and great ethical purposes have also been rendered possible only by reason. Consider the precept, "Do unto others as you would that they should do unto you." How would this have been possible but for the realization that others, even those who are remote from us in space or time, have feelings and purposes and desires and ends like our own? And how could this knowledge have been reached save by the intellect? It is true that here too the basic drive towards altruism comes from nonrational sympathy. And reason alone could never operate as a motive to action. But the sympathy of the animal is rudimentary and confined to a few other animals of its own family or kind in its immediate physical neighborhood. That of man has become enlarged till it can become, in certain cases, a universal love of all mankind. This enormous development has been rendered possible solely by man's intellectual or rational nature.

I should myself maintain that it is man's rationality which has rendered the artistic consciousness possible—without denying that here too nonrational elements must always be present. But the relation of art to conceptual thought is a highly controversial issue at the present day. And I refrain therefore from adding this as an instance to my list.

Third: The third function of reason is *to integrate purposes.* In the life of the animal or the animal-like man there were but a few purposes, and one might say that these were disconnected from one another and not woven together into systematic patterns and wholes. The animal now desires to eat, and now again to mate, and now again to sleep or rest. But the relation between the desires is merely additive. There is this desire *and* this *and* this. There is no subordination of one to another, no co-ordination into long-range plans. By its second function reason merely increases the number of these disconnected ends. Its third function is their integration.

In the first place, of the many ends sought by the will, reason discovers those which are consistent and those which are inconsistent with one another. It thus helps to rule out and suppress minor aims which are inconsistent with major aims. This is the work of inductive reason. For instance, suppose I desire both to hold a high post in the government and to steal the wife of a prominent citizen. It is an inductive generalization from experience that running away with the wives of influential people often leads to the loss of high positions. I thus discover that I cannot achieve both my ends at once, in other words, that they are inconsistent with one another. In this sort of way men are enabled to select from among an indefinitely large number of possible ends those which do not clash.

The sort of examples which Plato gives of what he calls the rule of the appetites by reason really come under this third function of reason. Thus the immediate appetite of thirst is judged inconsistent with the more important long-range purpose of maintaining health, and is accordingly rejected.

The purposes which are left after minor and inconsistent aims have been eliminated can further be woven into systems by tracing various relationships between them. Some which were originally ends in themselves can nevertheless be used as means to further ends, so that, by connecting them together in this way, we kill two birds with one stone, as the saying is. By tracing relationships between many ends they are woven into chains and networks of means and ends and into long-range plans. The process of integration is never complete. If it were, the entire life of a man could be said to have but one single purpose. Actually, in the best-integrated lives we find some one great major purpose to which the great majority of activities are subordinated. But there are always bound to be numerous activities leading to ends, often of trifling importance, which are to all intents and purposes unconnected with the major aim of the life.

The tracing of relationships, without which this integration of personality cannot be achieved, is always and everywhere the work of reason. For it depends on the discovery of regular sequences and uniform recurrences of events. The eating of certain foods is found to lead to health, of certain other foods to ill-health. The connections between wealth, power, luxury, hardness of heart, vanity, conceit, the disposition to help or to injure our fellows, must be noted by the man who, while aiming at riches, wishes not to be demoralized thereby. The mental function involved is that same inductive reason which traces relations and laws among natural phenomena.

These being the functions of reason in the sphere of our practical activities, what conclusions are we to draw regarding the original issue between the Platonic theory of the primacy of reason and the Schopenhauerian theory of the primacy of the will?

I think our first conclusion must be that the two antithetical ideas, one of reason ruling will and appetite, the other of will ruling reason and making a mere bond servant of it, are both much too simple-minded. Neither rules the other in any accepted sense of the word rule. We had better abandon altogether the picture of the potentate and his subjects, one ruling and the other ruled; and not seek to apply it to the functions of, and relations between, reason and will. It is nothing but a very misleading metaphor. The use of it leads us to take it for granted that one of them rules the other; and then to ask the absurd question, which is it that rules the other? Whereas the truth is that neither rules the other.

If we ask, in that case, what *are* the relations between will and reason, we can only answer the question by stating over again the conclusions we have reached regarding their respective functions. These may be summarized as follows. Reason and will co-operate in human action. Both are necessary, and each is complementary to the other. Will is the appetition of ends, and its function is to be the *urge* of action, the steam in the human engine. The functions of reason are to discover means to ends, to enrich life by opening up the possibilities of ever new ends, and to integrate purposes and personality.

Is there any sense, then, in which we can maintain the truth of the theory on which our civilization has rested, the theory of the primacy of reason, against the Schopenhauerian theory of the primacy of the will? For if not, we should have to conclude that the whole issue which we have supposed to exist between the ethos of western civilization and the ethos of the so-called new order of the totalitarian world, would seem to have rested upon a mistake. There would in fact be no issue.

The answer to this question must be, I think, along the following lines. Our discussion of the respective functions of reason and will shows that the essential insight of the Greeks was right. It is reason, and reason alone, which has lifted man above the animal, which has put so enormous a gulf between his life and that of the brutes. With no raw material save that of crude sensation it has produced the whole vast structure of human knowledge. With no raw material save that of crude desire and animal feeling it has produced the whole wealth of man's practical and purposive life. This life of man is higher than that of the animal, not in an absolute or cosmic sense, but according to the human scale, which is simply that of the more satisfactory, because the richer, life. And reason is higher than will in just the same sense. This is the true doctrine of the primacy of reason. And Plato's error was merely the use of an inaccurate metaphor, that of ruling. His insight was in essence true.

On the other hand Schopenhauer's doctrine was false in a much more serious way. Reason doubtless is, as he saw, an instrument of the will. That, indeed, is one of its functions. But Schopenhauer's disastrous error consisted in supposing that reason is *nothing but* such an instrument. How disastrous this was may be seen from the following. Suppose that from the beginning, from the first emergence of man out of the animal world, he had steadily refused to allow to his reason any voice in the direction of his affairs, but had confined it strictly to the office of ministering to the purposes which his will at that time had. The only purposes of the will at that time were the satisfactions of crude animal desires. Reason would therefore have had to be confined to the function of discovering means to the satisfaction of these alone. It would never have been allowed to suggest new ends. The result would have been that from that day to this man's purposive life would have been kept down to the animal level. Man would in effect never have risen above the animal at all. This is what would have been the outcome if men had from the beginning followed Schopenhauer's doctrine. And one may conclude that the literal adoption of Schopenhauer's theory now would result in the practical destruction of all that is valuable in human life. This is why the theory is not only erroneous but disastrous.

It may be thought that this is to paint an exaggerated picture of the life which man would live if he followed the Schopenhauerian rule. For are there not at the present day nations—in the totalitarian states—who have adopted, or at least been deeply influenced by, the doctrine of the primacy of the will? And however deeply we may dislike the way of life which they propose, it would be absurd to say that it is a mere return to the animal level. It is highly organized. It recognizes social demands, indeed enormously emphasizes them in its own way. It has its art and its literature. It embodies in its program all the fruits of modern science and civilization.

The first reply to this argument is that in so far as the totalitarian states are characterized by high organization, social life, art, literature, science, they are merely retaining possession of the fruits of that philosophy of reason by which they lived in the past and which they now repudiate. The ladder which they are kicking away from under them is the ladder by which they climbed. It is not the philosophy of the will which has produced these things. It never could have produced them. It is man's reason alone which has done so.

But there is another reply. The totalitarian states have not wholly rejected the philosophy of reason in their practice, whatever their theory may be. For to do so is in fact impossible to a human being. It *is* the function of reason to enrich life in the ways which have been described. And whatever men may say or think, reason *will* continue to perform its natural function, just as the heart will continue to pump blood. Men may adopt the theory of the primacy of the will, but in spite of it these very men will continue to use their reason to enrich their lives by the discovery of new ends and by the integration of personality. And even if the totalitarian states should decree that henceforth reason is to be nothing but an instrument of the will, they could not carry this out. For they cannot overturn nature. In these very states today reason continues to perform its ancient functions. For these men are after all human, and cannot wholly prevent themselves from behaving as human beings, however hard they try.

Yet though men cannot, by their false theories, wholly overturn the natural order, cannot wholly destroy their own humanity, they can go some way in that direction. And this is what is now happening. If men turn their backs upon the Platonic wisdom of our civilization, if they persistently belittle reason and extol the will, they will not indeed become animals or cease to be human. But they will tend in that direction. If they do not literally turn from men into brutes, they will at least turn into brutal men.

Consider only one point, which goes, however, to the root of the matter. What will be the chief ethical difference between the man who wishes to be guided by reason and the man who keeps insisting that he need consult only what he calls his will? The former will reflect that other men around him have minds, feelings, purposes, and ends essentially like his own, that they are as capable of suffering and happiness as he is, that they are in all these respects exactly like himself. Since these are the facts which his reason discloses to him, he will consider it irrational to act as if his own ends and purposes, his own sufferings and happiness, were the only ones in the world. It is irrational simply because it is contrary to the truth. He will accordingly endeavor in his actions to take account of these other selves. In this way rational reflection is the germ of all human morality. It is admitted that such mere reasoning will be ineffective in practice without the addition of a motive force of feeling, without sympathy. Yet reason alone will at least point the way to ethical action.

On the other hand, what will it mean, in practice, for a man to ignore the dictates of reason and to follow only his will? It will mean that he will seek to satisfy nothing except his own desires to the complete disregard of other selves. There is no difference here between will and self-will. And carried to its extreme conclusion the life of pure self-will is simply the life of the animal. For to be governed solely by its own will, in total disregard of the existence of other selves—this is precisely the principle of animal life. And those who in their philosophies set up the will above the reason, and who attempt to act upon this basis, though they will never, being human, cease wholly to live the rational and the ethical life, will yet tend in that direction. This is precisely what the totalitarian powers are now doing, at least in the international sphere. They advocate the complete rejection of reason, the complete domination of national self-will in international relations.

The doctrine of the primacy of reason is thus justified. Its insistence upon the ascendancy of reason over will is a correct analysis of human personality. It is only by keeping to this formula that human beings can remain human. The theory of the primacy of will cannot be completely put into practice so long as men do remain human. For this is simply contrary to nature. But in so far as men do succeed in putting it into practice, to that extent precisely they will have traveled on the downward road which leads from man back to the animal.

CHAPTER XII

NIETZSCHE OR CHRIST?

W E FOUND that western democratic civilization is based upon the idea of the infinite value of the individual. This in turn was derived from two sources, the Greek theory of the primacy of reason and the Christian theory of the primacy of sympathy. If then one could find a rational proof and justification of these two theories, one would therein be providing at the same time the ultimate justification of our civilization. In the last chapter I attempted to supply proof of the truth of the doctrine of the primacy of reason. There remains only the final task of vindicating the Christian principle of the primacy of sympathy. This I shall try to do in the present chapter.

The choice which lies before us is between the moral teachings of Christ and those of Nietzsche. Our civilization embodies the former. Totalitarianism, at least in its German form, tends more and more to the latter. We are at the parting of the ways. Which shall we choose as our leader, as the exponent for us of the good life, Nietzsche or Christ? Which conception of the good life, which set of moral principles, is true?

Our task is to prove, by rational argument, the truth of

the Christian ethics. It will be of no avail to appeal to our emotional preferences or our customary beliefs. For these precisely are what now come before us for judgment. It will be useless to express our horror of the principle of self-assertion, of hardness and brutality, and our instinctive feeling for the tenderness and beauty of Christian selflessness and love. For precisely what we are asked to do is to show that these feelings are founded in the nature of things, are *right*. We have to give reasons, not feelings.

To prove by argument the validity of its principle of the primacy of sympathy is something which Christianity itself has never undertaken. It has appealed always to intuitions. And it may be thought that such an undertaking is in the nature of the case impossible. For sympathy is an emotion. And how can one, by reason, justify any emotion whatever? Emotions, it will be said, are not true or false, right or wrong. They simply are, or are not. One may like them or approve them, or dislike and disapprove them. And there the matter must of necessity end.

But I do not agree to this analysis. Sympathy itself is an affair of emotion. But the *principle* of the primacy of sympathy is not. It is a principle, a proposition. And principles or propositions are either true or false. This means that their truth or falsity must be capable of rational demonstration. What then is it which the principle of the primacy of sympathy asserts to be true?

The principle of the primacy of the will asserted that it is the proper function of the will to determine all ends, and of the reason to discover means to these ends and to do nothing else. The principle of the primacy of reason asserted that reason has certain functions—discussed in detail in the last chapter—which give it the leading rôle in the development of human personality. We may be sure that the principle of the primacy of sympathy will be a proposition of something like the same fundamental form. That is to say, it will be a proposition about the proper function of sympathy in the control of human activities. And we have already seen at great length that propositions about the proper functions of the elements of personality may be true or false; and by what method they are to be proved or disproved. And it will be by such considerations that we shall meet the objection of those who say that sympathy, being an emotion or complex of emotions, cannot be justified by rational argument.

In attempting to state what it is that the principle of the primacy of sympathy actually asserts we shall be wise to be warned by certain considerations which were adduced in the case of the doctrine of the primacy of reason. It was a mistake, we found, to state this doctrine in terms of the metaphor of ruling, as Plato did. The elements of personality do not stand to each other in the relations of ruler and ruled. They have definite functions, and to state these functions as accurately as possible is to state the relations between them. And the *primacy* of reason meant, in fact, only that the practical functions of reason are of such paramount importance that they dwarf the functions of the other parts of the soul. Reason is paramount over will because its contribution to the enrichment of life is enormously greater than that of will. It is reason, not will, which has been the cause of nearly all that is by common consent of greatest value in human life.

We should interpret the doctrine of the primacy of sympathy in a similar way. But there is this difference. Sympathy, being a matter of feeling, is a direct cause or motive power of human action; which reason is not. We may therefore expect the principle of the primacy of sympathy to mean something like this: that there are a large number of kinds of human motive; for instance, a man may be impelled to an action by hatred, or by greed, or by self-interest, or by fear, or by anger, or by hunger, or by sex desire; among these kinds of motivation is sympathy or, what is the same thing, love; these different kinds of motive will have different degrees of relative importance in the living of the good life; and sympathy possesses primacy among them all in the sense that it stands out above all others as the supremely important motive of action.

We may put the same thing in another way. According to the humanist theory of morals which we have adopted, every element of human personality has a right to expression in the good life. It is accordingly right that fear, self-interest, sex desire, should operate as motives of action. For each has its proper function. The problem of the good life will be the problem of how to integrate them and what relative importance to give to each. Bodily desire must have its place. But should our lives be mainly devoted to the satisfaction of bodily desires, and only in a minor degree aim at—shall we say?—the satisfactions of the mind? Self-interest must have its place. But in what degree are we to follow its dictates? Are we to live ninety-nine per cent of the time pursuing our own interests, and giving only one per cent of our attention to the interests of others? Among all the different elements of personality where is the emphasis to lie? Which is to be given the prime place? Now the doctrine of the primacy of sympathy asserts, as I understand it, that the prime place is to be given to sympathy, that this is to be the leading motive of our actions, that the supreme emphasis is to be thrown here, and not upon bodily desire, nor upon fear, nor upon self-interest, nor upon any other element of personality.

It will be seen at once that the doctrine is, and must probably always remain, vague. It tells us that we are to attach much more importance to the dictates of sympathy than to those of self-interest. But exactly how much more it does not tell us. It does not attempt a measurement of values. But we can hardly expect that it should. No set of ethical principles in the world does so in any precise way. And this lack of precision, though it may worry the confirmed academic, will scarcely be a stumbling block to the practical man, for whose guidance, after all, moral codes were invented. To this man the Christian creed says: "Give to love and sympathy much more weight in your actions than you do now. Before acting on this advice, you need not wait to be told precisely what amount of weight you should attach to it in order to live the perfect life. For you are in no danger of ever being *too* unselfish."

What is the ultimate criterion which is to decide to what psychological element the primacy should be given? Why, in the last analysis, should we decide on sympathy rather than any other element such as lust or hatred or self-assertion? The ultimate criterion is, of course, the satisfactory human life. It is the same here as it is in the biological sphere. Why do we say that it is the proper function of the heart to pump blood? In the first place it is its function to do so because it actually does so. But why is this its *proper* function? Why do we say that it *ought* to do so, in addition to saying that it actually does? Because it is only *if* it does so that a satisfactory physical life results. If it fails to do so, we get a less satisfactory life, or no life at all. In the same way the ultimate ground for saying that sympathy must be given the leading place among our motives must be that this is what will lead to the most satisfactory human life.

We have now to attempt a rational vindication of the doctrine of the primacy of sympathy understood in the manner which I have just outlined. In this attempt I shall adopt a twofold procedure. We have before us as our practical choice the ethics of Christ and the ethics of Nietzsche. And these are, to all intents and purposes, opposites. The principle of the Christian ethics is sympathy and selflessness. The principle of Nietzsche is self-assertion and the repudiation of sympathy. I shall begin by trying to show that the Nietzschean principle is false, or at least ill-founded. The result of this will be, of course, merely negative. And I shall then be left with the far harder task of discovering the positive rational justification of the Christian ethics.

The philosophy of Nietzsche is, I believe, vitiated by the following fundamental defects:

First: It is derived from two premises, both of which are essential to it. One is the theory of evolution. The other is the Schopenhauerian doctrine of the primacy of the will. Nietzsche, like Schopenhauer, sets the will above every other element of human personality. And he too regards reason as the mere instrument of the will. It is on this that his ethical ideal is built. The ideal man is the man of will, the man whose will dominates all else. And this is the hard, self-assertive man, the strong man; not the man of reason, and not the man of love.

But the doctrine of the primacy of the will, from which these ethical conclusions follow, has been shown to be false. Hence there is no reason to accept the ethical conclusions which flow from it.

Second: Nietzsche further narrows and distorts even the small element of truth which informs the doctrine of Schopenhauer. Schopenhauer's theory of the will is a distortion of the truth. But Nietzsche's theory is a distortion of this distortion. For to Schopenhauer the will is the entire conative nature of man. It includes every possible human purpose and desire. It is simply our desiring nature as such. But Nietzsche arbitrarily narrows down the will to a single purpose, a single desire, the desire for *power*.

By this he does not mean, of course, mere physical strength. He includes every sort of physical, mental, moral, or psychical power. Nevertheless this is a much narrower conception of the will than Schopenhauer's. And if the doctrine that will is and ought to be supreme is false when will is taken in Schopenhauer's wide sense, it is bound to be even more false when will is interpreted in Nietzsche's much narrower sense.

It is true that Nietzsche sometimes seems to include under the term will to power almost every conceivable human desire or purpose. For he sometimes defines power as whatever yields a sense of the enlargement and expansion of personality. And it is plausible to maintain that the fulfillment of any purpose whatever does this. But in that case, why is the specific word power used? Quite clearly it is his intention to limit human purposes in some way. For instance, he contrasts power as an end with happiness as an end. He rejects the utilitarian end of happiness. The fact is that while power is defined in such a wide and vague manner as to *seem* to embrace almost all ends, yet Nietzsche, by using that particular word, succeeds in skillfully suggesting that the really important thing in life is power in the narrow sense in which that word is ordinarily used. Thus his ideal becomes in practice merely that of power in the sense in which the "strong man" possesses it. And it is this meaning of his doctrine of the will to power which has caught and inflamed the imaginations of his followers.

Third: The doctrine of the primacy of the will, as taught both by Schopenhauer and Nietzsche, is ultimately based upon a misuse of the Platonic method of arguing from the observed operations of the parts of personality to their proper functions. Schopenhauer's argument is that we do actually find will to be the driving force of all life, and that therefore it both is, and ought to be, the supreme part of personality. Nietzsche's argument is that the will to power actually is, and always has been, the driving force of all life; and that therefore it is, and ought to be, the supreme part of personality.

Now for Schopenhauer's statement of the facts there is *some* justification. For Nietzsche's there is none. Schopenhauer's statement is true in the sense that the propelling motive of all action is some kind of desire (never reason). But the suggestion of Nietzsche that all action is motivated by the desire for power is simply false. It might be true if power is taken to mean anything which brings a sense of the expansion of personality. For in that case the desire for power will mean practically any desire. But if power is taken in the ordinary sense—which it must be if Nietzsche's ideal of the strong man is to be reached—it is quite false. Only a very few men, and no animals, desire to be powerful. As to animals, what they crave is food, sex, and physical well-being. Among men there are some who desire to exert power—over nature partly, but chiefly over other men—for its own sake. They delight in the mere sense of compelling men and things to obey their commands. These are the ambitious men who become conquerors, tyrants, or perhaps captains of industry. They are relatively a very small band. The immense majority of men have no desire whatever to exert power as an end in itself, though of course they may often desire power to obtain other things which they want.

What they mainly want is to enjoy in peace and quiet the less spectacular blessings of life. Thus the alleged basis of fact upon which Nietzsche builds his whole argument is simply false.

Fourth: That Nietzsche commits an absurdity in setting up power as the highest good, the goal of life, is also evident from the fact that power is, in its own natural right, not an end, but only a means. It may certainly become an end in itself, as it does with ambitious men. But this is derivative only. Power, in this respect, is like money. The natural function of money is to be a means to the purchase of commodities, though for the miser it becomes an end in itself. And normally we desire power in the same way as a means to other things which we want. Hence men would never have come to desire power if they had not first desired other things. Therefore it is absurd to say that the desire for power has been, or is, the primary drive of life.

The foregoing criticisms of Nietzsche are concerned with his doctrine in so far as it is based upon the Schopenhauerian theory of the will. The remaining criticisms deal with its basis in the biological theory of evolution.

Fifth: From the time of Darwin till our own day we have had "the eternal law of struggle" dinned into our ears as justifying the exploitation and oppression of the weak by the strong. Nietzsche's ethics, and especially the version of it which has influenced Nazism, is full of this. Is it true, then, that the theory of evolution justifies any such conclusion?

We may throw the issue into another form. Struggle is the same thing as competition. And any ethics which, like that of Nietzsche, glorifies struggle, is glorifying the principle of competition. The Christian ethics, on the other hand, is based upon the principle of co-operation. The former means that individuals and races are to fight. The latter means that they are to help one another.

The argument from evolution assumes that competition has been the sole law of the animal kingdom and the sole cause of evolution. But both statements are untrue. Competition is *not* the only law of the animal world. Bee society, as everyone knows, is based upon co-operation. And the herd instinct among the higher mammals is a plain application of the co-operative principle. It is evident also that it possesses a survival value, and has been an instrument in the evolution of species.

Nietzsche professes a great contempt for the herd instinct among men. It is, he says, the main characteristic of the slave mentality as distinguished from the master mentality. But this attitude is entirely unjustified by the doctrine of evolution upon which it is supposed to be based. Nietzsche's fundamental principle is that whatever has helped forward the evolutionary process is good and should be encouraged. But the herd instinct is one of the things which has helped forward the evolutionary process. To condemn it therefore is arbitrary and inconsistent with his own principles.

Sixth: If we turn from the animal to the human world we find that Nietzsche's glorification of struggle and competition is even less justified. For human progress, as distinguished from the biological evolution of species, has resulted far more from co-operation than from competition. Doubtless in human life too the principle of competition is necessary and makes for advance. It is a commonplace that without it effort lags, incentive is wanting, and men become slothful and even effeminate. Yet the fact remains that if we ask what has been the prime cause of the enormous advance which civilized man has made upon the condition of the cave man—in the control over nature, in scientific discovery, in the development of social and political institutions, in art and literature—the answer is, in a single phrase, *organized co-operation*. This has been rendered possible, as we saw, by man's reason. But whatever may be the psychological source of the principle of co-operation, the fact that this principle has been the lever of all human progress is surely indisputable. Hence Nietzsche's theory that progress has been everywhere the result of struggle and competition is simply false. The very opposite is true. Human progress has been rendered possible precisely by the relative suppression of struggle and the introduction of mutual help in its place.

Seventh: This human capacity for co-operation is itself a product of evolution. Lower forms of life evolved new physical organs, such as eyes and ears and toes, to help them in the battle with their environment. Man has evolved no new physical organ. What he has contributed to the evolutionary process has been a new mode of life, the mode of co-operative living. This has a survival value, and a value as an instrument of progress, as great as any development of a new bodily organ, and is just as much justified by evolution as any such physical development could be. Nietzsche therefore commits an absurdity in attacking what is at once a product of past evolution and an instrument of further evolution on the ground that it is counter-evolutionary.

Eighth: It may be suggested that since, on our own admission, both co-operation and competition are necessary instruments of progress, therefore the moral ideal should encourage both. Christianity embodies only the principle of co-operation, Nietzschean philosophy only the principle of competition. Both are one-sided. The perfect ethical system would treat them as complementary and somehow combine them both. To this extent the Nietzschean philosophy would receive justification. It would be put on a level with, though not above, the Christian morality.

I do not agree with this conclusion, and for the following reasons. Suppose we make a distinction between nature and man by saying that whatever in life is peculiarly the work of man we will ascribe to man, but everything else we will ascribe to nature. In one sense, of course, everything that exists in the universe is a part of nature. And in this sense, works of engineering, such as houses and bridges, and works of the intellect, such as mathematical systems or systems of philosophy, are parts of nature. So are all social and political institutions. But there is another quite common sense of the word nature according to which we should say that all inanimate things, and all animals, and all the products of animal activity, such as the nests of birds and the dams of beavers, are a part of nature; but that cities, bridges, engines, works of art, institutions, and all other special products of human activity, belong, not to the world of nature, but to the world of man. This is the distinction between nature and man of which I propose to make use.

It is in this sense that, as we often say, morality is not natural, but human. It belongs to the world of man.

Now all human progress, the whole of the advance which man has made beyond the animal, has consisted in some way in an advance on mere nature. To give a few instances: Nature unassisted heals wounds and cures diseases. But medical science is an advance on nature. It adds antiseptics, drugs, surgery, to nature's means of restoring health. Again, nature keeps animals warm in the winter by thickening their furs. But man has invented artificial heat. Nature protects animals from the weather in various ways. But man builds houses and wears clothes.

Morality is an advance on nature in exactly the same sense. Hence its special function is to supply to human conduct that principle which nature has failed to supply. Nature from the beginning has ensured struggle and competition. And to do this is no part of the business of human morality. Therefore human moralists are right to make co-operation the sole principle of morality. Competition is not a part of morality, but a part of nature.

Nature can be relied on to continue to supply the element of competition to human life or any other life; and in doing so to provide automatically for the exercise and encouragement of those harder virtues which Nietzsche especially recommends. It is not necessary or suitable that moralists should assume this rôle. Morality is something which man has added to nature out of the stores of his own peculiar humanity. And what needed to be added to nature was the principle of co-operation. Therefore systems of morality rightly stress this *alone*.

We need not worry that Christianity, or socialism, or any other suggested system of living, will ever get rid of the principle of struggle and competition. You *cannot* get rid of it by any artificial means. Nature will eternally supply it. In pointing this out the Nietzscheans are right. But for this very reason they are wrong in making it the principle of their morality.

From this point of view it will be seen that the Nietzschean ethical code is a relapse to mere nature. In its attack on the Christian principle of co-operation, in its attempt to suppress sympathy, selflessness, humility, gentleness—all the peculiarly Christian virtues—it resembles exactly a doctor who should advocate the suppression of all surgical apparatus, of all drugs, antiseptics, medical appliances, and methods of disease control on the ground that these are not nature's methods of ensuring physical health.

Ninth: Nietzsche's philosophy is based upon a complete muddle regarding the nature of value. One of its absolutely necessary premises is the belief that whatever is higher in the evolutionary scale is also higher ethically. Thus man is higher than the ape, and the ape than the worm, in the ethical, as well as in the biological scale. Nietzsche must hold this because otherwise there is absolutely no ground for his contention that what favors the evolutionary process, such as struggle, is ethically good.

Now of course many people will agree with Nietzsche that man is, in this ethical sense, higher than the ape. But the point is that Nietzsche himself had no right to hold it because it is utterly inconsistent with other essential parts of his philosophy. For as I have pointed out in earlier passages in this book it cannot be maintained except on the basis of a belief in an absolute, nonhuman, and cosmic scale of values. But no one would be more horrified than Nietzsche to be told that he believes in a cosmic scale of values. He imagines himself to be an out-and-out relativist and humanist. He is loud in his protest against any morality which is supposed to be imposed upon man by gods or by any other external agency. That morality is a human thing is essential to the whole spirit of his *Weltanschauung.*

This convicts Nietzsche of inconsistency. Personally I should go further. I should say that he is not only inconsistent with himself in holding that what is higher in the evolutionary scale is also higher ethically, but that this belief is also positively false. For in fact morality is a purely human thing, and there is in truth no absolute or cosmic scale of value. I have already argued this at length, and shall not repeat my arguments here. The falsity of Nietzsche's position is involved in the whole humanist outlook which was developed in the first part of this book. And if Nietzsche was wrong in identifying evolutionary progress with progress towards the ethically good, his entire ethical philosophy collapses. There is then absolutely no ground for supposing that, even if struggle and competition alone have been responsible for evolution, they are therefore the principles of ethical action.

If on the ground of these various criticisms we reject the Nietzschean morality, as I think we must, we may now turn to the positive side of our undertaking. This is to find a rational justification of the doctrine of the primacy of sympathy, which is the essential principle of the Christian ethical system.

I shall take as one of the premises of my argument that the Greek doctrine of the primacy of reason has already been justified and proved true. I shall build on this basis. And the essence of the justification of the principle of the primacy of sympathy will be that it is required as a necessary complement to the principle of the primacy of reason. In other words, the doctrine of the primacy of reason will not work practically unless it is supplemented by the principle of the primacy of sympathy. In this sense it will be urged that the primacy of reason implies the primacy of sympathy; and that therefore if the former is true—and its truth has already been proved—the latter must be true also.

In this way we shall also solve the difficulty which was raised on the ground that, if reason were found to be supreme in the soul, sympathy could not also be supreme; in other words that the soul could not have two captains. The pragmatic solution was found in the fact that the primacy of sympathy and the primacy of reason both gave rise to the same deductions—the infinite value of the individual, equality, liberty, and individualism. The final solution consists in pointing out that, psychologically also, reason and sympathy work together, and not against one another; that the life of reason is also the life of sympathy; so that both may be regarded jointly as the crown of personality.

In order to understand the relation which reason and sympathy have to one another in the practical life, let us suppose, first, that there is a man in whom reason is developed but who is completely destitute of sympathy. Suppose that this man possesses the idea of his own infinite value, but still thinks of all other beings as mere means to his ends and as having therefore only finite and relative values. Reason alone will teach him, when he comes to reflect, that other men are like himself, that they possess feelings and purposes like his own. He will be able to reason that as he is they are, and that as he is a center of infinite value, so are they. That is, he will reach the conception of the infinite value of every individual. But lacking sympathy, he will possess no motive to *act* upon this conclusion of his reason. It will remain in his consciousness a mere ineffectual theoretical concept. For a man can only act on the impulsion of *his own* motives and *his own* purposes. He may know as a matter of theory that another man has a feeling or a desire or a purpose exactly like his own. But he cannot act from another man's motives or desires. The feeling or purpose of another is not steam in his engine.

It follows that, in order that this man may *act* upon the basis of the idea of the infinite value of the other man, the feelings and purposes of the other man must become his own. They must flow from this other man into him. But the transference of feeling from one person to another is

precisely the function of sympathy. Or rather, by definition, it *is* sympathy. Therefore it is only after this man
acquires sympathy that he can act upon the idea of the infinite value of all individuals. Thus sympathy is the necessary complement of reason in the sense that it supplies the
motive power which reason lacks.

Now suppose a man possessed of sympathy but without
reason. He too will start with the idea that he, and he alone,
is of infinite value. The idea will not be in the form of an
abstract concept, since he is without reason, but will be
implicit in his attitude, as it is with animals. But in his case
the feelings of another may flow into him since he possesses
sympathy. The purposes and motives of the other will become his purposes and motives, and will impel him to action. He will act as if the other were of infinite value.
Theoretically, if his capacity for sympathy were un-
bounded—which, of course, is never actually the case—he
would act as if *all* human beings were of infinite value. The
idea of the infinite value of all individuals would then be
implicit in his attitude, though unrealized as a concept. This
would have happened without any aid from reason at all.
Thus of the two principles on which the ethos of our civilization is built, reason and sympathy, sympathy is in a
sense the more fundamental and vital, in the sense, namely,
that it is capable of producing the characteristic ethical behavior pattern of that civilization without the aid of reason,
while reason is not capable of producing that behavior
pattern without the aid of sympathy. On the other hand
reason alone can produce the idea, in the form of a concept,
while sympathy is incapable of doing this.

Sympathy suffers from a serious defect which is absent
from reason. Sympathy, radiating from a human being as
a center, operates at maximum strength only at very close

range, rapidly decreases in strength as it moves away from the center, and then quickly fades out altogether. But the strength of reason is not diminished by distance. It streams out to infinity. Sympathy is like sound, which does not carry very far from its source. If there were a ray which, starting from a center, traversed all space without any diminution at all, such a ray would be the analogue of reason. If this contrast between reason and sympathy is not immediately clear to the reader, a few examples will make it so.

Instances of the fading out of sympathy through distance will be quite familiar. We sympathize strongly with those with whom we are in close contact, with those who are near us; but much less with those who are far away. If men die of hunger on our doorsteps our hearts are torn. If they die of hunger in the next town, we are genuinely concerned. If the tragedy occurs on the other side of the United States we are moved, but considerably less so. If it occurs on the other side of the planet, it means almost nothing to us. The starvation of millions in a famine in some remote continent moves us less than the starvation of a single family a few doors from where we live.

The distance which exercises this damping effect upon our feelings is of two kinds. It may be mere physical distance. Or it may be remoteness of relationship. We sympathize greatly with our fellow citizens, less with the citizens of other states. We are profoundly affected by the fortunes of the members of our own families, less by those of our neighbor's families.

It is because of distance of both kinds that a war between nations far away, however important it may actually be for us, may fail to move us deeply.

But distance is irrelevant to reason. The geometer proves

to us that the three angles of a Euclidean triangle are equal to two right angles. We never think of asking where the triangle is, here or in China. The proof will be as convincing to us if the triangle is fifty billion miles away in the depths of interstellar space. And so, if we become aware of the infinite value of individuals through the channel of reason, not sympathy, the idea becomes true for us however far away, in space or in relationship, the other individuals may be.

Thus as sympathy supplements reason by providing it with motive power, so reason supplements sympathy by giving it extension, by eliminating the narrowness of its range. Sympathy unaided can travel only a few yards from home. But it can be transported by reason across vast distances. It will still suffer diminution because of the distance it has traveled. But it becomes at least to some extent effective. If there is a flood or a famine twelve thousand miles away, the misery of the suffering cannot flow, through sympathy alone, into our souls. This is less to us than the death of a pet dog at home. But reason comes to our aid. It teaches us that these remote beings are human like ourselves, have feelings and needs like our own, are centers of infinite value. Thereupon sympathy flows, albeit somewhat thinly, across the gulf, and produces action. We send stores and supplies over the oceans. It has been denied by some that there exists any such thing as a love of mankind in general. I believe it, or something approaching it, can exist in some exceptional men. If so, it is an extension of emotional feeling due to the marriage of sympathy and reason.

Man is distinguished from the animals by the power of his reason. But it is almost equally true to say that he is distinguished from them by the enormous increase in his capacity for sympathy. The animal is incapable of sympathizing with any but a few fellows of its own kind in its own immediate neighborhood, and then only in respect of a very limited number of the more violently emotional feelings. A man is at least potentially capable of sympathizing with all the hundreds of millions of other men on the planet in respect of almost any of their feelings. And his sympathy may even extend beyond the borders of mankind into the animal kingdom. This extension has been produced by the operation of reason.

This fact alone gives to some extent a rational justification of Christian ethics. For if the mere fact that reason is what is specifically human is a good ground for giving it a leading rôle in our conception of the good life for man, the same argument can be used to show that sympathy should likewise play a leading rôle. The ethical ideal must give expression to all man's psychic elements. But it must give the strongest expression to those elements which are characteristically human, and which distinguish man from the animal. And these are both sympathy and reason.

But the main point is not this. It is rather that this enormous enlargement of the power of sympathy in man is the direct result of the fact that he is a reasoning animal. With beings who are extremely like ourselves, and also extremely near ourselves, that is, with the very few, we enter into sympathetic relationship through mere intuitive or irrational feeling. But with more remote beings we cannot sympathize at all except on the basis of an intelligent understanding of them. We must first come to know, by the exercise of our intellects, that they have feelings at all, what their feelings are, what their environments, circumstances, needs, and purposes. Only when we know these things does feeling begin to flow between us. And to produce this preliminary understanding is the work of reason.

Mere brute instinct, without any reason at all, will cause a man to sympathize with his child or even with a stranger whom he actually sees suffering in his immediate presence. But that sympathy should extend any further than this, that it should embrace people in remote lands, is not possible on the basis of mere animal feeling. It has to be preceded by operations of the reason.

We can now see how intimately reason and sympathy are actually bound together in the practical life, how they complement one another, and how both are essential ingredients of the moral ideal.

First, though reason leads to the same cluster of ethical ideas as does sympathy, it is completely incapable of translating them into action. Sympathy alone can provide the necessary emotional drive.

On the other side, emotional sympathy by itself is incapable of that all-embracing character which alone can make the idea of the infinite value of the individual a universal human ideal. If sympathy were left to itself, the conception of the equality of all men could never have emerged. Men would have been valued not equally, but more highly as they were nearer the valuing individual, less highly as they were further away. A man's family would have seemed to him of supreme value, his neighbor's family of far less value. And we do, of course, still feel and act as if this were so. That is because we fail to put our ideals fully into practice. It is reason which insists that in the ideal life this process of valuational fading out must not occur, that those who are far away must be treated on the same principles as those who are near at hand.

Thus we see that the Greek spirit and the Christian spirit were alike incomplete. It required both to bring to birth the peculiar ethos of our civilization. The Greek spirit in contributing to civilization its rational character lacked the side of emotion. It was this which the Christian spirit supplied.

Reason and sympathy may thus be said to amalgamate into a single force in human personality. This single spiritual force has two aspects or facets. It appears now in the form of feeling, now in the form of the concept. Sympathy is practical reason in the form of feeling. It is intuitive reason. Practical reason is sympathy which has become conceptual. It is intellectualized sympathy. And herein we see how the apparent contradiction of declaring first that reason is the crown of personality, the captain of the soul, and then that sympathy holds this place, is resolved. It is the single spiritual force, compact of both, which is supreme. This idea of a single force is, of course, only a metaphor. Reason and sympathy are in fact as distinct as any two elements of personality can be. But the metaphor expresses how they work in unison in the practical life.

And the rational justification of the doctrine of the primacy of sympathy, the final proof that it is true, is this. That the doctrine of the primacy of reason is true we know from our inquiries in the previous chapter. We take that as our premise. It implies that the ideal life is the life of reason. But we cannot live the life of reason without a motive in the form of feeling. The necessary feeling motive is supplied by sympathy. So that the life of sympathy and the life of reason are in fact one. Thus the primacy of reason implies the primacy of sympathy. And since the former is known to be true, the latter must be true also.

I must now draw attention to the fact that it is the Christian principle of life which provides the fundamental feeling basis not only of our civilization but of all human society. It is the foundation of pre-Christian societies, of non-Christian societies, of societies which have never heard of Christianity. This may sound paradoxical, but it is not. For the Christian principle, which is sympathy, was not invented or discovered by Christianity. To suppose this would be like supposing that the Greeks invented man's rationality. Sympathy and reason both exist permanently in all human nature everywhere. What the Greek spirit did was to give to reason its proper place in life, to emphasize its proper function. What Christianity did was to give to sympathy its proper place in life, to thrust it into the foreground as the ruling principle of life. Hence there is no paradox in the assertion that the Christian principle of sympathy is in fact the basis of all society, whether the society be nominally Christian or not.

It is so because what is commonly called social feeling is in fact nothing else but the sympathy which human beings have for one another. It is remarked that man is a social animal by nature, that the idea of a completely nonsocial man is an impossible abstraction. Such a being, if he existed, would not be human. This is because what joins men together, what prevents them from being self-enclosed atoms, windowless monads wholly cut off from one another, is the fact that feelings flow from one into another. And this means that personality is not discrete from personality, but that they interpenetrate one another and merge into larger wholes. These larger wholes are societies. And the flow of feelings which renders this possible is, by definition, the psychological fact of sympathy. Or to change the metaphor, sympathy is the cement of society, that without which an aggregate of men would be nothing but a heap or pile instead of an organic entity.

In this way the so-called organic character of society is explained. It consists, as we saw, in the fact that the social relations between *A* and *B* alter the internal natures of *A* and *B*. This is not a mystery. The reason for it is obvious. Social relations consist in, or are produced by, social feelings. And this means simply that *A*'s feelings, purposes, and ends pass over into *B*. *B* is of course altered thereby. He now possesses feelings, purposes, and ends which were not in him before. His personality is changed.

Thus Christianity, in emphasizing the principle of sympathy, in assigning to it the leading rôle in life, is simply emphasizing and giving the leading rôle in life to man's social nature. Nietzsche in contemning sympathy is contemning the basis of society. His philosophy is antisocial. It is strange that totalitarianism should have failed to see that, in allying itself with Nietzschean ethics, it contradicts itself. For totalitarianism emphasizes above all else the social character of man, the organic character of society. But the Nietzschean ethic, inasmuch as it despises that human sympathy which is the cement of society, is atomistic in tendency, if not in intention. Democracy is the genuine product of the organic theory of society. Thus the tables are turned. Totalitarianism professes that its theory of society is organic, while the democratic theory is called atomistic. The shoe is really on the other foot.

And this constitutes a second proof of the doctrine of the primacy of sympathy. For what the doctrine really asserts is that the best life for man is that in which his social nature is developed to the utmost, so that it predominates over and controls the antisocial forces in his nature. And to deny it is to assert that the best life for a man is that in which he lives solitary and unsocial, in a state of enmity and war with his fellow men. And who is there who will believe this?

The final test as to whether the set of rules which a dog trainer recommends for the living of dogs is true is whether the rules do in fact yield, if followed, the most satisfactory dog life. And the final test of a set of human moral rules is whether they do in fact yield the most satisfactory human life. The question then is: Would the Christian moral ideal, if men truly followed it, ensure to the men who followed it the best, most happy, healthy, and satisfactory life? Should we ourselves be more satisfied with our lives than we are now if we lived lives more nearly approaching the Christian ideal? If the answer is yes, then the Christian moral ideal is the best and truest. But if no, then it is a false ideal or at least an ideal less true than some other.

Perhaps it cannot be proved that each individual man, taken as a separate unit, must necessarily feel his life satisfactory and happy if he lives according to the Christian ideal. Perhaps it cannot be shown, as Plato tried to show, that each individual good man must necessarily be a happy man. For there are so many other things in his environment which may bring disaster upon him. And a single man who follows the ideal in an environment of bad men can scarcely reap the fruits of his goodness. Moreover, to put the question in this way, as Plato did, implies a too atomistic conception of man and of society. The question should be asked, not about the individual man, but about the social group. And I do not see how it can be doubted that a society of men would as a whole be happier if all its members applied to their lives the rules of Christian morality; or that the society of nations would be happier if all the nations applied these rules to their conduct towards one another instead of the laws of the jungle. And if so, the Christian morality must be held able to meet the final test, which is whether its principles are really those which, if followed, would lead to the best, most happy, healthy, and satisfactory human life.

To us who argue thus it is sometimes replied that there is no empirical proof of what we say. But this is because there never has been a society which, in a high degree, in all its actions, has followed the Christian rule of life. Nor has this ever been tried in the affairs of nations. But that civilization which has, more truly than any other, attempted to embody Christian ethical ideas in its institutions is precisely the civilization of the western world. And I cannot see any reason to deny that it has in doing so found a happier and more satisfactory way of life than that of other civilizations which are based upon other ideas.

If the substance of the last two chapters is true, we can conclude that the struggle of our western democratic civilization to maintain itself against the menace of its antagonists is justified by the nature of man. We are fighting for our ideals not merely because they happen to be ours, not merely because our fathers handed them down to us, not merely because we have become accustomed to them and have developed personal prejudices and preferences in favor of them. We might sympathize with men fighting for their way of life on account of even such irrelevant reasons alone. But we should have to admit that their action was in the end irrational, unless it could be shown also that their way of life was in itself good.

And this is what we have tried to show of the democratic way of life. If we have succeeded, then we can believe, on good and rational grounds, that our ideals are rooted in reason and goodness, that they are worth defending because they are right and true, because they are actually the noblest and greatest ideals which human beings have yet found in the world. And we may further fortify our faith that in the end our cause must triumph, not because it is ours, but because it is just.

INDEX

A

Absolute, 22
  Hegelian, 182-183, 208-210
Action, life and, 47
"Adventures of Ideas," Whitehead, 19 *note*
Animals, good life, 47-50
  morality and, 10-12, 30-41, 51-
  54
  personality, 54
  sympathy, 110, 304-305
Anthropology, morality and, 12-13
Antirationalism, 173-201
  Bergson and, 194-197
  Plato's view, 33-41, 264-268
  reason and, 94-95
  science and, 228
Aristotle, 106, 193
  humanism, 39-41
  intellectual virtue, 178
  moderation and, 100
  organic relations and, 240
  researches, 180
  view of man, 242
Art, civilization and, 3-4
  morality and, 59

Asceticism, evaluation of, 69
  morality and, 258
Assembly, liberty of, 159
Atomism, democracy and, 210-
  211, 244-245
  Hobbesian, 242, 245

B

Barnes, J. S., 205-206
Behavior, natural principles, 10-
  17, 30-41
Bentham, Jeremy, 41
Bergson, Henri, 109, 145-146
  antirationalism, 194-197
Body, soul vs., 5-6
Buddhism, individual values, 147-
  148

C

Callicles, 189
  laws and, 11-12
  moral viewpoints, 18, 30-31
  Nietzsche and, 87
Calvin, John, 194
Ceylon, child sale in, 147-149

313